Taking Baby Steps

Taking Baby Steps

How Patients and Fertility Clinics
Collaborate in Conception

Jody Lyneé Madeira

UNIVERSITY OF CALIFORNIA PRESS

University of California Press, one of the most distinguished university presses in the United States, enriches lives around the world by advancing scholarship in the humanities, social sciences, and natural sciences. Its activities are supported by the UC Press Foundation and by philanthropic contributions from individuals and institutions. For more information, visit www.ucpress.edu.

University of California Press
Oakland, California

Library of Congress Cataloging-in-Publication Data

Names: Madeira, Jody Lyneé, author.
Title: Taking baby steps : how patients and fertility clinics collaborate in conception / Jody Lyneé Madeira.
Description: Oakland, California : University of California Press, [2018] | Includes bibliographical references and index. |
Identifiers: LCCN 2017030457 (print) | LCCN 2017033914 (ebook) | ISBN 9780520966314 (ebook) | ISBN 9780520293045 (cloth : alk. paper) | ISBN 9780520293052 (pbk. : alk. paper)
Subjects: LCSH: Infertility—Patients—Counseling of—Moral and ethical aspects. | Fertility clinics—Evaluation. | Infertility—Alternative treatment. | Infertility—Psychological aspects. | Patient education. | Human reproductive technology. | Conception.
Classification: LCC RC889 (ebook) | LCC RC889 .M33 2018 (print) | DDC 616.6/92—dc23
LC record available at https://lccn.loc.gov/2017030457

Manufactured in the United States of America

27 26 25 24 23 22 21 20 19 18
10 9 8 7 6 5 4 3 2 1

Contents

Illustrations

Acknowledgments

My thanks and appreciation extend to so many people who have encouraged me, listened to me, and provided invaluable advice. Chief among them is my husband, Matt, and our children for always being there with love, understanding, patience, hugs, and back rubs during this project. They understand it is never possible to "do it all" well.

I'm deeply indebted to the women and men who took the time to sit down to complete a lengthy survey or telephone interview, to return to emotionally difficult subjects, issues some hadn't thought about for a long time, details that for others were a hell they endured every day. I've lived with their stories for several years now—accounts that still warm and chill me, make me laugh and make me cry, and fill me with gratitude for their experience and willingness to share. I'm also grateful to the reproductive medicine professionals—physicians, nurses, administrators, staff members—who spoke to me over the telephone or within a quiet room in their clinics. Their openness and interest in this project reveals their commitment to their patients and to reproductive health.

This project would never have come to fruition without several organizations' assistance. Projects like this take a great deal of time; the Federalist Society's generous award of a Searle Young Legal Scholar's Research Fellowship provided crucial interviewing time. Financing this research would have been very difficult without a substantial research grant from the Indiana University Faculty Research Support program. The Indiana University Maurer School of Law provided resources to hire additional research assistants. I am also grateful to organizations like RESOLVE (the National Infertility Association), the National Organization of Mothers of Twins Clubs, and clinics that allowed me access to forums and wall space. These organizations' tireless advocacy and the relationships they facilitate help individuals connect over reproductive issues, give voice to important matters, and effect needed reforms.

Finally, others have provided invaluable assistance in conversation or reading manuscript drafts, engaging and challenging me in critical and productive ways. Pamela Foohey and Rachel Guglielmo read and commented on the entire manuscript—a task beyond the boundaries of friendship. June Carbone tirelessly fielded questions throughout and provided invaluable remarks on drafts. Basia Andraka-Christou helped me to untangle research findings and also provided excellent draft contents. Debra Unger read drafts and talked me through some tough parts, and Laura Helper-Ferris delivered top-notch developmental editing. Hannah Eaton provided excellent research assistance. I would also like to thank (in alphabetical order) Susan Frelich Appleton, Gaia Bernstein, Naomi Cahn, I. Glenn Cohen, Susan Crockin, Judy Daar, Dov Fox, Michele Goodwin, Jim Hawkins, Kimberly Krawiec, Seema Mohapatra, Dara Purvis, Rhadika Rao, Rachel Rebouché, John Robinson, and other participants in the "Baby Markets" conferences over the years. Last but not least, I'm so thankful for my colleagues at Indiana University Maurer School of Law, whose constant curiosity, support, and engagement over the years has helped me to fill a scholar's shoes.

Prologue

Few topics are as compelling or contentious as how we create families—including reproductive decisions involving adoption, abortion, and reproductive medicine. Assisted reproductive technologies like intrauterine insemination (IUI), in vitro fertilization (IVF), and surrogacy generate particular controversy. Just as we make assumptions about many other "hot" issues, we often assume that people actually make or should make reproductive decisions in certain ways, or to achieve certain outcomes. One of our conventional assumptions is that emotions overwhelm patients and often hamper decision making. From this vantage point, emotions allegedly make patients more vulnerable, and it's dubious whether they can be trusted to make family-building decisions. Another conventional assumption is that doctors' profit incentives negatively affect their treatment decisions, prompting uncertainty over whether medical professionals can be trusted to put patients over paychecks. Finally, we assume that informed consent doctrine and documentation provide adequate protection against both strong emotions and predatory providers. But there are two problems with these assumptions: we confuse them with the truth, and we're often wrong. When we're wrong in the reproductive context, our mistakes have grave consequences for millions.

Taking Baby Steps asks readers to rethink conventional assumptions about how patients and their medical professionals collaborate in conception, allowing hundreds of men, women, and reproductive experts to explain in their own words how they negotiate key stages within the infertility experience. It is about infertility's associated emotions and stereotypes, and how they influence when and in what ways the public and professionals think about fertility treatment, decision making, and the meaning of consent. It is about the impact these emotions and choices have on friendships and marriages, how patients' friends and family sometimes don't understand or grow weary of discussing infertility. It is about how women in particular may face loneliness and stigma in the shadows of disempowering popular stereotypes of the "desperate" or "demanding" woman battling infertility. It is about women and men who turn to fertility professionals for emotional support as well as medical care, and about the enduring treatment partnerships they form that motivate patients to appear educated, cooperative, and in control, and spur doctors to inspire and be worthy of patients' trust.

Finally, it is about the legal framework that protects both doctors and patients addressing infertility. Relationships that progress to treatment trigger the safeguards of informed consent, a ritual involving documentation, explanations of procedures and risks, agreement to a plan of action, and signatures. Though experts believe (at least tacitly) that consent documentation diminishes medical paternalism and exploitation, patients experience it as legalistic, bureaucratic, generic, and cold; they prefer informative and personal conversations with providers. Though the vast majority of patients affirm they have read and understood these consent forms, they dislike forms that apparently protect doctors over patients. Instead, they find solace in the broader treatment relationships in which the acts of informing and consenting take place. Thus, this book attempts to turn the infertility experience inside out, exploring how women, men, and fertility professionals together negotiate infertility's rocky terrain and navigate the personal, medical, and ethical minefields inherent in creating life and building families—and move forward in the event of defeat.

. . .

I've experienced these treatment relationships and informed consent processes—and unexpected consequences—firsthand.

It was early (very early!) on a morning in mid-March 2007, a few weeks after my partner, Matt, and I had undergone IVF and transferred back three three-day-old embryos. In a fertility clinic on the outskirts of a major northeastern metropolis, I reclined on an examination chair resembling a dentist's, only with hair-raising equipment at my feet. In the sonographer's hands, an ultrasound wand shifted back and forth like an automotive stick shift, seemingly going from first to second gear, then back to first again, looking for the pregnancy that bloodwork had confirmed two weeks before. First and second gear were both fine with me—I feared being stuck in neutral, or, now that I was finally pregnant, being thrown abruptly into reverse.

"*I see two heartbeats*," enthused the ultrasound technician from somewhere near my feet.

This revelation caused *my* heart to temporarily relocate to my throat.

"I see another gestational sac down here, but there's nothing in it," the sonographer continued.

"What does that mean?" I asked.

"Oh, that happens when one embryo starts to implant in the uterine lining, then stops developing," the sonographer explained. "It's quite common."

"*Twins!*" I enthused to Matt some moments later, after I'd been reunited with my clothing. We pored over the ultrasound pictures we'd received. Each showed what looked like three black birds' eggs: gestational sacs, two of which had strange lines we'd been told were "fetal poles," the first measurements of our nascent offspring. The third was a black hole, a realm of mystery that, honestly, we ignored in our obsession with our twins. I still couldn't believe I was pregnant, but at the same time wasn't surprised to be expecting multiples. One week after our embryo transfer, a home pregnancy test had glowed positive seconds after I took it, and I'd been feeling breathless and dizzy for two weeks. Two weeks post-transfer, my fertility clinic administered a blood pregnancy test measuring the level of hCG, or human chorionic gonadotropin, the "pregnancy hormone" that embryonic cells generate after the embryo implants within the rich uterine lining. My results were extremely high; while the clinic expected a viable pregnancy's hCG levels to exceed 100 mIU/ml, mine had rocketed to 725 mIU/ml.

"Why don't you go in to work, hon?" I said to Matt, who had a long trek back to his office. "The important part was the ultrasound—I'll stay here to meet with the doctor and go in to the city after that."

"Are you sure?" he asked. I nodded.

"Okay," he agreed. After a final hug, he left the office, and I sank into a chair in the waiting room and stared in joyful disbelief at my ultrasound pictures until I was called back to see my reproductive endocrinologist, or RE—a fertility specialist. Though I calmly seated myself before his desk, I really wanted to throw myself into his arms.

"Sooooo . . ." intoned my RE. I beamed in anticipation.

"Twins!" I exclaimed, awaiting his response.

But my RE's words were far from the congratulatory statement I'd been expecting. "Triplets, actually. Two viable fraternal twin embryos, and a third gestational sac. We'll have to keep a close eye on that one."

. . .

When Matt and I first considered having children, we never imagined needing fertility treatment. But how many of us do? I knew my mother had had trouble conceiving me, enduring several miscarriages. But I was healthy, in my late twenties, and in great shape. Yet, here I was. The problem wasn't getting pregnant. In fact, my problems began after I miscarried my first pregnancy shortly before Christmas in 2005. When bleeding signaled that our baby was endangered—and our hopes and joy along with it—I was frantic, especially after learning there was nothing to be done. *Miscarrying. Mis-carrying.* That word cruelly intimated I'd done something wrong, like negligently jostling my child's nascent form or abandoning it. It suggested I was somehow a bad mother before I even gave birth. That day, Matt found me sobbing as if the world was ending—which it was, in a sense, for our poor baby, who had never seen it and now never would.

The following year, each month was another infertility battle, and I was getting worried about losing the war. Having miscarried my baby, I guess I misplaced my period as well, because I couldn't menstruate. No unfertilized egg burst out of its watery ovarian home and bumbled down my fallopian tube each month, triggering a shedding of uterine lining. Medical tests confirmed that I wasn't ovulating, but couldn't explain why. But without eggs, there couldn't be a pregnancy. I became increasingly cynical, furious that my body had failed me, my baby, and my partner. My world seemed newly populated by pregnant women and unwanted pregnancies. I dreaded trips to my OB/GYN, who merely reassured me time and again that miscarriages were "perfectly normal" and that I should "just relax." *Ha.*

Spring and summer came and went with no period to end my sentence of barrenness. My physician finally prescribed Clomid to stimulate ovulation, but the only thing it awakened was my inner Mr. Hyde, whom my more kindly Dr. Jekyll struggled to subdue. The most trifling things drove me to the refuge of our walk-in closet, where I would scream into a pile of sweaters.

Per our OB/GYN's orders, we waited one year before seeing an RE. Because our particular northeastern state mandated that health insurance cover infertility treatments, our fertility care would be paid for, but with two caveats: patients without male factor infertility had to complete three rounds of intrauterine insemination (IUI) before undergoing IVF, and there was a lifetime cap of three IVF cycles. Before my long-awaited Fertility Clinic Consultation (believe me, it merited capital letters), I solicited friends' recommendations on clinics and REs, researched clinic success rates, made an appointment with the best I could find, and waited.

I'll skip over much of what happened during the first few months of treatment, when I was on a merry-go-round of tests and consultations: testing, bloodwork, provider conversations, followed by more testing, more bloodwork, more conversations. Matt and I dutifully proceeded through three IUIs, accompanied by lengthy consent documents and shopping-spree-sized bags of fertility drugs, leaving trails of discarded syringe needles in our wake. We completed our third IUI early on Christmas morning, inventing some lame explanation for our absence to our holiday houseguests. When January 2007 brought confirmation that there would be no New Year's baby-to-be, I was more than ready to move on to IVF.

We began our first IVF cycle in February. The IVF regimen was almost identical to the IUI protocol, but with closer monitoring. Our egg retrieval proved successful, netting twenty-one mature eggs. The night of retrieval, I pictured those eggs frolicking with sperm in their petri dishes and awaited the next day's fertilization report. But our nurse delivered devastating news: only five embryos had fertilized, and we'd try to transfer the survivors back into my uterus on day 3 instead of day 5, per clinic policy. Crestfallen, I thanked the nurse and hung up. The expected fertilization rate for IVF embryos was approximately 75%; my rate had been closer to 25%. Sure this first cycle was a bust, I sobbed on Matt's shoulder. He tried to reassure me, reminding me *five* embryos gave us an excellent chance of having *one* baby. But I wasn't consoled; fertility math is notoriously unpredictable. Confident I knew better (I'd done a ton of Internet research, after all), I expected the worst.

The next three days crawled by. We wouldn't know how many embryos we had to transfer until that morning, and it was possible that all would stop dividing, leaving us with nothing. But our phone stayed mercifully quiet, and on the morning of transfer we drove to the clinic, wondering what we'd find. When we were ushered back into the surgical prep area, we saw what a difference three days could make.

On day three, viable embryos are six to ten cells in size. Embryos are graded according to their quality on a scale from A to D or 1 to 4, and are also evaluated for fragmentation, or how many portions of cells have broken off during their division. A high-quality embryo will have little to no fragmentation, and its cells will appear uniform in size. Any embryos that are not transferred are left to develop until day 5, and then, if they are still active, are frozen (or cryopreserved) for future use. We had two grade-A embryos and one grade-B, each with minimal fragmentation; two were eight-cell and the third had seven cells. One embryo, however, had an "M" in front of it; a query to the embryologist revealed this meant "mutation," conjuring up images of embryonic X-men invading my uterus. Seeing my look of consternation, the embryologist explained, "It means the embryo is dividing more rapidly than we'd expect."

But three embryos created another problem: we'd agreed beforehand to transfer only two embryos, and we didn't want to freeze a third embryo by itself, or endure a second IVF cycle. Sensing my hesitation, the embryologist pointed to the third embryo marked "M" and quipped, "This one might be happier in you than outside of you." It was ridiculous to anthropomorphize embryos as if they could be happy or sad, or indeed feel anything. Yet, that remark somehow resonated with me; part of me embraced the idea that M *needed* me. My first act of maternal love could be transferring it, rather than dooming it to a cold and uncertain cryopreserved future. And we only had a few more moments to make this decision.

"What are the odds of triplets if we transfer three instead of two?" I asked.

"Oh, about 3%," said the attending physician.

To me, those sounded like pretty good odds, given the likelihood that M wouldn't implant. That made the decision easier. Deliberately having triplets seemed irresponsible; dooming one of the three seemed heartless. Transferring all three and allowing nature (or God) to decide felt much better. The doctor had just said the odds that all three would implant were miniscule, and we were still not convinced we could get pregnant at all.

"Let's do it," I said.

. . .

Back in the RE's office, I shook my head in disbelief.

"Triplets?"

"Not a viable triplet pregnancy yet, but yes, you have three gestational sacs."

A stunned silence ensued. Despite transferring three embryos, I had never considered such a possibility.

"Would you ever consider selective reduction?" my RE asked.

"I suppose so," I responded, though I didn't even know what that meant. (Selective reduction is a procedure terminating one or more of the fetuses at approximately twelve weeks into the pregnancy.)

After I left the RE's office, I made a *very* memorable phone call to Matt.

"Hey, honey? It's not twins. It might be triplets."

One week later, after an episode of bleeding and an emergency ultrasound, a technician reassured me I was still pregnant—in fact, very much so. For now we had three heartbeats—and a *viable* triplet pregnancy.

. . .

Despite our initial shock, we didn't undergo selective reduction. Though I believe my RE felt I made the wrong decision, he deferred to our decision and remained supportive. He explained the risks we faced in carrying a "higher-order multiple" gestation. He even set up an appointment with Dr. Michael Evans, the New York physician who had pioneered the reduction procedure. But after seeing our three wiggly lima beans via ultrasound and contemplating yet another fertility-related procedure, I knew I couldn't go through with the reduction. Quite honestly, after three IUIs and one IVF cycle, I just wanted to be left alone.

I strongly believe everyone in this position must make this decision for themselves, according to what they feel is right. I'm thankful for this freedom. I also feel we couldn't have anticipated that all three embryos would implant and thrive, and so attach no blame to my RE, his staff, or for that matter, to us. We had researched IVF thoroughly and repeatedly read over every consent form that we received, and our RE ensured we understood what we read. So much of fertility treatment is still a black box, making reproductive medicine as much an art as a science. Nor was a single-embryo transfer a customary medical practice in 2007, at least for a three-day transfer; transfers ideally occur at the five-day mark with more developed embryos called blastocysts, hulking brutes hundreds of cells in size.

. . .

Our triplets—three boys—were born at exactly thirty-three weeks on September 15, 2007, after I'd been on bed rest since the twenty-fourth week of pregnancy, thanks to an "incompetent cervix" (a preposterous term) that was reluctant to support a triplet pregnancy. Nonetheless, modern medicine handed us three breathing, bleating, squirming newborns to bring home after three weeks in the neonatal intensive care unit, or NICU. I felt simultaneously giddy and guilty; many of the other pregnant triplet moms I met instead brought home heartbreak.

Our IVF cycle and treatment decisions have had lasting effects on me, my marriage, my career, and every other aspect of my life. That fateful phrase approving the embryo transfer—"Let's do it"—has come to mean an affirmation of life, love, and a willingness to encounter the unknown. As a result of making this affirmation, I also developed a strong and enduring appreciation and respect for REs and high-risk obstetricians, and a fascination with how medical decisions are made, which led me to incorporate reproductive technology and its legal consequences into my own teaching as a law professor. While preparing lecture materials for a related course, I was stunned that some experts suggested that women and couples experiencing infertility were "desperate" to conceive, implying that emotion imperiled their capacity to consent to treatment. Others suggested that fertility professionals exploited their vulnerable patients. But none of these characterizations matched my own experiences or those of other women I knew.

It wasn't that I hadn't been desperate—of course I had. It is nigh impossible to miscarry a wanted pregnancy and experience subsequent infertility without some feelings of anxiety, anguish, hopelessness, and despair. Instead, I suspected that experts' definitions of desperation didn't match mine. Far from the stereotypical desperation experience of paralysis and powerlessness, my emotions galvanized me, pushing me to seek answers, research treatments and providers, and speak to others about their experiences. Other women I had met described similar experiences.

The more I examined these characterizations of infertility and affected individuals, the more curious about their accuracy I became. Mainstream stereotypes of women with infertility depict a conglomerate of broken souls: selfish older career women, whiny and annoying mothers of multiples on reality television, and sensational stories about a woman on public assistance who birthed IVF octuplets, adding to a brood of six—a woman who is often denied her name—Nadya Suleman—and referred to as "Octomom." I didn't see my own face in that crowd, or those of my friends. These images increased my determination to investigate their accuracy, if necessary replacing them with fresher, more accurate and diverse portrayals of what infertility was, whom it affected, and how it changed lives. I wanted to destigmatize, even normalize infertility and its treatment, moving it from its social margins to the center of mainstream discussions about family and reproduction. In an echo of women who sought the right to terminate their pregnancies, I wanted to be unapologetic about my own choice to initiate one through reproductive medicine. Thus, in addition to triplets, my IVF cycle sowed the seeds of this research project, of which this book is the fruit.

. . .

This book begins with my own story, but focuses primarily on those of others, representing the diversity of experiences and perspectives that both enriches and challenges those who experience and explore this subject. Conceiving a child, watching it grow in the womb, and ultimately giving birth can rank among life's wonders. For many, pregnancy simply happens, often in unplanned or unexpected ways. But for others, an inability to conceive creates anxiety, frustration, and sometimes despair, and for centuries, people simply had to live with those emotions. Since the birth of Louise Brown in 1978—the first baby born through IVF—the reproductive medicine industry has flourished, injecting hope into reproductive attempts—hope that one's failure to conceive can be overcome, hope that it just requires sufficient determination, money, and medical skill.

This hope is increasingly in demand as more women defer childbearing. And these technologies, and the hope they create, are subject to few safeguards. In America, the reproductive medicine industry is still largely unregulated, and there are few federal or state restrictions on embryo transfer or cryopreservation.[1] Though many clinics belong to professional associations like the Society for Assisted Reproductive Technology (SART) or the American Society for Reproductive Medicine (ASRM) and agree to follow their clinical and ethical guidelines, these guidelines lack legal effect, with minimal consequences for noncompliance. If there are few policy incentives to regulate ART, there are even fewer motives for popular culture to accurately represent its patients. As women become more likely to defer childbearing, more celebrities, media characters, and public personas—from Celine Dion to *Friends'* Monica and Chandler, from Kate Gosselin to Nadya Suleman and her octuplets—represent what fertility treatments might offer. These representations matter to individuals seeking medical intervention to achieve motherhood, whether they're professionals who have surmounted every other life challenge, or women whose primary ambition has always been starting a family.

Although IVF is more affordable and available to a wider range of women (hence the importance of this book), it is not right for everyone. Deciding to try IVF involves a series of potentially gut-wrenching decisions, starting with the question of whether to try at all. IVF is expensive. The initial consultation often costs hundreds of dollars, and the first round of treatment will amount, on average, to $8,158, with medications costing an additional $3,000 to $5,000.[2] Insurance likely won't cover many expenses, even in the fifteen states mandating insurance coverage,[3] and out-of-pocket costs may be high. Deciding to undergo IVF may therefore compel people to mortgage a house, max out credit cards, or use savings for a down payment on medical treatments instead. It may involve going hat in hand to relatives, describing reproductive troubles and then asking to borrow money. It may mean postponing other dreams—starting a business, switching jobs, or reaching the point where monthly bills don't produce anxiety. And it may mean mortgaging the future, using funds intended for college tuition or retirement.

Treatment decisions also include which fertility interventions to pursue and what risks are acceptable—and these choices are influenced by informed consent disclosures. These treatments may involve surgery, drug regimens with potentially serious risks for mother or child, and novel procedures with uncertain consequences. Even routine treatments and medications have side effects; treatments may entail discomfort and sick leave, and medications alter hormone levels, change moods, and unsettle emotions. Some doctors recommend procedures of undetermined safety and efficacy. And there are no guarantees that these efforts will yield the longed-for pregnancy or live-born, healthy child.

Even standard treatments may pose difficult ethical choices. IVF increases the odds of getting pregnant with twins, triplets, or more and having to decide whether to undergo selective reduction. Some religions like Catholicism oppose IVF altogether; others mandate that believers follow guidelines, like using all fertilized embryos. Some couples who have no objection to producing embryos in a lab find it difficult to choose among those they create, or object to letting a doctor choose for them. Others might find that they can't reproduce without using donor eggs or sperm, meaning any resulting child is genetically related to only one of its intended parents. Then there's the question of what to do with surplus frozen embryos: should they be destroyed, transferred to another couple for reproductive purposes, donated to research, or frozen indefinitely?

Working through these choices raises profound questions about decision-making capacity, encompassing not only a patient's ability to choose appropriate treatment, but the nature of the industry guiding that choice. Doctors providing emergency services or advising cancer patients may not know the cost of recommended treatments or payment mechanics. But fertility specialists can't afford to ignore such matters. Most patients pay out of pocket, and Congress bars the use of federal research dollars for the very procedures that would most advance reproductive treatments. The reproductive medicine industry has been called the "Wild West" of the medical profession and, while not all criticisms are deserved, clinic professionals need to compete for patients and must remain cognizant of what their clients are willing and able to pay.

At its best, therefore, the world of reproductive medicine brings together distraught patients and business-minded professionals. It is little wonder that some critics, particularly those who counsel against deference to professional expertise, worry about women's exploitation. Will those who can't become pregnant on their own experience such despair and desperation that they become easy marks for the unscrupulous? Should someone else make certain choices for them, like how many IVF cycles they can afford, or what procedures offer the best prospects for success? Other critics direct their skepticism at patients, counseling hesitation before allowing an overambitious career woman access to a gestational carrier she might try to control, and worrying that a "desperate" woman might agree to marginal treatments that bankrupt her family or endanger her child's health. Critics on both sides of the political spectrum often draw upon these stereotypes to support limited access to reproductive procedures, reflecting deep-seated cultural wariness over trusting women to make good decisions about their bodies and reproductive capacities.

Here is where informed consent comes into play, in all its many incarnations. To safeguard patients from predatory providers, courts and lawmakers have created this legal doctrine to require medical providers to tell patients about a proposed treatment's material risks, benefits, and side effects, as well as other treatment options, before obtaining their consent.[4] But in practice, informed consent has acquired a much broader meaning, encompassing not just consent forms but conversations. The informed consent project is connected to the four moral principles of medical ethics: autonomy (respect for persons), beneficence (do good), nonmaleficence ("first, do not harm"), and justice (be fair).[5] Done correctly, consent may protect physicians from legal liability, but it also promotes patient autonomy, encourages the development of safe and high-quality procedures, helps to make care patient-centered, and improves patient-physician relationships. Receiving information may even be therapeutic for patients, conferring a sense of control, although some patients may find information emotionally threatening because of its content or ambiguity.[6] Thus, informed consent comes in several nested layers: informed-consent-as-ritual, informed-consent-as-relationship, and their combination, the informed consent project. Informed-consent-as-ritual is consent-as-bureaucratic-ritual, including the act of signing consent documents. Informed-consent-as-relationship represents consent-as-treatment-relationship, including interpersonal consent encounters. Together, informed-consent-as-relationship and informed-consent-as-ritual form the informed consent project, a merger of relationship and ritual. The informed consent project represents every potential consent purpose: a complex interpersonal encounter, a clinical process, a legal doctrine, and an ethical imperative, all of which are affected by concerns of emotion, trust, and profit.

Providers and patients often think of consent in these categories as well, as one provider stated,

> We've got informed consent for intrauterine insemination that's like a page long that I don't think I've ever discussed with a patient. It's nonsense; they can go home and sleep with each other for crying out loud. There's some circumstances in which the consent form is almost like a *pro forma* piece of bureaucratic paperwork, and there are other times when it's really critical and real and deserves the respect and time. . . . I shouldn't probably be allowed to distinguish . . . the bureaucratic [forms] from what's real . . . but in fact I do. (Dr. Bret Sternberg)

Here, Dr. Sternberg is distinguishing informed-consent-as-ritual—"bureaucratic paperwork"—from informed-consent-as-relationship—what's "critical and real." Moreover, his willingness to forego an IUI consent in a clinical situation where he believes it's irrelevant illustrates how providers can use informal treatment relationships to make informed-consent-as-ritual more meaningful, improving the entire consent project.

Informed-consent-as-ritual is legally and ethically required; informed-consent-as-relationship is not. But mandates that informed-consent-as-ritual must occur in certain ways that impose distance between patients and providers or that harm the treatment relationship within informed-consent-as-relationship undermine the entire project.

Informed-consent-as-relationship and informed-consent-as-ritual are both integral to a successful informed consent project. Without the trust and interaction characteristic of healthy treatment relationships, patients will likely dismiss consent tools, including documents, as bureaucratic, untrustworthy, and too generalized. But the consent forms, the consent ritual, and the signature requirement create the necessary opportunities and incentives for consent interactions to occur. Informed-consent-as-relationship humanizes and individualizes the consent project; informed-consent-as-ritual keeps it orderly and official.

According to patients, informed-consent-as-relationship begins far earlier than signing consent forms—often when they began to research infertility, during their first consultation, or when they commit to IVF or pay for a cycle, demonstrating the connection between consent and treatment relationships. And it lasts until the termination of treatment. But informed-consent-as-ritual typically occurs in a more predictable, focused, and short sequence. A patient is first given information, usually within a document, that describes material information about a treatment method, with or without an explanatory conversation with a care provider. Second, the patient signs a form giving consent to this treatment. Ideally, before signing, the patient can ask questions or request changes to treatment procedures, though emergency circumstances curtail time for reading forms and asking questions. Unfortunately, this traditional consent process often fails to significantly improve patients' understanding, so that some may consent to treatment without being informed, undermining autonomy and exposing care providers to legal liability. Patients may find forms overwhelming and may believe they protect doctors at patients' expense.

Most professionals take a broader view of the informed consent project, extending far beyond legalities to ethics, material information, what the consent experience is like, and why consent is essential, emphasizing professional responsibilities, patients' corresponding obligations, and the interaction between them. They regard *informed consent* as an umbrella term incorporating several behaviors and concepts, including conversation, patient education, personal capacities for explaining and understanding consent information, and evaluating these capacities.

Providers frequently regard informed-consent-as-ritual as the medical equivalent of Santa Claus or the Tooth Fairy—something that doesn't exist. Instead, they presuppose that patients generally don't read forms, that forms are largely unintelligible, and that documentation exists to satisfy a sue-happy society, not safeguard patient autonomy. Medical professionals have described consent forms as "make-believe papers,"[7] mere "rationality badges" that reassure their audiences all is "under control."[8] They believe that something has become lost in translating informed consent principles from theory into practice. Critics assert that courts and medical scholars have typically emphasized consent's legal aspects—the "obligation to make disclosure"—over the medical—the "meaning of informed consent,"[9] transforming consent into a bulwark against malpractice litigation. This is the same as confusing informed-consent-as-ritual for the entire consent project. But morally, informed consent concerns patients' autonomous choices, not professionals' liability for nondisclosure.[10] These dimensions of informed consent—legal doctrine, medical information, and moral viewpoint—are in tension, with profound implications for the consent experience, including undermining informed-consent-as-relationship.

Taking Baby Steps disentangles this complex web of personal emotions, relationships, and legal and ethical requirements. It interrogates how patients and reproductive medical professionals work together to build families, using patients' and fertility professionals' experiences and reflections upon emotions, decision making, and interpersonal relationships, against a backdrop of social norms, cultural attitudes, and market forces.[11] Their observations teach us how emotions, healthy treatment relationships, and effective legal protections for patients and providers are inextricably connected. An inability to conceive creates intense emotions, and individuals seek outlets not only in existing social relationships with partners, friends and relatives, but also within reproductive medicine, with gynecologists, REs, and fertility clinic personnel. Provider-patient relationships might become especially important for patients who lack other social supports, see these matters as too private, or have friends who have become pregnant or turned away from endless fertility-related conversations. These treatment relationships are hybrids of commercial and personal dynamics. While these relationships are founded upon trust and communication, their goal—fertility treatment—carries both benefits and risks, which in turn trigger a need for the informed consent project. Trust within these professional relationships depends on effective communication—something that most consent forms don't achieve. But the adversarial and litigious winds that blow informed-consent-as-ritual into treatment relationships, and its distanced and clinical language, might seem rude and unwelcome intrusions into the interpersonal warmth and hope that treatment relationships kindle.

Lawyers, not doctors, police informed consent doctrine and draft forms that supposedly both insulate professionals from liability and protect and inform patients. These contradictory goals often produce Frankenstein-like documents that recite laundry lists of risks and side effects, allowing clinics to prove that providers have warned patients—of *everything*. Understood for what it is—a legal process designed to both educate patients and shield doctors from liability—informed-consent-as-ritual likely breeds cynicism, not trust, encouraging patients to put more stock in providers' discussions of risk. While consent conversations might include the same disclosures as consent forms, they can also be tailored to individual patient needs and relational nuances.

And not all forms of trust are equivalent; interpersonal trust tends to run much deeper than the shallower (but perhaps more visible) institutional forms of trust shored up by legal protections. Thick trust—grounded in strong and supportive personal relationships—can be distinguished from thin trust—a social form of trust that depends on "shared social network and expectations of reciprocity."[12] Thick trust is what prompts me to donate a kidney to save a friend's life; thin trust allows me to permit the surgeon I have just met to extract the kidney. Thin trust, in turn, is different from institutional trust, like that in government or hospitals.[13]

Most patients already place trust in their providers because they are socialized to believe that medical professionals play healing and caring roles. Though consent documents can reinforce this trust, it is different from the thick trust that sustains healthy provider-patient relationships. More personal and robust, this thick trust likely replaces and eclipses the thin trust anchored by consent documents. Thus, in patients' eyes, strong provider-patient relationships and growing trust in treatment teams can weaken consent forms' significance. Documents are only one part of the consent process, which extends throughout treatment and incorporates many other aids, including conversations. Patients may therefore be skeptical of consent forms, yet retain faith in the process.

In essence, infertility-related emotions and provider-patient relationships coexist in largely unregulated, heavily commodified, and profoundly intimate environments. Both create dilemmas that may require legal intervention and provide frameworks that structure and constrain solutions. Emotions and conceptive desires affect patient vulnerability, but also motivate patients to form effective relationships with doctors and other fertility clinic personnel. Though these relationships are very much business associations, neither party usually experiences them as distanced or arms-length. And the more interpersonally successful these relationships are, the more problematic they may be for purposes of informed-consent-as-ritual.

This creates two paradoxes. First, although informed consent doctrine supposedly facilitates trust by outlining what providers can do to patients, it also seeds *dis*trust, because of the need to set these boundaries in the first place. This distrust is communicated more explicitly in consent forms. Second, the deeper the interpersonal bond and trust between provider and patient when consent forms are signed, the more likely patients are to discount these documents as routine or ritualistic. And provider-patient relationships are probably quite strong by then, since IVF consent forms are usually signed late in the game, after a couple has committed emotionally and financially to undergoing IVF. Thus, informed consent (as conventionally understood) in effect harbors a viper in its bosom: the biggest threat to informed consent may not be poor patient comprehension or failure to read consent documents, but the successful doctor-patient relationship this doctrine ostensibly exists to promote.

To date, these dynamics have gone largely unrecognized; critics have instead focused on other consent problems like poor reading, comprehension, and recall. *Taking Baby Steps* explores their dimensions, inviting readers into the lived experience of receiving and providing in vitro fertilization (IVF), privileging the voices of 478 participants, including 127 interviewed patients, 267 surveyed patients, and 84 professionals: doctors, nurses, clinic staff, and mental health experts. It seeks to understand how men and women undergoing fertility treatments make decisions, how medical professionals frame available choices, and how doctor-patient, patient-family, and family-clinic relationships contribute to the quality of reproductive decision making. In doing so, this book places great emphasis on emotions and their roles in guiding both patients' conduct and relational dynamics between providers and patients. Effective decision making unites reason and emotion, and relationships, including profoundly emotional ones, affect individuals' ability to weigh alternatives and reach reasoned conclusions.

Part 1 of this book focuses on infertility-related emotions, from women's first inklings that something might be amiss to the moment they pass through a fertility clinic's doors. Chapter 1 chronicles infertility's emotional contours and their effects on friendly and romantic relationships, chapter 2 explicates the complicated politics of desperation that underlie many popular stereotypes of individuals struggling with infertility, and chapter 3 examines how infertility-related emotions can both help and hinder treatment goals. Part 2 follows individuals into the fertility clinic as they become patients, documenting the concerns they and their providers encounter. Chapter 4 explores how and when individuals decide to seek fertility treatment, how they choose a provider, what they expect from treatment experiences, and how they approach treatment relationships. Chapters 5 and 6 address patients' and providers' perspectives on treatment relationships, including stereotypes of ideal and difficult patients, whether patients should be assertive or aggressive, the importance of trust and bedside manner, how emotions affect decision making, and what happens when one party doesn't meet the other's expectations. Part 3 turns to the more bounded ritual event of signing forms, exploring how both emotions and provider-patient relationships influence informed consent. Chapter 7 discusses how bureaucracy influences the entire consent project, in particular treatment relationships, and chapter 8 delves into the experience of informed consent, explicating how emotions, rituals, and relationships affect providers' and patients' perspectives on informed consent interactions, protections, and tools. Finally, chapter 9 explains why these factors prompt patients to view IVF consent forms differently from other documents requiring them to select embryo dispositions in the event of their deaths or divorce. This book concludes by suggesting ways to reenvision the informed consent project.

All three parts of this book engage popular infertility stereotypes that have very real effects on individuals' decision-making behaviors. Part 1 tackles emotion-related stereotypes like the "desperate" woman, explaining how real women experience infertility-related emotions and their reactions to this politicized portrayal. Part 2 addresses the related stereotype of the "difficult" patient, usually the desperate woman in treatment, who becomes overly deferential or aggressive in clinical settings. Seeking to earn providers' approval, many patients try to avoid this stereotype, adopting "ideal" behaviors like being informed, responsive, cooperative, and professional. Finally, part 3 confronts the stereotype of the "detached" patient, who wants to proceed with IVF while bypassing informed-consent-as-ritual or other critical treatment steps. To avoid this stereotype, patients emphasize that they read and understand consent materials, and strive to appear knowledgeable in provider conversations. Thus, although these stereotypes don't match most individuals' treatment experiences, they still exert a strong, stressful, and often destructive influence upon patients' and professionals' expectations, presenting yet another complication they must overcome. And overcome it they do, through resilience, creativity, and support from their reproductive medical providers.

PART ONE

Infertility as an Emotional Experience

CHAPTER I

Consent and Sensibility

Emotions, Decision Making, and Informed
Consent in Reproductive Medicine

Let's not forget that the little emotions are the great captains
of our lives and we obey them without realizing it.

—Vincent Van Gogh, 1889

Emotions affect everyone undergoing infertility; women experience infertility as a chronic medical condition, and have psychological symptoms equivalent to those of patients with cancer, cardiac issues, and hypertension.[1] Infertility had pronounced emotional consequences for 91% of patients interviewed and 82% of those surveyed. But emotional effects are starkly different from person to person and often unpredictable.

Sonya Saunders has lived this unpredictability. Before Sonya married her husband, James, they knew he had varicocele, a condition in which enlarged scrotal veins cause low sperm production and decreased sperm quality. But after trying to conceive for six months, they learned that James actually had a sperm count of *zero*—something his urologist hadn't seen in thirty years of practice. After James underwent corrective surgery, his urologist reassured them they still had plenty of time to conceive and should wait a year before trying. But six months later, James's sperm count still hadn't improved. Distraught, Sonya visited an RE for her own workup, only to have her doctor tell her, "You have a genetic condition where you'll never be able to have kids." She was devastated for the second time in as many years: "I hyperventilated, couldn't stop crying during that meeting, I felt like I just got hit by a freight train." She felt helpless in the face of infertility: "How much money are we going to spend on this? How far are we going to go? What are we going to do?"

Advised to try "natural IVF"—where patients don't take medication to stimulate their ovaries and increase egg production—Sonya and James completed four cycles over the following year. One cycle was cancelled, and three resulted in embryo transfer, but none resulted in pregnancy. These experiences took a terrible emotional toll. "By the third negative, I was having a major breakdown. . . . I wasn't getting the help I needed, and I was in big trouble," Sonya said. "It just starts to build up and you don't realize how much it's unraveling. . . . At that time, I would talk about suicide all the time." Eventually, she found a RESOLVE support group and counselor. "Being with people that have gone through the same thing helped the most," Sonya reflected. "I don't think the isolation can ever be overrated." By this time, infertility had wreaked havoc on her personal relationships. "The majority of my friends are on [their] second or third kid; you feel so far left behind," she explained. "Nobody can grasp [infertility, so] you lose the ability to talk to your best friends about something that can be so incredibly painful. . . . Your external support system is just crushed . . . so your marriage has an incredible strain."

The emotional dynamics in Inez Griffith's conceptive journey were markedly different. When she was 33, Inez consulted her gynecologist for severe bleeding, only to be told she should already have had children and might need a hysterectomy. "I came home and cried about a bazillion tears and thought it was the end of the world," she recalled. Soon after Inez began dating her husband, Chris, the two discussed starting a family. Anticipating difficulty, they visited an RE to formulate a game plan: first attempt IVF with Inez's eggs, then move on to donor eggs, and finally try adoption. This strategy helped Inez to cope: "we wouldn't just put ourselves into desperation trying again and again and again." Inez determined she'd not allow infertility to dominate her: "I went to a couple of support groups. . . . there was this one woman who you can tell she's been through a lot of failed cycles, and she had this angry, miserable look on her face. . . . I can certainly understand feeling that way, but I'm like, 'I don't want this to be my end result.' That's when my husband and I really sat down and said, 'We're not just gonna keep beating something and start throwing something in and just keep being disappointed.'" It took only one IVF cycle for Inez to became pregnant with her first child; she conceived her second with a frozen embryo transfer. She credited her emotional equanimity to conceiving easily: "we did luck out, and I don't know, if we hadn't, [we might've said], 'Then let's just keep trying; the next time it'll work.'"

Both Sonya and Inez had to confront an infertility diagnosis, and each made the same choice—to seek fertility treatment. But this choice yielded two wildly disparate outcomes and two strikingly different narratives. Whereas Inez was all too aware she'd need medical intervention to conceive, Sonya experienced an unforeseen series of painful setbacks as each proffered remedy proved unsuccessful. And while Inez ultimately conceived twice, Sonya was still stranded in IVF hell at the time of her interview and felt victimized by bad advice and misfortune. How can infertility produce two such radically different emotional accounts?

As these two narratives illustrate, infertility is an umbrella term covering a multitude of causes, contexts, emotions, and outcomes. People speak of an infertility "journey," a flexible metaphor implying that these sojourns can have different durations, don't always progress in a steady or orderly fashion, and can be easy or difficult (or both, at different times). Infertility journeys aren't only about getting from Point A to Point P(regnant), but also about the experience of traveling itself; like all journeys, this one takes people to new destinations, requires planning, and changes lives.

Emotions often spark infertility journeys, which in turn change personal identities; begin and end relationships with friends, family, and medical professionals; and trigger medical and ethical decisions. Emotions supposedly disrupt individuals' lives and pose problems for decision-making capacity. But for better or worse, they also play key decision-making roles. Thus, emotions are like compass points that help individuals to orient themselves and find direction within the infertility experience—but unlike these points, they can change in unpredictable ways throughout this disorienting journey.

CAPACITY INCAPACITATED?

As history goes, it's been a mere heartbeat since a radical transformation took place in medicine, from the "commonsense" assumption that doctors are logical treatment decision makers to the conviction that such choices should be left to competent patients. Patient autonomy is now the watchword for doctor-patient interactions—unless questions about patient capacity arise.

But in reproductive technology, patient autonomy is far from commonly accepted. Many voices have challenged the presumption that women generally make informed reproductive choices, from religious and political leaders to scholars and even feminists. The criticism is often phrased the same, regardless of the reproductive choice at issue, and goes something like this: "She wants desperately, blindly to _____" (get an abortion, become a mother, donate her eggs, become a surrogate, or get her tubes tied).[2] One scholar has claimed that patients undergoing IVF "have difficulty absorbing medical information and rationally evaluating the risks and benefits of various treatment options," and that "the power of wishful thinking obscures rational deliberation. Infertile women will often opt for any treatment option presented, regardless of the physical, psychological, or financial price."[3]

Other voices challenge whether the reproductive endocrinologists who help patients make treatment decisions can maintain professional ethics and prioritize patient care in the face of profit motives.[4] One author, for example, asserted that "the underlying principle of fertility treatment is the right of the paying consumer to reproductive freedom," and described ART as "relentlessly profit-making."[5] A high-risk pregnancy physician remarked that reproductive medicine "has become a consumption specialty," and claimed that REs, like their patients, will "do anything": "[t]here [are] so many of them out there, they compete among each other to see who gets the patients, so they'll do anything to maximize the chances of achieving a pregnancy."[6]

In most areas of practice, insurance providers or hospital associations provide a buffer between professional compensation and patient payments. An emergency room doctor doesn't need to worry whether she'll be paid, even if she provides care to indigent patients. The typical RE, however, does need to be concerned. The pervasive lack of insurance coverage for treatments like IVF makes most fertility processes elective, to patients' consternation, more like cosmetic surgery than cancer care. Within reproductive medicine, independent, private providers or university clinics provide most services. These entities (and often the REs they employ) must be aware of their practices' bottom lines, lest they find themselves out of business.[7] Clinics' financial health depends on their ability to attract patients who can afford their services. Given these incentives to treat as many paying patients as they can handle, critics question these clinics' motives, citing highly publicized abuses to demonstrate that reproductive medicine professionals are untrustworthy.[8] Patients' vulnerabilities compound these issues, making professionals' profit motives seem especially dangerous. Providers benefit from the freedom of choice fertility patients supposedly enjoy and also, critics allege, "from transferring practical, psychological, and moral responsibility for decision making to patients."[9]

These critiques of patients and professionals aren't necessarily inaccurate or inappropriate. Reproductive decisions *do* fundamentally alter individuals' identities, whether they concern running a business or deciding to genetically test embryos. Reproductive decision making *does* engage emotions. Patients often *are* vulnerable. Doctors *do* have to balance clinic practices, profit margins, standards of care, and patient needs. But these statements are also true throughout medicine and, indeed, for many other important life decisions. What *is* troublesome is when media, policymakers, and scholars misrepresent decision making's emotional consequences to suggest desperation and greed are practically universal, experienced in the same ways, with virtually the same consequences: undermining rationality, ethical values, and professional standards of care. This skepticism prompts critics to propose placing reproductive decisions in others' hands. Politicians and experts have suggested restricting IVF for certain populations,[10] limiting how many embryos can be transferred per cycle, mandating greater psychological screening for patients, or supervising reproductive medicine providers. Some regulatory oversight might be appropriate if informed by professional standards, but claims that patients undergoing fertility treatment lack normal decision-making capacity violate patient autonomy and demean their integrity. Instead, fertility care should start with the same presumptions of patients' and providers' decision-making capacity as other health fields, with reforms tailored to specific abuses or evolving medical practices.[11]

Characterizations of patient and provider capacity matter because medical care takes place within a legal, rational bureaucracy. Under the rubric of informed consent, this bureaucracy provides guidelines for what doctors can do to patients and when. Usually, *consent* means that patients sign forms that doctors give them, sometimes after discussing them. But there are serious doubts as to whether this transaction really does inform patients and ensure their competent consent. The first part of this book questions whether consent *can* be informed within reproductive medicine, whether patients are capable of making good treatment decisions despite strong emotions.

A BUMPY RIDE: INFERTILITY AS DISRUPTION

When you begin planning your family, you get excited because it's something that you've always wanted and the time has come to make your dreams a reality. As with anything, you begin with anticipation, you hope the outcome is successful. For example, you've waited to

travel to Europe and the time has finally come. . . . You go on the
trip and everything you have waited for, that you anticipated, that
you dreamed, was crushed as your flight was canceled, your hotel
burned down or someone hacked your bank account and you don't
have the money to go. However, you don't give up because . . . it's
been a lifelong dream. . . . Meanwhile, all your friends have gone
and traveled there and experienced great things and you're still stuck
at home.

—Sheri Lopez

Reproductive decision making takes place in a unique emotional, psychological and physiological context. One way to understand what this might
be like is to imaginatively step into the shoes of an individual confronted
with an infertility diagnosis, making her a "we" instead of a "she."

For most, conceiving a child is fairly easy—perhaps too easy, if pregnancies are unwanted. If we can't conceive, we can seek medical assistance, but at steep prices, leaving many stranded without access to fertility technology. If we're lucky enough to access these treatments, we must
submit to complicated monthly treatment routines, including anything
from ovulation-stimulating medications, to timed intercourse, to IUI or
IVF. This is a very stressful time; we might learn smack-dab in the middle
of our IVF cycle that we have too few mature eggs or unusually low
embryo fertilization rates. And at its end, we face the interminable "two-
week wait" before the final pregnancy test. Even a positive pregnancy test
doesn't grant us respite from anxiety and heartbreak, since miscarriage
is still possible. Infertility disrupts our lives in varying ways, depending
on our personalities, relationship dynamics, coping skills, doctor-patient
relationships, medical history, prior conceptive attempts, and just plain
luck. We likely endure these journeys alone, or with our partners.

Infertility also forces us to negotiate difficult decisions—whether to
continue treatment, what interventions to pursue, how to finance care,
and sometimes how to get through the day—all while wrenching emotions may destabilize our core feelings of identity and competence. In
infertility, as in many other life circumstances, we must make complex
choices among numerous options with conflicting advantages and disadvantages and uncertain outcomes.[12] These decisions often require us
to weigh religious and personal values, ethics, financial assets, short-
and long-term goals, and partner preferences. Deciding what to do may
change our sense of who we are and what we believe.

Infertility's impact starts with diagnosis. Cultural expectations about
what's "normal" in certain life stages can structure our lives; trying
and failing to meet these expectations is disruptive, especially when

unanticipated.[13] We may think we have a "normal" potential to conceive until infertility catches us unawares. Afterward, we might feel broken. Even those of us who anticipate difficulty conceiving find an infertility diagnosis unsettling, a crossroads where we must halt to determine what comes next.

Infertility first compels us to choose whether to accept a childless future—a decision that entails others, like how much we really want children, what we might give up to have them, what risks we're willing to take, and whether our children must be genetically related. For many of us, this is the most momentous decision we've encountered as adults. Accepting childlessness might be a predictable and "safe" option, but may over time be the most painful. Undergoing treatment means seeking a future with children at unknown cost, a willingness to make the necessary sacrifices, and facing the real risk of not having children anyway. Which path is most attractive depends on our personalities, needs and desires, support skills and systems, and physical, emotional, and material resources.

Adjusting to and negotiating infertility, then, requires that we learn how to tell this event within our life stories.[14] Telling stories about disruptive events is a healthy coping mechanism. We revise our life stories to include events we need to make sense of—to understand, redefine, resist, and ultimately own their effects on our identities, relationships, careers, and life plans. This, in turn, helps us to work through these events, solve the problems they pose, endure them, and even defy them. Emotions are undeniably important to these storytelling processes.

How disruptive infertility feels depends on how easily we're able to include it within our life stories. Before we suspect that something might be wrong, we often use our family medical histories to create and structure our family-building expectations—sometimes to our detriment. "I never really even thought of the possibility that it wouldn't be easy for me," Kathryn Patton reflected. "My grandmother had seven kids. . . . and my mom had us very quickly and young." Difficulty conceiving is particularly shocking for those experiencing "secondary infertility"— when a person becomes infertile after successfully having children without medical intervention. "That was something that never entered my mind," said May Weiss. "I was that person which we all hate now." Those who anticipate difficulty conceiving find it easier to adjust. Given her medical and family history, Shannon Ward wasn't surprised when she couldn't conceive: "I'd had irregular periods for my whole life; it had occurred to me that we'd have trouble getting pregnant, and we knew that [my husband]'s brother had had male factor infertility as well. . . . When we were trying month after month after month and not getting pregnant, . . . so I think, in some ways, that emotional difficulty was kind of a bit abated for us."

Those who have supported a friend or relative through infertility may also feel more prepared. Shannon Ward took heart because her sister had conceived using donor eggs: "watching her go through it just a few years before me is where I learned a lot about IVF and also the donor egg option. . . . So, it was very emotional, but . . . I knew the end result was still possible."

Patients' reflections on their initial reactions to infertility diagnoses testify to its strong impact on life stories. But how exactly do emotions shape our adjustment and decision making, and with what consequences?

BACK TO THE FUTURE: EMOTION'S ROLE IN COPING AND DECISION MAKING

A popular saying advises, "When life gives you lemons, make lemonade." But when infertility sours life plans and threatens bitter disappointment, making lemonade requires us to roll up our sleeves and engage our emotions.

After a diagnosis of infertility, we need to take stock, look ahead to what may come, and choose how to react.[15] Here, as in other life situations, our emotions influence our interpretations, judgments, reasoning, and decision making. The conventional wisdom that emotion weakens our ability to make "rational" decisions is far too simplistic; emotion always affects our decisions, whether it helps or harms them. Infertility, a threatening event, can demand our attention and influence how we react, what seems relevant, how much we focus on this issue, how carefully we consider information, and whether we use stereotypes and other shortcuts to evaluate options, or opt for deeper reflection.[16] Emotions also affect why we make decisions in the first place and which options seem most attractive. Making decisions about infertility generates additional emotions; time constraints or uncertain outcomes can create anxiety, and time delays can produce anger and frustration.[17]

Deciding what to do about infertility means working through many highly uncertain and complex choices with great personal and social stakes. We don't make infertility-related decisions like a computer, mechanically analyzing each option's mathematical risks and benefits, comparing their immediate and long-term consequences.[18] This would be impossible; even if we can identify all possible options, we don't know what will work or each outcome's precise likelihood.[19] This would also take too long, strand us in impossible calculations, force us to work with impossible amounts of information and chains of events,[20] and require us to compare incommensurable outcomes[21]—and most of us are already notoriously bad with probabilities and statistics to begin with.[22]

Instead, we rely largely on our gut feelings about infertility and particular treatment options to make these kinds of decisions.[23] "Bad" gut feelings can direct our attention toward negative outcomes and serve as "alarm bells" or "red flags"; maybe we don't want to voluntarily accept childlessness and opt for treatment or adoption. "Good" gut feelings can steer us toward positive outcomes;[24] if we have enough money to pursue IVF *or* adoption, we might opt to adopt, since its outcome is more certain. Our emotions play key roles in forming these gut feelings, and even in making them seem inherently "rational."[25]

Thus, when confronting infertility and making decisions, we project ourselves into the future, choosing among options from Clomid to IVF to childlessness. To do so, we weigh possible outcomes, their likelihood, and their financial, emotional, psychological, and social "costs" and benefits. Our gut reactions to each option and outcome help us determine what steps to take. Our emotions usually improve these decision-making processes, so long as they are not extreme or overwhelming.[26]

Just because our emotions can improve decision making, however, doesn't mean we always choose well, particularly about uncertain events—not because of emotion, but because we don't have the right information or simply because we're human, subject to human biases.[27] We might be misinformed, overestimate how intensely certain events (like childlessness or an unsuccessful cycle) will impact our lives, or assume our current wishes will apply to future situations.[28] We even selectively remember the emotions that past events generate, remembering only how we felt during an event's most intense moment and at its end.[29] For instance, assume we experience more negative than positive emotions throughout six unsuccessful IVF cycles. But if we conceive on our seventh try and birth a healthy child, we may well remember our treatment experiences quite positively. Nor can we do much to ensure emotion influences our decision making in healthy ways; trying to suppress our emotions often intensifies them.[30] It might help to think of setbacks like an unsuccessful IVF cycle as just one step in a longer process of trying to conceive, or as a learning opportunity.[31]

Medical challenges like infertility and treatment decisions cause especially strong emotions, especially given medicine's inherent risk and uncertainty.[32] Strong emotions can prompt us to make a decision too early, without adequately considering other options, or too late, when treatment becomes impossible.[33] At other times, stress may motivate us to carefully research options, knowing we've only one opportunity to make the best possible decision. But medical decision making can also be therapeutic, too, when it provides strategies for dealing with infertility.[34] Even undergoing testing can reduce anxiety and stress, provide answers, and make us feel as if we're doing *something*, and therefore aren't entirely helpless.

Specific emotions also influence our behavior in particular ways. Anger can motivate us to take treatment risks,[35] attempt to change providers, or fight against infertility.[36] When we're sad, we're more likely to blame fate or situational circumstances, attribute infertility to divinity or destiny,[37] believe we'll never conceive,[38] and avoid pregnant women.[39] Anxiety, on the other hand, makes us feel that infertility threatens our future and can motivate us to learn more.[40] We experience disappointment when our choices turn out worse than we expected,[41] and we might withdraw from problematic situations or people.[42] Fear renders us more pessimistic about the future,[43] makes riskier events seem more likely,[44] and prompts us to choose the "sure thing" or avoid a decision altogether.[45] When we feel guilty, we blame ourselves for bad outcomes, focus more on the decision at hand, and narrow our choices. Happiness encourages us to expect or even overestimate[46] that we'll get pregnant,[47] and hope makes us feel a little personal control over what happens,[48] but surprise makes us feel that others are responsible for certain outcomes and that positive outcomes are unpredictable.[49] Finally, we feel regret when we realize later that another option was better.[50]

Making infertility-related decisions can unleash all of these highly charged and interdependent emotions. Understanding how they influence our decisions reinforces that these emotions aren't random, but linked to particular options and outcomes. Ideally, we'll choose options that make us feel good and that protect cherished goals, values, and relationships. Once made, our choices become courses of action with real-world outcomes that carry their own emotional consequences.

REASONED EMOTIONS: PROVIDERS' REACTIONS TO PATIENTS' AFFECT

With this brief glimpse into infertility's disruptive and emotional experience, we can step out of patients' shoes and into providers' to gauge their reactions to patients' emotionality. Most providers expect patients' emotions to affect decision making—"almost everything about having babies is emotional" (Dr. Errol Walter)—and grow concerned only when these emotions effect harm.

Patients' desires and life goals—like having a family—are both cognitive and emotional, and it's difficult to contemplate changing them even when odds become slim. "If they've thought their whole life they wanted to have three babies and they have two, they just can't put that away. There's somebody missing, and I think that's an emotional type of reaction," explained Nurse Melanie Simons. Indeed, why should reproductive medicine *not* be emotional, in keeping with other medical treatments? "I would actually be worried if there was no emotion at all," opined Dr. Heike Steinmann, "that kind of person, like an automaton, . . . I mean, it's not like taking out your gall bladder." As Dr. Denzel Burke said, "It's impossible to remove emotion from anything in medicine . . . [especially] when you start talking about . . . family and your future, the idea of you continuing on your family name or your family genetics and then all of the social expectations and family expectations of you having children." Thus, the concern isn't patients' emotions, but their effects.

In providers' experience, emotions affect patients in complex and contradictory ways, steering them toward or away from treatments. Intense feelings might motivate some to pursue more aggressive treatments early on. In these situations, patients usually feel stressed, frustrated, and think they have no other options. Patients who are "just tired of getting disappointed" (Dr. Stefanie Burgstaller) will "want to do the most aggressive treatment this afternoon" (Dr. Cary Priestley). Or they might want to be aggressive with embryo transfers: "I have a hard time convincing somebody to put in one embryo. You can show them the statistics" (Dr. Rory Fontaine). Or patients could attempt to cycle too soon after an unsuccessful attempt: "you say, 'I'm very sorry but the pregnancy test was negative,' and . . . they say, 'Oh, what do I do next? Let's do another cycle.' Once they've thought it through, most patients become more rational" (First Year RE Fellow Dr. Yazmin Kuhn). Or they might attempt any treatment option: "If they're tearful, emotional, willing to do anything, . . . if you say, 'Well, you can do these three therapies, but there's really no proven utility,' they sometimes want to try them anyway, because they don't want to have regrets" (Dr. Jie Hu). Patients are eager to dot every "i" and cross every "t."

Conversely, emotions also deter patients from using certain medications or moving on to more advanced treatments, and may even drive them to prematurely cease treatment. Patients who undergo more cycles "have a different kind of capacity for stick-to-it-iveness and pain than maybe the one who can only do the one" (Psychologist Valerie Ness), and certain patients, "if they're depressed and they're tired, . . . can give up prematurely" (Dr. Teagan Shepherd). "I think patients just get burned out. A lot of them just get to the point where the stress is so much that they decide they just got to take a break," Dr. Gerard Gabler explained. "Unfortunately, when they're 38, 39 and decide to take a break, that can certainly be detrimental to their overall chances."

But whether emotions encourage patients to prematurely begin or end treatment, they are particularly problematic when they distort perceptions of what providers are saying. "You try to encourage people to come to closure . . . and they often will kind of refuse to listen because in their mindset they aren't done yet," remarked Dr. Wes Hoffman. "It makes it hard to kind of convince them from a medical standpoint that they need to think about other things, and emotionally they aren't ready." This closure is a process patients must work through themselves. Significantly, competing needs and desires might diminish emotions' influence on treatment decisions. "Every once in a while, I'll get patients that say, 'Well I'm not terribly [eager] to have a child. I'm doing this to make my husband happy or what not, . . . I don't really want to do anything all that involved,'" explained Dr. Corwin Summers.

EMBARKING ON THE INFERTILITY EXPEDITION

Being diagnosed with infertility is like becoming stranded upon an exposed, rocky precipice at twilight with no obvious paths to safety. We can easily identify with the horror of being trapped in that new base camp as darkness falls, left to figure out the safest route down, knowing nothing of the terrain and trying to avoid injury. An unknown fate awaits at the bottom—there could be a child or no child, stronger or weaker relationships with partners and friends, bankruptcy or manageable levels of debt. Medical professionals, like Sherpas, create paths for us and provide guidance and support along the way. This descent can be terrifying, tiresome, and costly, but there also might be beauty along the way.

Jessica Frazier found herself on that precipice after her OB/GYN misdiagnosed her with blocked fallopian tubes. She had a panic attack: "I was sweating and had to sit down on the pavement and felt really dizzy and freaked out. . . . That initial shock was pretty intense." Others, like Tracey West, went "through the stages of grief." But some found it empowering to have answers. Eva Davidson said, "Once someone said, 'You know what, you've gotta do IVF, . . . this is the only way you can get pregnant,' I said, 'Okay, let's do it.'" A specific infertility diagnosis can be a turning point that means new information, treatment possibilities, and hope. To Brittany Watson, her diagnosis was "the light at the end of the tunnel": "When it all finally clicked what was wrong, it was this emotional, cathartic experience. I think I cried a good bit."

Living through infertility—descending from the precipice base camp—can seem like a long journey comprised of smaller stages, like monthly attempts to conceive. If infertility is analogous to being trapped on this rocky outcrop, we can call the overarching process of adjusting to and negotiating infertility an "Expedition" and the descent's shorter segments "Attempts." Ideally, each Attempt allows us to move our base camps farther down the slope, getting closer to Expedition goals like conceiving. Because infertility's topography obscures the landscape, we might not know how far we've come until we're almost at the bottom.[51] This Expedition isn't so much a progression as it is a continual readjustment to new terrain. This analogy captures the infertility journey's individual legs, during which we continually adjust to outcomes and reassess next steps. If we could chart what an Attempt feels like, it might resemble a succession of peaks and valleys, displaying a "roller-coaster" pattern of emotional highs and lows. Attempts are the building blocks of our infertility experience, the moments we live in and through. In contrast, we're most aware of the Expedition at its beginning and end, or when we pause to consider our journey thus far.

Emotional Baggage: Packing for the Infertility Expedition

Our emotions affect decision making differently in Expeditions and Attempts. Throughout our Expeditions, they help us to choose among viable options, particularly whether and how to seek treatment. In Attempts, our emotions assist us in working through our choices and their outcomes and evaluating our decisions so we can make better ones in the future. How long we stand on the precipice after receiving an infertility diagnosis varies widely. Eventually, we must choose a course of action, accepting involuntary childlessness, attempting to conceive through first-line fertility treatments like Clomid, or proceeding to more advanced treatment options like IUI and IVF. Upon stepping off the precipice, we set off on our Expedition and into our first Attempt and begin to live our choices, experience outcomes, and negotiate their emotional consequences. What are the emotional experiences of the Expedition and Attempt like?

At first, infertility-related emotions can seem indistinguishable from one another, especially when they wash over us with such frequency and strength. Time and reflection allow individuals to disentangle and deal with these emotions and identify which outcomes are most important. Emotions can race between highs and lows as individuals adjust to infertility and seek treatment. Sometimes, these tumultuous emotions are linked to treatment outcomes and change as treatment progresses. For Brittany Watson, "Every month it was just the high of 'OK, maybe this is the month,' and then the low of 'No, it's not again.'" Lauren Mack found this downright traumatic: "in the beginning . . . I felt more peaceful, [as if] this is going to work. . . . I felt a lot more in control and more hopeful. Now I feel like I have developed post-traumatic stress disorder, and every time I start, I'm ready to break myself again." Like Lauren, most interviewed patients (71%) felt that undergoing fertility treatment gave them more control; 54% believed it was important to be proactive and have a plan.

It is here that the emotional distinctions between Expeditions and Attempts become more apparent. In the Expedition, sadness and other "negative" emotions largely define patients' overall infertility experience. But in Attempts, positive emotions supplant negative ones, at least until a negative pregnancy test. Thus, in many ways, the Attempt is the emotional inverse of the Expedition. Anticipating a potentially happy cycle outcome, individuals feel excitement, hope, and happiness, even if these emotions jostle against confusion, nervousness, and sadness. (See Figures 1–4.)

Moreover, in treatment, patients' emotions are linked to specific IVF cycle phases. Individuals undergoing IVF for the first time generally feel most daunted in the beginning. "I think some patients get overwhelmed by the process; [they say] 'I don't know if I can take my shots, . . . I don't know if I can be sedated,'" Nurse Gabi Simpson explained.

This roller-coaster pattern is evident in Figures 3 and 4, which aggregate hundreds of patient responses. Patients experience "positive" emotions most strongly from egg retrieval to embryo transfer, peaking at that point. Men are more nervous than women at this time, but they tend to become more hopeful following embryo transfer, whereas women remain nervous throughout the cycle, even after a positive pregnancy test. For

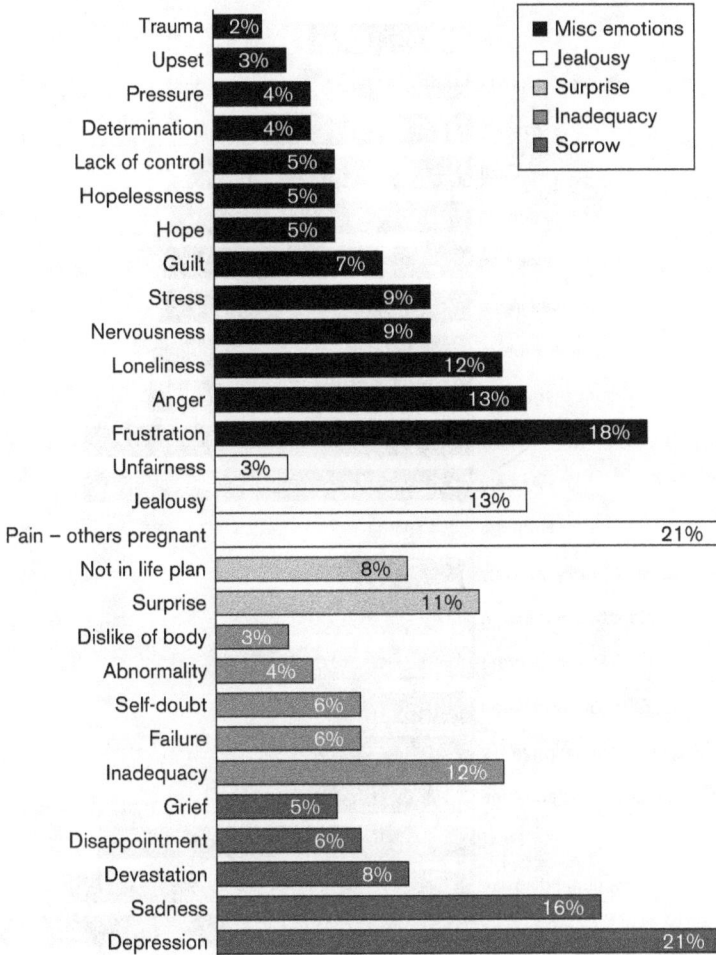

FIGURE 1. Expedition Emotions: Qualitative Interviews (by % of participants indicating each emotion). Source: Jody Lyneé Madeira

both, excitement peaks following embryo transfer, during the agonizing time known as the "two-week wait." Predictably, both men and women are saddest following a negative pregnancy test. Surprisingly, women's anger and frustration generally remain low until a negative pregnancy test, belying the stereotypically wrathful and bitter infertile woman. Thus, the Attempt more accurately captures this emotional "roller-coaster" than the Expedition, although both layers are necessary to fully illustrate infertility's emotional complexity.

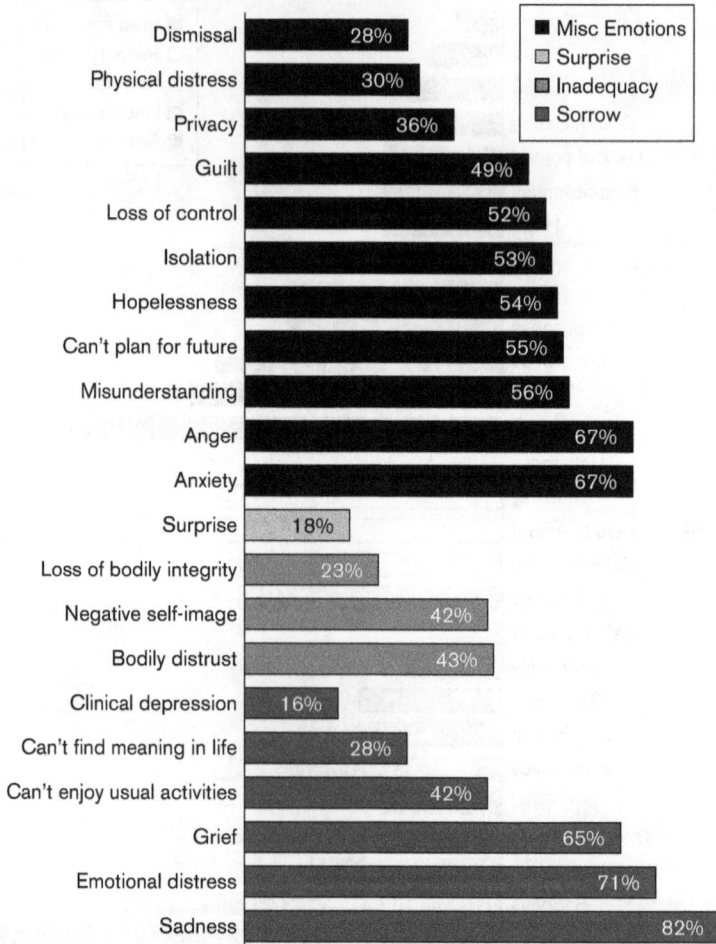

FIGURE 2. Expedition Emotions: Quantitative Surveys (by % of participants indicating each emotion). Source: Jody Lyneé Madeira

Sinking Feelings: From Diagnosis to Descent

Standing on infertility's precipice, most individuals feel many more negative than positive emotions and often experience emotions in "clusters"— from most to least common, they are sorrow, jealousy, inadequacy, and surprise. The sorrow cluster (which 71 individuals, subsequently represented as "n," reported) is comprised of depression ($n = 27$), sadness ($n = 20$), devastation ($n = 10$), disappointment ($n = 8$), and grief ($n = 6$). Jealousy ($n = 47$) encompasses pain from seeing pregnant women

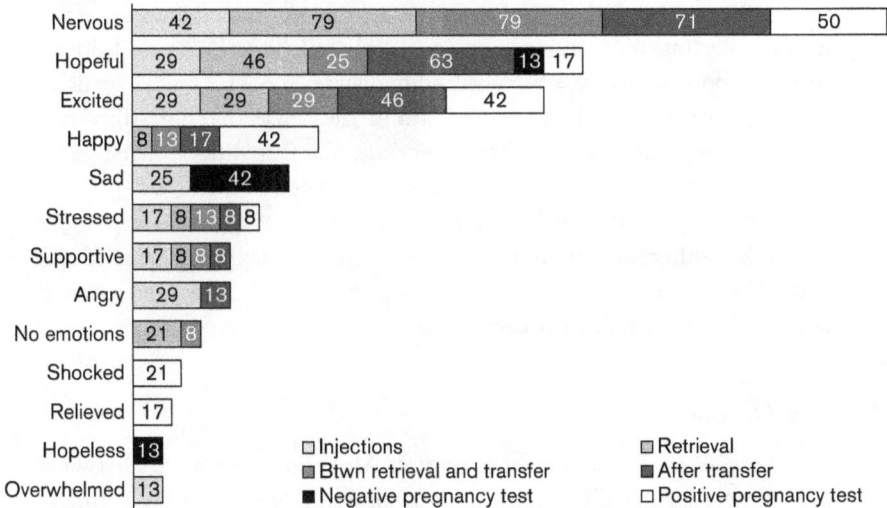

FIGURE 3. How Men Feel across an IVF Cycle, Qualitative Interviews (by % of participants indicating each emotion during each cycle component). Source: Jody Lyneé Madeira. Note: Emotions indicated by fewer than 5% of participants during each cycle component are not reported.

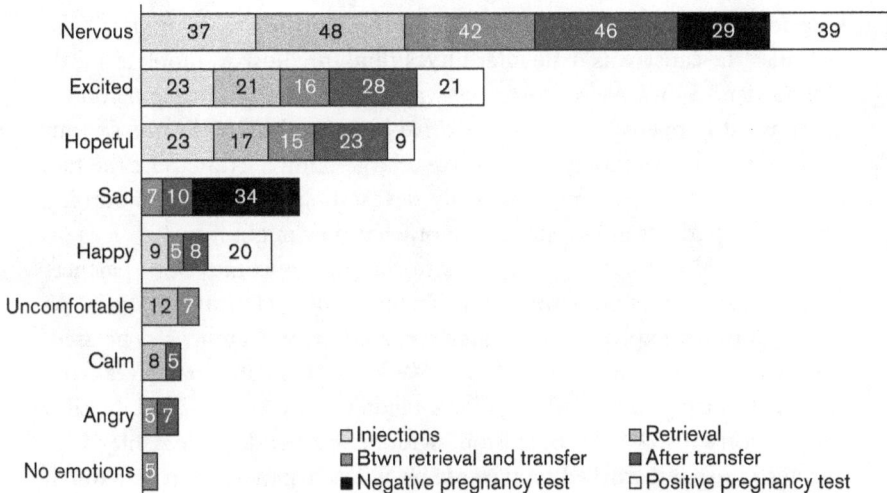

FIGURE 4. How Women Feel across an IVF Cycle, Qualitative Interviews (by % of participants indicating each emotion during each cycle component). Source: Jody Lyneé Madeira. Note: Emotions indicated by fewer than 5% of participants during each cycle component are not reported.

(n = 27), envy (n = 16), and unfairness (n = 4). Inadequacy (n = 39) includes feelings of insufficiency (n = 15), failure (n = 8), self-doubt (n = 7), abnormality (n = 5), and bodily dislike (n = 4). Finally, surprise (n = 24) consists of shock (n = 14) and the sense that infertility has hijacked life plans (n = 10). Other emotions like frustration, anger, guilt, and determination also play significant roles. Figures 1 and 2 depict the emotional experiences of both interview and survey participants; these charts list different emotions because survey participants selected all applicable options from a lengthy list, while interview participants described emotions in their own words.

1. Sorrow

a. Experiencing Sorrow on the Precipice. Most individuals are sorrowful following an infertility diagnosis. Grappling with infertility's consequences brings sadness, an umbrella concept often encompassing frustration, anger, jealousy, introspection, and anxiety. As Maria Craig described, it was "not like a clinical depression, but maybe a little bit sad or depressed. Like, why me?" Women frequently describe this reaction as grief over the delay or potential demise of their hopes, life intentions, parenting identities, and, often, pregnancies. Tracey West recounted, "Right after we got the actual diagnosis, . . . you kind of go through the stages of grief. And because the cause was male infertility, I think my husband took it a little bit harder." Sylvia Nelson's sorrow was quite intense: "I have no control over what happens. . . . I'm one of five kids, my husband's one of four kids; we'd always thought we'd have a large family. I think just the fact that that might not happen is really devastating." These are mourning reactions; patients are keenly aware of what they might lose.

Sorrow also affects romantic relationships. Sometimes both partners experience depression, either as a mental state or clinical diagnosis. As April Gonzalez explained, "I became very anxious and, at times, depressed. Started going to therapy myself. . . . We kind of isolated ourselves from some of our friends . . . feeling like we didn't really fit in." For Lily Ellis, depression caused "a lot of tension" with her husband, while Ashley Carpenter's husband worked to alleviate his wife's depression: "it was tough to . . . keep both of us focused and more upbeat about it." Coping with infertility is especially difficult if one's partner is also in need of support.

b. Experiencing Sorrow during the Expedition. Sorrow's root causes persist in Attempts, only now the most sorrowful experience isn't diagnosis, but failed treatment cycles or miscarriages. If a positive pregnancy test proves elusive cycle after cycle, disappointment is all but inevitable. As Darla Clarke asserted, "I supposedly have these follicles, I get all these shots and do all this stuff, and I don't get pregnant, and then it wears into, 'OMG we're spending all this money with no return.'" Individuals had to manage their own disappointment alongside their partners'. Even friends can trigger sorrow; Shelley Lawrence felt let down by "how people in my life responded" to infertility. These feelings often overlap with isolation.

Sorrow compounds over time, as sadness from an infertility diagnosis acquires layers of grief from unsuccessful treatment attempts. For Rochelle Rowe, infertility was "the most devastating thing that's happened to me, including my mother having cancer and everything else. It's definitely changed my world view." Deep sorrow reflects individuals' profound commitment and efforts to conceive. Lauren Mack observed, "[A]ccording to my insurance, I have four IVF cycles for a lifetime. . . . all my girlfriends who have infinite chances the rest of their lives, I have four, and when one fails it's just devastating. . . . You work so hard, and you've put so much effort and hope into something." Here, even though Lauren had insurance, jealousy still crept in, deepening this emotional pain.

Depression can be both a synonym for sadness and an actual clinical diagnosis. For many, depression is a mental state; Nicole Bell said she'd "slip into" depression, and Brittany Watson described how infertility "spiraled me into a bit of depression." Depression can be debilitating, particularly in combination with other emotions and events. For David Reid, "there have been times I've been so angry I can't see straight, so depressed I can't barely lift a pen, . . . our first IVF cycle was around Christmas, . . . we got a positive result, and I kept singing in my head 'All I Want for Christmas Is You.' And then came New Year's, and we had a bad beta/HCG, and we had everything fall apart."

Infertility experiences might also aggravate clinical depression; as Marisa Sims related, "I've had problems with depression most of my adult life, and I think the infertility certainly exacerbated that." Patients in this situation might not be as surprised at infertility's effects and may have preexisting resources to cope with them in healthier ways.

2. Jealousy

a. Experiencing Jealousy on the Precipice. After receiving an infertility diagnosis, women and men most commonly experience jealousy from seeing others conceive without apparent effort. Their worlds seem suddenly overpopulated with pregnant women and unwanted pregnancies, engendering envy, feelings of unfairness, and pain. Tanya Rivera explained, "[F]or a year at least while I found out I was infertile and then had to wait [for insurance coverage], I was possibly more resentful to women that it came easier to and especially for those that didn't appreciate it."

Comparing one's self to others who conceive easily makes personal failure seem more pronounced. It is particularly difficult when friends and family become pregnant—particularly in less than ideal circumstances. Patricia Burns recalled, "[M]y brother and sister get pregnant every other second. . . . It was horrible. And you don't want to make them feel bad, but I also don't want to hear from them they're pregnant, because nobody wants to hear . . . your sister cry. . . . I got to the point where actually I was having panic attacks, and had to actually go on medication." Because of jealousy, individuals might feel like Dana Gibbs: "a heartbeat away from being bitter."

b. Experiencing Jealousy During the Expedition. After individuals begin treatment, feelings of jealousy can intensify as physical, emotional, and financial resources dwindle. Lola Lewis acknowledged growing envy of "all those people [who] don't have all those problems and get to have kids and a typical life."

The pain of encountering pregnant women and children prompts many to socially withdraw: "I just isolated myself, because I either didn't want people to know what we were going through, or those that did know didn't understand" (Brittany Watson). Kay Elliott emphasized, "[E]ven if you're at home, it's always on your mind. You don't want to see that physical reminder that's outside." Thus, even one's home isn't a place of peace.

Socially withdrawn individuals often become lonely. Isolation presents a profound problem for many; 49% of interviewed individuals noted that others could not understand what they were going through, 46% found it hard to see others building their families, and 31% reported troubled relationships with former friends. Though 20% observed they felt alone and didn't know others experiencing infertility, 26% formed new friendships. "I had a lot of depression, anxiety, and feeling very alone until I got to a support group to find out that other people were feeling that way," recalled Danielle Green.

But it is impossible to stay inside all the time; workplaces and daily routines inevitably bring individuals into contact with painful reminders of what they lack. Joyce Harrington found it particularly difficult "seeing co-workers' pictures of their kids and hearing about relatives who had a baby or things like that. Just seeing someone with a child in a supermarket can cause anxiety." Diane Barrett described these encounters as "daggering your heart," noting it was "torture even stepping out of my house, practically. . . . it just destroyed me until I got pregnant." Men also experience jealousy; Clay Padilla confessed, "[Y]ou just don't feel like you can measure up there, in that department."

At these moments, jealousy also provokes the feeling that life is unjust: "this one thing that's supposed to be natural doesn't come to you, and it seems very unfair" (Lana Houghton). Unfairness captures the maddening abyss between the childbearing "haves" and "have-nots"; as Phoebe Paul put it, "Why can everyone else get pregnant and not me? . . . I just was wondering why we had to go through these trials and tribulations and a lot of people don't have to." These words echo with loneliness, underscoring the need to befriend others enduring similar struggles.

3. Inadequacy

a. Experiencing Inadequacy on the Precipice. During the Expedition, many individuals (18% interviews) feel physically inadequate, perhaps even "broken." An infertility diagnosis often makes women and men believe they are less feminine or masculine. Christine Zimmerman noted, "I do feel less of a human . . . incomplete, like I'm not even a real girl." Marie Boyd told her husband "that he was still within the lemon law to exchange me for a wife that actually worked." Infertility may produce a physiological breach not only with friends, family, and even complete strangers, but also with one's ancestors: "you can't do a simple function that women's bodies have been able to do for gazillions of years" (Amber Butler). Men facing male factor infertility also experience inadequacy; as Nathaniel Sims related, "I felt like . . . I kind of let her down and didn't feel like as much of a man after."

Feelings of inadequacy accompany self-doubt; infertility "shakes your self-esteem" (Jeannie Lindsey). Victoria Santos wondered "a lot of emotional things . . . are you sexy, or . . . does he not want kids, does he not want to be married anymore." Cynthia Gardner's infertility "made me doubt my body, and . . . some of the choices, because I started to believe that maybe it was because I'd waited too long." Inadequacy, then, ushers in many new fears.

b. Experiencing Inadequacy During the Expedition. Once treatment begins, protocols can reinforce feelings of abnormality and brokenness. Victoria Santos explained, "There's a degree of separateness knowing that you had to conceive a child in separate rooms, and that you really didn't do this together. It's not normal. Or what you concede is normal." During IVF cycles, individuals have to monitor life choices in ways others don't, from everyday decisions about diet, exercise, and stress management to more consequential ones regarding vacations: "It's irrational [that] they say, 'If you do all these things, you'll get pregnant,' but then people who drink and smoke get pregnant on a whim" (Darla Clarke). Unfairness is always close at hand.

Self-doubt can easily intensify after an unsuccessful treatment cycle. Lena Coleman encountered "Inadequacy. Failure. As if God has decided for me that that's not the path I get to take, being a mother. I felt like . . . a burden on my husband for having to bring him through this with me as well." Many are frustrated because this helplessness is altogether new. "Both of us have never failed at anything in our life and so this is kind of the first thing," Anne Kelley noted. "[I]t's not something you can work harder and succeed at. . . . it's either going to happen or it's not going to happen." It's especially painful when individuals regard infertility as a personal failure.

At times, feelings of inadequacy can bleed into anger, frustration, and anxiety. Women and men refer to IVF as an anxiety-inducing process of "learn[ing] to be afraid" (May Weiss). "You always want some sort of outcome, whether it's follicle growth, or this or that, or estrogen building up," Juanita Poole explained. "[It made] me completely anxious, in a way far more than I ever was before." June Barber had "a high level of stress" because "you couldn't really plan things in life, just because you didn't know if you get pregnant or if you'd be in treatment." This fear and anxiety in turn heighten stress, which most patients internalize and a few vent on others, including partners and clinic staff.

4. Other Emotions—Surprise, Frustration, Anger, Guilt, Determination

a. Experiencing Other Emotions on the Precipice. The "surprise" emotional cluster encompasses both the shock of an infertility diagnosis and its unforeseen disruptions. Very few individuals make room for infertility in their life plans, and those who can't easily conceive must face (perhaps for the first time) their lack of control: "I think that was . . . the biggest wake-up call. I can't control when this happens, which was very hard for me because I'm one of those planner type[s] of people" (Kathryn Patton). This sense of helplessness was "really devastating" for Sylvia Nelson, especially given that "it's kind of like a basic part of my life." Women and men are often surprised at infertility's emotional currents, including frustration ($n = 23$), anger ($n = 16$), loneliness ($n = 15$), nervousness or fear or anxiety ($n = 12$), stress ($n = 11$), guilt ($n = 9$), hope ($n = 6$) and hopelessness ($n = 6$), lack of control ($n = 6$), determination ($n = 5$), pressure ($n = 5$), being upset ($n = 4$), and trauma ($n = 2$).

Stranded upon the precipice, individuals become frustrated, particularly at delays in seeing providers, obtaining testing, or managing others' judgmental reactions to their diagnosis or choices. "The infertility heightens the frustration, heightens the aggravation, because we were married 11 years before we got pregnant . . . and we never intended to wait for that long," Marisa Sims said. Monica Hansen was fed up with friends' reactions to her choice to undergo fertility treatment: "[T]hey'd say things to me that were bothersome to me like, 'Well, why don't you just adopt?'" Even waiting to begin treatment was frustrating: "When you're in a cycle, you're hopeful. When you're after one and in between, you can't start the next one, there's this lag time that really feels tough" (Nicole Bell).

Several are angry at themselves for being on the precipice in the first place: "Being male factor was difficult for [my husband] to accept, so he was very angry" (Brittany Watson). Anger and frustration bring self-blame and guilt; Luis Torres described a "whole battle with insecurities and frustration, which would then circle back around and put more pressure on me, and I would feel guilty about it." Shelley Lawrence felt she was "standing in the way," and Francis Foster felt "that I kind of let [my wife] down." Men even blame themselves for being unable to perform sexually under the pressure of trying to conceive. Some can't help but be angry at their partners; May Weiss admitted, "I feel guilty to even say this, but I was mad at my husband [who had male factor infertility]."

b. Experiencing Other Emotions During the Expedition. An infertility diagnosis's emotional impact may startle many. Rodney Hodges recalled, "I didn't expect things to be this difficult . . . emotionally on both my wife and myself in different ways." But other emotions can increase individuals' resolve to forge ahead and meet infertility's challenges head on. "I knew I had to keep going, and through it all, there was that determination," remarked Nicole Bell. "[A]s long as I had a plan of action, as long as I was doing something, I felt good. I felt proactive." Yet, this determination can become compulsive: "[I]t becomes kind of like this obsession and it almost becomes like a goal to reach" (Anne Kelley).

Thus, infertility's emotional experience changes from diagnosis through treatment. Its effects are pervasive, influencing how readily individuals cope, what course of action they choose, and how they react to outcomes. Emotions' onset, intensity, and duration all determine whether they help or harm individuals—or both, at varying points in time. Most important, however, these emotions have very real physical and social effects: drawing couples and friends together or driving them apart, prompting individuals to seek new social connections or isolation, immediately seeking fertility treatment or considering other options, and continuing to pursue certain interventions or cutting losses and ceasing treatments.

AT EXPEDITION'S END: THE INFERTILITY EXPEDITION'S LONG-TERM EFFECTS

Individuals with lengthy infertility Expeditions that last through several treatment cycles occasionally assess where they are and what has changed thus far. They consider how infertility has affected their daily routines, personalities, values, romantic relationships, and friendships, noting personality changes, redefined life priorities, religious doubts, introspection, and vulnerability. Friendships are lost and won; couples' relationships are strained and strengthened; new sources of support are identified and tapped.

An infertility Expedition rapaciously devours individuals' emotional, physical, and financial resources. It takes over life routines. Sylvia Nelson explained, "[I]t's also really all-consuming. . . . between pregnancy and miscarrying and having surgeries and fertility treatment, it's very hard not to think about it every day. And there are times when I'm at the doctor more than half the month . . . at least once a day." It proves physically exhausting. Kay Elliot observed, "We're no longer active. We don't go out. We used to go out all the time. And [it] just rarely happens now. . . . you're always tired." It prompts deep introspection. Sheri Lopez recalled, "[I]t just caused us to question everything that we'd thought or known."

Moreover, infertility shakes up spirituality and challenges religious convictions. Doreen Fernandez said, "We're both pretty religious; my husband is actually a pastor. We had a lot of anger towards God for a while." Often, individuals wonder if infertility is a spiritual message. Kendra Figueroa was perplexed: "I guess it's just wondering if maybe God is really saying you don't need to have children or just like am I supposed to have children." Other times, faith provides support, as Madeline Lowe found: "Our faith helped a lot. . . . God kept telling me, 'Hey, you're supposed to conceive,' so we kept trying." Infertility expectations thus prompt introspection as well.

Individuals often realize they have undergone temporary or permanent personality changes from their Expedition, which they often attribute to medications that "change your whole demeanor" (Juanita Poole) or the length of time they've dealt with infertility: "You're so pumped with hormones; almost every emotion that you're feeling is pretty much a false one, probably, or magnified" (Stella Madison). Infertility's emotional roller-coaster often produces turbulent moods: "I was short-tempered, I would fly off the handle, I was very sensitive to other people's pregnancies, I would get really upset. . . . It was just like manic-depressive" (Bridget James). And personality changes can be more long-lasting; Jenna Moreno felt as if she "kind of checked out for a while. I got to a point where I really wasn't happy. I wasn't smiling. I wasn't myself. And I almost felt like a sort of shell of who I actually am."

There is often no going back to who one was beforehand—a bittersweet discovery. "I definitely feel stronger with what I've gone through, but . . . I feel like part of me, like an innocence will never come back" (Sasha Goodman). "In the long term, . it's left me a little more bitter," reflected Delores Weber, "and a little more patient and understanding of other people's issues." But infertility forced Adam Woods to mature: "Miscarriage was a very adult experience, and I've found I don't feel like a kid anymore, in pretty much anything, and that wasn't true before we started this." Individuals complete their descents from the precipice as changed individuals, arriving at different destinations than they had originally mapped.

Unfortunately, it's at this time of instability and doubt, when support is most needed, that infertility can jeopardize relationships with friends and family members. It's painful to keep others apprised of the latest treatment developments, and so silence seems safer: "Every time it didn't work, I didn't want to have to call my mom. . . . So the less people that knew, the less people are going to be asking me questions" (Antonia Hughes). Marital and romantic relations take the brunt of infertility-related stress. "It weighed heavily on our relationships," Brittany Watson noted. "I know a lot of people have said that it only made them stronger but for us it was really trying." Adam Woods explained, "[W]e'd fight all the time, some nights we'd cry, we'd feel very alienated, and of course you can't hide from this." Changes in a partner's personality exacerbated marital strain: "I wasn't being my normal self; we didn't enjoy the time we had together the way that we should" (Jenna Moreno).

Intimate relations are also strained, most often from having sex to conceive rather than for pleasure—"baby dancing," in infertility forum lingo. Kay Elliot said, "It's no longer about 'We want to have sex,' it's 'Is it time to have sex?'" Sex is no longer sexy: "[not] a natural thing between man and wife [but a] biological experiment or something. Just a process" (Tyrone Crider). Futile conceptive attempts lead to performance issues, particularly for men: "[T]here came a point where he couldn't even get aroused, 'cause he just knew that there was nothing that he could do" (Victoria Santos). And if men can't perform sexually, their partners may feel unattractive or even unloved. As Logan Hunt recalled, "[W]e were butting heads because she was putting pressure on, like, 'We need to [have sex] tonight at 11:00 p.m.' She had it all mapped out and timed out, and it actually ended up causing my inability to even . . . ejaculate. And I never had that problem. . . . Psychologically I was locking up. And therefore she was starting to say, 'It must be me; you don't like me.'" Eventually, one or the other partner might throw in the towel: "[My wife] became depressed and distant, and didn't want to be sexually active anymore and just wanted to mope around" (Francis Foster). One or both partners' refusal to "baby dance" might mean leaving the reproductive dance floor altogether.

Moreover, conflict ensues when partners want to pursue different treatment plans. As Sean Gray recalled, "[M]y wife wanted to immediately go the in vitro route, and I didn't want to do that. . . . being Catholic . . . that was my challenge, and so I at first was reluctant to do it, which of course made her very angry." Sometimes one partner wants children more than the other. "It's been extremely trying on our marriage," related Patrick Shields. "[S]he feels very strongly identity-wise as far as being a mother, being pregnant, having children, . . . I don't identify quite the same way. . . . I can be happy in life without kids." Finally, husbands find it painful to watch their wives endure treatment procedures. "It really had a significant impact on my husband's emotional state as well," Jenna Moreno observed. "[H]e tried as much as he could to understand what I was going through, but because it wasn't his body, he couldn't." In short, running the infertility gauntlet leaves couples exhausted: "This whole thing has really pushed our marriage to a breaking point. We're very lucky that we're good at communicating, but it's been really rough" (Kelley Bates). Relationships, like individuals, emerge from the Expedition changed.

Marriages can also be wellsprings of support. Most often, infertility simultaneously stresses and bolsters romantic relations: "It's very straining on a relationship . . . ; in another way you're forced to find strength in each other" (April Baldwin). Men often become emotional anchors for their wives and try to "to be strong for my partner" (Christopher Franklin). As Aaron Schneider explained, "[O]ne of us has to be the level-headed person. . . . I couldn't just sit there, and [lie] on the pillow and cry with her all the time about it because it wasn't going to be helping either one of us, so I had to be . . . the strong shoulder, . . . [reassuring her] it's going to get better, things are going to happen. . . . it was taking a toll on her; it was taking a toll on me."

And as old relationships sour, individuals often find solace with new friends who have undergone similar experiences. Danielle Greene recalled, "I had a lot of depression, anxiety, and feeling very alone until I got to a support group to find out that other people were feeling that way." These new friends model new ways of negotiating infertility and exchange advice on coping strategies. "I was in the support group with other women that were going through infertility as well that probably showed a lot more emotion and had a lot more difficulty," said Maggie Copeland. "I would say it wasn't as bad for me."

Thus, old relationships and routines are stretched and sometimes broken under infertility-related stresses and schedules, and new patterns and partnerships emerge, for better or for worse. However an individual's Infertility Expedition unravels, it always leaves its mark. If individuals' remarks communicate nothing else, they convey that infertility is an arduous experience—but perhaps not always an intolerable one. Those diagnosed with infertility choose next steps while mired in an emotional swamp, but the vast majority somehow manage to find their way to solid ground.

CONCLUSION: "ARE WE THERE YET?"

Patients' and providers' comments reveal two separate layers of emotional experience: Expeditions, or long-term adaptive periods lasting from suspected infertility to either successful conception or treatment cessation, and Attempts, shorter segments when individuals try to conceive.

This model illustrates how emotions change both over monthly cycles and throughout the course of an infertility career, documenting the stages of descent from the precipice and revealing otherwise hidden positive emotions. Emotions play fundamental roles in treatment decisions and personal relationships, spurring their growth, death, and change. Eventually, for individuals who seek fertility treatment, these relationships grow to encompass doctors, nurses, and clinic staff, and they set in motion family-building efforts that trigger the informed consent project.

As of yet, however, we haven't heard much about desperation, the emotion popularly thought to be most problematic. In reproductive contexts, desperation is a politicized cluster of other emotions—sorrow, preoccupation, restlessness, heedlessness, intense motivation to act, and so on—that critics strategically use in ways that fuel infertility-related stereotypes of individuals who can't make good choices. These stereotypes exert real influence over individuals' infertility experiences. But are they accurate?

CHAPTER 2

"The Heart Wants What the Heart Wants"

Patients' and Providers' Reflections on Desperation

I would define desperation the same way the Supreme Court did when ruling on obscenity back in the '60s: I know it when I see it. Or, rather, when I feel it. It's when I have no other options, or when none of the options available to me are realistic or helpful. It's when things seem impossibly tough, but I know that there's no cavalry coming to save the day, so I pin all my hopes on something that might have low odds of success. It's when there's no Plan B—or when Plan B has been exhausted in favor of Plans C, D, E, and F and I'm wondering how far down the alphabet I can go before I give up. . . . I've been desperate for a crystal ball to find out whether this story would have a happy ending, for my baby's health and life and for my own mental and physical well-being. . . . I've been desperate for time to pass so I can put miles between where I'm now and where I started this process, and I've been desperate for time to slow down since I fear that the worst is yet to come.

—Jade Jones

In 1978, the birth of a baby girl named Louise Brown produced a seismic shift in reproductive medicine. Louise was no ordinary baby, but the first child to be born through IVF. No longer was infertility an automatic life sentence to involuntary childlessness, to be negotiated only through adoption or donor sperm and IUI. For those with resources, like insurance, savings, credit cards, and generous relatives, IVF offered new opportunities to get pregnant. Intervening decades have brought new technological breakthroughs, but fairly stable (and high) prices. But with these reproductive medical advances come the emotional, psychological, and financial realities of unequal access. Others who can afford such treatment may find it's not successful. For many, the dream of a biologically related child still shimmers on the horizon, seemingly just out of reach.

For decades, many have used the term "desperate" to describe individuals caught up in conceiving.[1] If emotions like anger, frustration, and sadness are thought to warp decision making, then desperation is allegedly the worst of the lot, ostensibly robbing individuals of rationality and even competency. The "desperate" label has become highly politicized, used to create (or have the effect of creating) a power relationship, in which individuals experiencing infertility are subordinate to others, most often medical professionals. "Desperation" signals unease with emotion's role in decision making—and with reproductive decision makers. Unsurprisingly, it is a label almost exclusively applied to females, like the "hysteria" diagnosis used to marginalize women in the nineteenth and early twentieth centuries.[2]

Legislators, policymakers, and the entertainment media frequently use a discourse of desperation and emotional extremism to justify proposals for ART regulation. As Dr. Stefanie Burgstaller observed, "it seems like movie stars and people in *People* magazine are frequently conceiving by infertility treatments, and they're kind of portrayed as being devastated if it's not happening and ecstatic if it does." It gets to the point where it's hard for clinics to get magazines for their waiting rooms, since "patients . . . complain that . . . almost every cover is about whether or not someone's pregnant" (Dr. Burgstaller). Other critics use the term "desperation" as shorthand for concern about infertility's emotional repercussions, the commodification of reproductive processes and products, and the potential for coercion and exploitation. Meanwhile, this characterization has fueled negative stereotypes of women experiencing infertility, who appear selfish, obsessed, and rude on the one hand or helpless or pathologically depressed on the other. Perhaps the most desperate of desperate women are those, like Lisa Montgomery or Korena Roberts,[3] who murder other women who are pregnant and nearly full-term, cutting the babies from their dead mothers' wombs.

These arguments also come into play in related contexts like abortion.[4] Here, advocates champion women's right to choose to terminate a pregnancy—an option that, like trying to create a pregnancy through IVF, is a reproductive decision. Sometimes, women undergoing IVF are labeled desperate, and those choosing abortion are not. But why should we trust women's decisions in one context, but not in another? Shouldn't we trust all such choices, without good reason to believe such trust is misplaced? Why are emotion-related rationales necessary for regulating reproductive technologies in the first place, when such calls could logically come from IVF's scientific, medical, and ethical risks, like multiple births?

DESPERATE MEASURES, MEASURING DESPERATION

"Desperation" might not even be an identity that many women actually own in conventional ways. When interviewed, several were surprised when asked whether they felt desperate, and instantly denied that it (or related stereotypes) applied to them. For instance, Jackie Carson would've gone to great lengths to conceive, but she found "desperation" offensive: "Anything legal I would've done, probably, . . . if you had given me herbs, I would've taken them; I would've stood on my head for 20 minutes. But . . . I don't like when I see in the tabloids like, 'Claire Kardashian is *desperate* for a baby!' Why does she have to be 'desperate'? Why can't she just be 'ambitious'?"

Jackie doesn't just reject the desperate label; she transforms it, reframing such activities as agency, not weakness. This suggests that intense emotions do not necessarily translate into deficient decision making. And far from viewing themselves as passive or paralyzed, individuals overwhelmingly (83% interview, 91% survey) described themselves as assertive while obtaining fertility treatment.

A deeper exploration of "desperation" illustrates why and how emotions are central to informed reproductive decision making.[5] Instead of paternalistically labeling patients, we must comprehensively understand their experience of desperation and identify what factors trigger its rarest and most harmful forms to improve treatment experiences for all patients. Many individuals consider themselves desperate and even describe this emotion in stereotypical ways—but very few report that it interferes with decision making. As they describe it, desperation is usually an internal drive, invisible to others. This explains why providers believe that only a handful of patients—5 or 10%—are desperate; they simply don't *see* desperate patient behavior very often. Moreover, as in other medical fields, if desperation becomes problematic, it offers opportunities for doctors and nurses to help guide patients, providing information and counsel—one way in which patients and reproductive medicine professionals collaborate in conception. Thus, the desperation label paints with too broad a brush. Even if this label implies that commenters have an appropriate, even thoughtful concern for women's welfare, it ultimately undermines the very autonomy it supposedly protects, since concerns over capacity actually apply to very few.

Understanding the term as political, we can see that each individual makes infertility-related decisions within her own complex web of personal and societal relationships, values, and norms as well as conflicting perspectives on sex, gender, love, marriage, reproduction, childbearing, family structures, lifestyles, and health needs. For better or worse, part of the infertility experience is acknowledging the desperation label and negotiating its fallout. To recognize desperation's political contours, set it aside, and explore the emotional truths it obscures, we must explore how patients define and experience desperation and how medical professionals think it affects treatment decision making.

Patients' and providers' comments illustrate how desperation is simultaneously helpful and obstructive. Intense emotions can undermine decision making, but although desperation is a conglomerate of strong feelings, it doesn't usually interfere with these activities. Instead, patients say, it motivates them to research infertility or seek treatment (perhaps effectively becoming fertility consumers[6]), surfaces temporarily in extremely distressing situations like receiving negative pregnancy tests results, or doesn't come up at all. Fertility professionals report that very few patients are desperate, and they often characterize this term as stigmatizing. Although (and perhaps because) it is often inaccurate and demeaning, both patients and fertility professionals recognize that desperation nonetheless influences their infertility experiences, intensifying infertility's emotional burden and affecting the development of provider-patient relationships.

A LABEL OF LAST RESORT: DESPERATION AS A POLITICAL CATEGORY

Conventional definitions of desperation highlight an intense hopelessness and despair that might encourage recklessness,[7] a "state of anguish accompanied by an urgent need for relief,"[8] and a feeling of entrapment accompanied by powerlessness.[9] All of these emphasize disruption[10] that alternately motivates action and induces paralysis.[11] The other health needs that create desperate patients and scenarios tend to be life-and-death experiences, like running out of standard treatments for an illness and turning to experimental ones, being on a ventilator, being extremely ill and entirely dependent on others, and awaiting "the last hope of rescue."[12]

In reproductive decision making arguments, desperation is attributed to both internal and external sources. "Internal" desperation stems from an individual's conflicted emotional state, and "external" desperation from factors in the outside world. Who is said to identify as desperate and why differ with historical and cultural factors, in line with this label's politicization. For instance, this term has long been used by both abortion advocates and opponents. Before *Roe v. Wade*, abortion advocates characterized women with unwanted pregnancies as internally desperate, emphasizing "women's vulnerability" due to external factors like abortion's illegality and "the dangers of back-alley abortions, unsanitary conditions, and unscrupulous and unlicensed providers."[13] Now, they use desperation to describe women's reactions to different practices that restrict access, like state regulations. Here, desperation addresses not the *quality* of a woman's options but her *ability* to effectuate her choice. Conversely, groups such as Feminists for Life, Life Resources Network, and others initiated a "Women Deserve Better" campaign, arguing that women would be better served if external abortion alternatives like adoption or social supports like maternity coverage, flex time, and quality child care were easier to access.[14] A more widespread opposition trend is to assert the "women-protective"[15] claim that women are internally desperate and thus uninformed, undecided, and untrustworthy, eviscerating their decision-making autonomy.[16]

Abortion opponents' arguments closely resemble the (often dubious) claim that women negotiating infertility are likely to make bad treatment decisions. But real external factors limiting treatment access, like weak institutional support for fertility services, *do* affect patients' emotional states, along with pressure from partners, peers, and family members, employer inflexibility, financial obstacles, and other difficulties. Each barrier to autonomous and independent decision making requires a different solution. For *external* desperation, effectuating autonomy means removing obstacles to aid women in implementing their decisions; for *internal* desperation, it means improving their capacity for autonomous choice. Regulations mandating infertility insurance coverage effectively remove financial obstacles, allowing some men and women to access fertility treatment; other processes like informed consent can educate patients and reassure providers, improving decision-making ability.

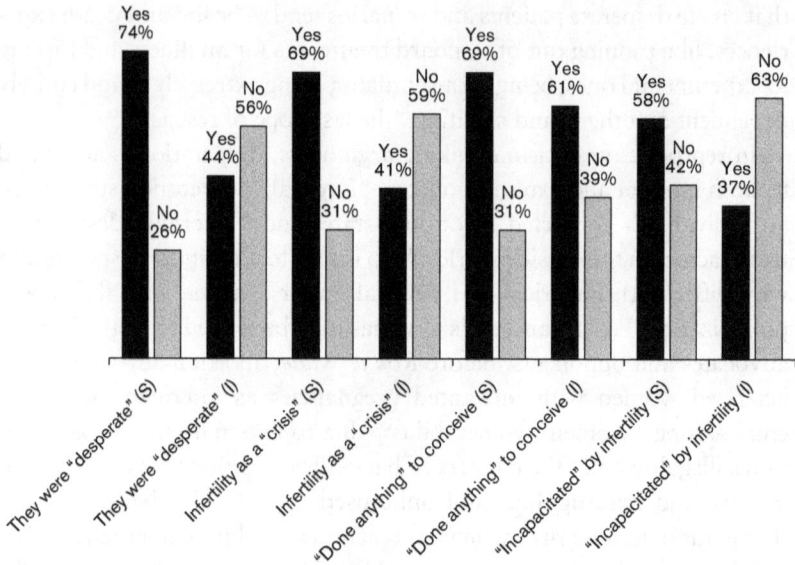

FIGURE 5. Patients' Perceptions of Their "Desperation" (by surveys [S] and interviews [I]). Source: Jody Lyneé Madeira

Notwithstanding its negative connotation, the term "desperation" resonates with many experiencing infertility—but usually not in conventional ways. It's immediately apparent in Figure 5 that high percentages of individuals considered themselves desperate, viewed infertility as a "crisis," would "do anything" to conceive, and believed that infertility "incapacitated" them at some point. But these statistics represent the tip of the iceberg; the truly interesting explanations of what desperation actually means have lain invisible, under the waterline.

Individuals experiencing infertility must grapple with desperation as a political or cultural tool, pushing aside existing cultural stereotypes of bitter, demanding, spineless, hysterical, or bitchy women to make room for their own family-building stories. Consequentially, desperation has evolved along two contradictory paths. In one sense, the term is popularly identified with extreme and impulsive behaviors. But in the context of women's actual experiences, desperation is less politically loaded and usually describes healthy, if harried, attempts to negotiate infertility's diverse consequences, including fitting rigorous treatment protocols into busy schedules, pervasive life changes, shifting relationships, and loss of control. Importantly, individuals also identify this kind of desperation in many other significant and challenging life events, like job loss or career changes, seeking a loving life-partner, and non-infertility-related health conditions.

Many patients never feel desperate; they identify options, won't "do anything" to conceive, aren't obsessed with infertility, and adhere to treatment limits. Patients find other family-building routes should treatments fail. Kendra Figueroa intended to use donor eggs, but realized success wasn't guaranteed: "[I thought], 'Okay, here I'm doing what the doctor has said gives us the highest percent chance to conceive, and if this doesn't work, then that's just God's way of saying you're done, . . . you're meant to do other things.' And other things in life can be fabulous." Patients who aren't desperate have lives, limits, and options. "I had other stuff going on; it was just one component of my life, not my life," explained Stella Madison. Similarly, Jenna Moreno reflected, "If we never have kids there's always adoption, but we'll have each other. We both have good jobs; we'll have a good life." Allison Perkins's religious faith deterred obsessive thoughts: "I have a huge desire to have a child with my husband, and would have to go through a grieving period if we can't conceive, but I know that this isn't the end of the world. . . . I know life isn't going to stop if we can't have a kid." Marie Byrd knew IVF with her own gametes was her "last resort": "one, for the Catholicism, and also because my cousin did it. He and his wife used donor everything, and ended up with triplets. And I didn't want to go there."

And those who do experience desperation can create strategies to mitigate it: treatment limits like not using donor gametes, or caps on numbers of cycles or dollars spent. As Jackie Carson remarked, "I don't think I was desperate to conceive. I was very driven to conceive, I had a lot of ambition to get pregnant. . . . I wasn't going to steal a baby or anything." Several reproductive professionals affirmed that most couples choose the most appropriate treatment rather than the most aggressive: "I think patients are very accepting in our practice of the results of their testing and that guidance from their physician. . . . In almost every case, we're starting with the least invasive treatment, the least costly treatment that's appropriate for the patient" (Head Nurse Melina Draper).

Like other emotions, desperation can make patients vulnerable and thus potentially easy marks for unscrupulous providers.[17] But patients, too, have responsibilities, like making reasonable efforts "to seek technically competent help [from] . . . a physician and to cooperate with him."[18] So-called "desperate" behaviors like researching infertility, investigating infertility clinics, and strictly complying with treatment protocols are how most patients attempt to fulfill their end of this bargain.

As a political label, desperation includes certain emotions and mental states that allegedly heighten coercion and warp decision making. If an individual who intensely desires a child chooses IVF, the presumption is that her choice is hastily made or ill-considered. But *what* choice an individual makes—like whether or not to undergo IVF—often matters less than *how* it is made. Choices based on critical reflection more likely reflect patients' actual interests and desires, while "desperate" circumstances, like "fear, low expectations, and unjust background conditions," can deform decision making.[19] But it's important to distinguish between choices that are coerced and those that are merely constrained. Conceiving a child through IVF is a "Plan B"—what couples decide to do if their "Plan A" doesn't work.[20]

Righting wrongs (and reconstructing individuals' autonomy) requires us to reject the idea that desperation is *only* a response to a "bad" or "wrong" situation. Rather, devoting one's self to making a decision and scrutinizing all options can be an inevitable and healthy response to tough choices, a sign that someone is circumspectly and competently identifying and evaluating all options to a sticky problem. Here, desperation is the by-product of empathy and awareness of how infertility, like other troubling issues, affects one's self and others, and of how a decision is difficult and implicates many cultural stereotypes. Perhaps, then, we should be more concerned by desperation's *absence* than its presence.

According to patients' reflections, desperation rarely paralyzes them. It might take over their lives, frustrate them, prompt them to rethink life goals or treatment limits, or make them ever more determined to find a successful treatment. But even in the face of severely constrained options, individuals most often treat these points as decisions that require engagement, not moments to act carelessly. Rather than signaling imperiled decision-making capacity, then, desperation often summons agency or autonomy. A woman choosing whether to undergo IVF is likely aware of and weighing important considerations; she recognizes the factors at play and the decision's complexity. In the most troubling situations, she makes *no choice*; it's most worrisome when patients can't decide what to do or don't review an informed decision to undergo IVF before starting another cycle. Desperation becomes most problematic not when a woman doesn't understand its root causes, but when she's frozen in indecisive contemplation or action. But indecision and "decision by default" happen to almost everyone in other life circumstances. Patients' experiences with desperation illustrate how this emotion both advances and hinders their infertility journeys.

DESPERATE MEASURES, MEASURING DESPERATION:
HOW PATIENTS EXPERIENCE AND DEFINE
DESPERATION

Desperation has predictable causes and contours, depending on when and how strongly individuals experience it. Such feelings often follow memorable events like diagnoses or unsuccessful cycles that entail new decisions, raise different options, and trigger tumultuous emotions.

When individuals feel desperate after being diagnosed with infertility, it often comes as a shock, feeling overwhelmed, or a willingness to consider all options—and as a driving force to seek medical assistance.[21] "It wasn't really that strong until we found out we couldn't [conceive]. . . . That's when it was kind of like, 'Okay, I'll try anything now,'" Tracey West reflected. Kelley Bates would never forget "that first conversation where IVF was on the table": "I didn't realize it was going to be that serious of a talk. . . . It was a 'come to Jesus' meeting; it was like, 'Holy shit.'" Clay Padilla's male factor infertility diagnosis made it "hard to even know or to think what the expectations were. I think we were very demoralized initially." One particular diagnosis—unexplained infertility—only made individuals like Nicole Bell more desperate: "If someone said, 'This is what's wrong with you,' I might be able to accept something. But unexplained [infertility], it threw me over the edge. . . . I couldn't wrap my brain around there being no answer really. That was hard."

Desperation acquires different dimensions as patients pursue treatment, time wears on, and pregnancy remains elusive. Here, desperation is the product of treatment.[22] Francis Foster felt desperate after learning reproductive medicine is as much an art as a science: "By the way that the medical community talked, and the boards talked it up, and the doctor talked it up, it's almost a sure thing, and then you come to find out that that's the furthest thing from the truth. . . . You think modern medicine is more than it actually is. . . . This is the best thing that medical science has to offer. . . . And then we did [IVF] twice. . . . So how can this keep failing? It's so god-awful expensive, how can it not work?"

Cecelia McBride and Philip Barnett each grew desperate after three unsuccessful IVF cycles, and Nicole Bell reached that point after "four or five IVFs." After her first and fourth IVF cycles, Nicole asked herself, "how many more times can you do this to yourself? One more, one more, one more. When do I stop? I don't know." Women in their late thirties are especially likely to feel desperate, largely "based on my age and time passing by" (Josephine Palmer). Desperation also accompanies pregnancy loss. Dora Adkins felt desperate during a frozen embryo transfer after losing a twin in a previous pregnancy: "I may have felt a little more desperate just because I was very much wanting to get back the sibling that we lost."

Whether patients already have children also affects desperation; those patients with secondary infertility might still feel desperate, but their experiences are qualitatively different. "We have kids, and so . . . the necessity for us to actually get pregnant wasn't desperation I guess because we always had a fallback," Nick Hall recalled, "but there was some desperation because of our age, and we already had the kids and we didn't want to space them too far apart. We did kind of rush through the infertility." Similarly, Antonia Hughes reflected, "I have an older son, so in some ways it wasn't as big [a] deal to me"; after she remarried, "she "felt more pressure to give him his own child than . . . a desire to want one myself."

When individuals acknowledge feeling "desperate" after several unsuccessful treatment cycles, they're usually using this term as a synonym for an intense emotional barrage. This type of desperation has several different components—the feeling that infertility consumes their lives, a determination to conceive that occasionally becomes preoccupation, feeling that there aren't other options, reconsidering limits on fertility treatment, and a willingness to "do anything" to conceive. Though individuals' descriptions can sound like stereotypical desperation, only a few felt that desperation had worrisome consequences. For instance, Danielle Greene felt she was "really not able to move past being obsessed with it [infertility]"; her desperation provoked depression, not decision-making effects: "not being able to move on to other emotions and not being able to have joy in other parts of your life." When patients can no longer reflexively weigh risks and benefits, doctors must occasionally step in and play guide or gatekeeper.

Infertility can seem all-consuming when patients have to schedule all else around treatment protocols: "Everything revolves around it. And this went on for years, two or three years. . . . Your whole life is really at a standstill until you become pregnant" (Nicole Bell). "All-consuming" also means that infertility routines absorb all of patients' internal resources—their attention, mental and emotional stamina, patience, and creativity. Adam Woods was intensely focused on conceiving:

> I would've cut off my own leg. If it didn't endanger the child's future, I would've done pretty much anything short of hurting someone else. You make those deals with the universe. . . . . So the desperation comes from just

being held in absolute check by it. You can't think about anything else, you'd do anything to make it happen. . . . As a biologist, I mean, part of the definition of life is something that replicates itself. If a person can't do that, they don't actually satisfy the definition of a living organism. So at times I've felt like I'm just a walking zombie, that I don't matter anymore.

It was certainly unhealthy when individuals' lives revolved around their infertility.

Or desperation can be a boundless determination "to have a child no matter the cost" (Nick Hall); therefore, individuals "w[ere] willing to try anything and spend any amount necessary to do so" (Deanna Douglas). "A lot of my girlfriends were . . . trying to get pregnant, but a lot of them were scared off from IVF or fertility treatment," Gillian Matthews reflected. "They don't want it that bad. We wanted it bad. We were the type of people that would mortgage our house." At times, individuals even seem to take pride in the strength of their determination.

Finally, several who feel desperate think they have no other options, "like you've nothing left to lose" (Cameron Ellis) or you're "at the end of your wits, you've nobody and nothing to turn to, . . . it's the end of the line" (Clay Padilla). This outlook can blind individuals to important information about treatment risks and consequences: "I think I had blinders on a lot of the times of just getting to point A to point B to baby-in-my-arms. . . . I'll sign whatever I had to; I do whatever I had to" (Amber Butler). As these comments illustrate, in almost all "desperate" situations, individuals feel that infertility has backed them into a corner.

AT THE END OF YOUR TETHER: DESPERATION AND TREATMENT LIMITS

Desperation is frequently associated with reconsidering limits on fertility treatments. Fearing they might become too deeply involved, many patients stick firmly to their treatment limits, measured in use of donor gametes, numbers of cycles, embryos transferred, or dollars spent. Lena Coleman never wanted to use only one set of donor gametes: "if the babies couldn't be all of ours, then it was going to be neither of ours biologically." Christine Zimmerman, who already had one child, chose not to purchase a plan covering multiple IVF cycles because she "didn't want to do it that many times." And Nathaniel Sims and his wife stopped after their first IVF cycle: "the answer was pretty clear: four unfertilized eggs. And that was the line; that was when we stopped digging a ditch."

Patients' finances often impose treatment limits by default. Stella Madison told her physician up front they'd attempt only one IVF cycle because of dwindling finances and drained emotional resources: "I told the doctor, . . . 'Look, outside of having only limited funds left, . . . I don't have it in me too many more times to miscarry. . . . I need to put all my money in one betting hand here, and to me that's one last round of IVF.'" Christopher Franklin agreed: "I was kinda like 'Well, I'll do $30K, and that's it. Or I'll do $15K a year, but once that's out, we'll wait till next year.'"

Most patients who keep to their limits are wary of becoming desperate. On the cusp of starting her first IVF cycle, Allison Perkins was determined not to let treatment control her life and financial priorities: "I don't want us to get to a place that every year we save up enough money to do a fresh IVF cycle the next year, and that it's just this never-ending cycle." Racquel Kennedy took a six-month hiatus from IVF to become more grounded: "it's kind of taken over our lives at some point. We were determined not to let it, but it becomes like the most important thing that's going on. So we actually took a six-month break to save for the in vitro and for me to get my cool back, just to make sure we were focusing on ourselves and not just on this project." Similarly, Inez Griffith said, "The one thing I didn't want this process to do was to turn me into someone that had no enjoyment in life and that narrowed my worldview to think the only way to happiness was a child. I just wanted to hug those women and tell them that they were more than their infertility."

But desperation can make it harder to stick to treatment limits, and patients frequently link it to reconsidering and then exceeding their personal restrictions: "I would define desperation as doing the absolute last thing that you thought you'd do, [IVF]" (Lindsey Burton). Early on, it can be hard for patients to place realistic limits on switching or stopping fertility treatment, especially when new treatments reveal new information and novel options. Christy Hoffman's willingness to try IVF evolved gradually: "At the beginning, I said I would never inject myself with needles, and then I did. I said I wouldn't undergo more than three treatment cycles with needles, and then I did. I said I would never undergo IVF, and then I felt like I *had* to. I finally had to realize that it was *possible* that I would never have my own biological child and only then did the anxiety and desperation go away."

For this reason, patients acknowledge their treatment limits are often elastic and are often adjusted for reasons other than desperation. Simone

Henry reflected, "Where I draw the line in the sand is consistently changing, and I think part of it is the feeling of being out of control, and part of it is now I have information that I didn't have. . . . I once heard someone describe it [as] like a drug, because you think 'Okay, we'll do this and then we'll stop, let's do one more.' And so I think the more I do it, the more I want it to work." But even patients who set limits can feel desperate as they approach these upper bounds. Joyce Harrington described how desperation suffused her final IVF cycle:

> I would describe "desperation" as a feeling of anxiety trying to tamp down hopelessness. It means that everything is on the line, and it conjures sweaty palms and a pit in one's stomach. We felt increasing desperation as our treatments continued with negative results. It reached an apex with our latest round of IVF, which we decided would be our last due to financial and emotional concerns. The entire process was loaded with the knowledge that this was our last shot and that we were on the cliff. We felt tremendous relief when this round produced a positive result, and we're now seven weeks along. The desperation is still there, however, as we know that nothing is guaranteed. I guess hopeful desperation has replaced the hopeless variety.

Some have great difficulty pausing to weigh risks alongside benefits. Patricia Burns urged, "at one point my husband even said he felt like I would keep trying to conceive even if I didn't have him. . . . he could've left me, and I would've gotten donor sperm." It was as if, when the going gets tough, the tough get tougher: "The harder it was, the more I wanted to persevere through it; to keep trying what we could try. But I don't know if the difficulty of it is what drove me" (Brittany Watson).

The question of when to take a break or cease treatments frequently causes tension between partners. Bridget James was so eager to conceive she began another IVF cycle immediately after miscarrying: "I felt like the way for me to help cope with the loss was to get right back into treatment, and he [my husband] wanted to take some time off, and maybe even explore other avenues." Nicole Bell acknowledged, "I was so afraid he [my husband] was going to say 'stop' because I never wanted to stop. I was obsessed." She continued, "[A]s long as I had a plan of action, as long as I was doing something, I felt good. I felt proactive." For their part, men often feel besieged when they try to discuss limits: "I'm willing to do anything my wife wants, and if my wife wants to continue, I've learned not to question," Rodney Hodges noted. "[W]hen the third time came up, I was like, 'So, are we stopping?' Honestly, I could've said I was going to murder her mother." Occasionally, these tensions can destroy marriages: "if I was willing to accept and to be childless, then . . . we'd still be married, and happy. But I think we just spent so much time on this and we've been through so much pain" (Kay Elliott).

THE DEPTHS OF DESPAIR: WHEN DESPERATION BECOMES PROBLEMATIC

As it grows more extreme, desperation often comes with costs—physical, emotional, relational, and financial. It can even progress to the point where individuals plead with doctors to take unhealthy risks. "I've been spending money likes it grows on trees, asking for off-label drug therapies that might help me to get pregnant, doing one FET cycle after another, not even giving my body a rest from hormone therapy," opined Lola Lewis. "I think all of these things are acts of desperation."

When they reconsider treatment limits, individuals' views of appropriate risk levels change, like their willingness to chance conceiving twins or triplets: "we weren't sure about multiples. By the time we got to the second one [cycle], we were so kind of desperate, you know, how many [do] we get, let's just do it" (Joyce Harrington). Desperation can encourage individuals to prioritize the odds of success of IVF, not its risks and side effects: "I don't think that we really considered or talked about too much of what we were signing [on the consent forms]. . . . I didn't want to hear about the bad stuff that could happen, it was just a 'let's get this show on the road' kind of thing." And they might lobby for treatments that they feel will work faster: "We did one IUI, and I was like, 'I'm done with that. I want to go straight to IVF.' . . . So even though he always makes you take a month off, I never want to take a month off. And I push and I want to have more, even when it comes to the transferring. I always want to transfer more embryos" (Deanna Douglas).

Whether perceived benefits outweigh perceived risks is a subjective determination on which individuals differ. Patients may well be in trouble when they consider compromising their financial security, personal integrity, or religious creeds. But when a decision entails a deliberate assessment of information, possible outcomes, and emotions, it's not "desperate" as popularly conceived. For instance, exceeding expected treatment limits needn't always compromise values: "when it looked bleakest, we were considering adoption as the next step rather than pursue fertility treatments that would be distinctly against our beliefs/morals" (Marie Byrd).

Fertility professionals also encounter patients who articulate firm treatment limits on ethical or religious grounds. Many patients don't want to face ethical dilemmas: "The biggest sort of roadblock that we come across with IVF is 'I don't want surplus embryos created.' So we try to work with them. We'll do limited insemination, . . . just to make two embryos and then freeze the rest of their eggs if they want" (First Year RE Fellow Yazmin Kuhn).

In the infertility context, then, desperation is most intense and problematic when individuals believe they are entrapped—out of options, out of money, or out of time—and they are urgently seeking ways to escape. Again, these dilemmas aren't unique to IVF. Life situations, from problematic careers to troubled romances, can also make individuals feel desperate, unsure what to do when plans fail or possibilities grow increasingly futile.

Critically, the vast majority of patients experiencing desperation experience these strong emotions when IVF cycles fail, not at their outset, during informed-consent-as-ritual, when they are presented with risks and benefits. This suggests that they can effectively weigh these factors and that desperation doesn't undermine their consent to IVF. This accords with patients' own descriptions of how desperation affects their decision-making capacity. Nicole Bell defended the capacity of individuals undergoing IVF: "there was a level of desperation, but it didn't cloud my judgment on making good health decisions for myself and my potential child and my husband. I think that anybody that does pursue this isn't an uninformed person. I'm sure they've gone through . . . some struggle. They're not uninformed about what they're going to put their bodies through." Thus, unless their desperation becomes extreme, most individuals do not see themselves within conventional infertility stereotypes of incapacity, *even if* they consider themselves desperate.

IN CRITICAL CONDITION: HOW PROVIDERS DEFINE DESPERATION

Patients' and providers' views about desperation are influenced by personal relationships, treatment outcomes, and social, cultural, and political contexts. But providers' perspectives are also influenced by different factors. Because they work in clinics and hospitals that have structures, practices, and policies (like short appointment lengths) that directly bear upon patient care and interaction, these factors might affect their opinions of desperation.

Providers have understandably complicated reactions to this label. Many despise the term, but they can discuss which groups of patients might be desperate and describe how they behave. Several professionals find this term offensive. Dr. Heike Steinmann thought it a "harsh word," and Head Nurse Melina Draper deemed it "fairly extreme." "When you use the word 'desperate,' you've already loaded the conversation," Dr. Bret Sternberg asserted. He preferred the term "motivated": "'desperate' . . . is an emotionally loaded term because [it] describes a situation of . . . life or death. You could say somebody who's just jumped off the bridge in a panic is in a desperate situation. But it also has the connotation of someone who's misinterpreting something as desperate when in fact it isn't life-threatening, in which case we're making a psychological judgment about them."

Because they make decisions with patients and put these decisions into action, reproductive medicine professionals have unique insight into whether and when patients experience desperation. The vast majority admit to having some "desperate" patients, but apply this term to very few; most spontaneously estimate 5% (8) or 10% (13), rather than 20% or 30% (6) or higher (3). Specifically, 54% stated a "few" were desperate—a higher percentage than those estimating that this label fit "some" (4%), "quite a few" (7%), "most" (14%), or "all" (6%).

But several providers believe that "desperation" is too extreme a label. Dr. Denzel Burke felt it implied "somebody [was] starving or doing anything to get food for their children or somebody has a drug habit." It might impugn patients' desires and emotional needs, unfairly punishing a behavior—desiring children—that society strongly encourages. Other professionals are reluctant to pathologize patients' strong desires to conceive, because some so-called "desperate" behaviors indicate informed decision making. "They're asking millions of questions. They want to know everything. And that's not something a desperate person would do," Donor Program Assistant Tori Krausse explained. "They're very well aware of what they're choosing, what they're doing, and what they want."

In addition to allegedly "desperate" behaviors that actually reflect patient engagement, other stereotypically "desperate" reactions come from (and reinforce) problematic perceptions about women's "natural" emotionality and parental inclinations. For example, Dr. Oliver Evans asserted that women are more "hard wired" for parenthood and thus more likely to become desperate when parenthood is thwarted:

> [W]e can certainly see that woman have some sort of biological wiring, for a lack of a better word, a deeper sort of sense of person that's tied to having children. Whereas men can be more rational and say, "You know, I can

envision life without children." But for women, I think there's a more innate sort of, just human nature in having children, and you can see this caring for children. You stick a crying baby in a room full of guys, and they're all gonna bump into each other and [say] "what are we going to do?" . . . Whereas women go into [it] more naturally. . . . I think those types of things come into play with the treatment as well. The woman actually has fought a battle, not just with herself and her own emotions, but often times her physician [who] may or may not fully understand fertility and prescribed basal body temperature charts. . . . And she probably has had a battle with her husband, who doesn't want to spend money on this because it's not that important. So from that standpoint, that's sort of a different meaning of desperate. . . . This poor woman has just had nothing but barriers to pregnancy and I don't think the husbands comprehend how important they are in that.

Providers may think such opinions are less problematic if they appear to be biological and not sexist.

Beyond so-called "desperate" behaviors that aren't really desperate (but reflect engagement or sexism), professionals' perceptions of which patients became desperate overlap in many respects with patients': individuals without children, "doctor shoppers," patients from some ethnic backgrounds, older or repeat IVF patients, or those in their last cycle. Culture and ethnicity matter; Dr. Bret Sternberg said, "[M]y Latino patients who don't get pregnant are essentially disenfranchised. . . . they'll have no social standing in their community." Treatment history and experiences also factor in: "My 'last chance' kind of patient . . . they're just drowning and . . . they're very intense and . . . overwhelmed because this is gonna be it" (Nurse Elihu Brant). The length of time patients have pursued treatment is also a significant influence: "When they hit about the three to five year mark, I would say, probably about 50% of them [are desperate]. Because most people don't come in the first year of trying. They're not worried about it. But after they've been through a few fertility treatments, I think they become more desperate" (Psychologist Geoffrey Bourke).

A "desperate" patient "often has [had] a lot of difficult things happen," like miscarriages, said Physician's Assistant Nora Stanton. Even older patients "in their mid to late forties" might be desperate if "they think, 'My fertility is so good,' and I show them all the numbers," reflected Dr. Connor Gibson.

The handful of patients whom providers consider desperate exhibit behaviors and emotions that match conventional infertility stereotypes: anger (8%), extreme anxiety (12%) or continual crying (9%), a perceived lack of control, extreme deference (5%), distrust (9%), failure to listen (10%), obsession, denial or medically "unsound" requests (46%), and excessive clinic phone calls (7%). These extreme behaviors are easy to observe; several professionals claim they can tell whether a patient is desperate even "when you're talking to them over the phone . . . by their voice, their type of questions" (Nurse Jaylen Abbott). "Desperate" patients also exhibit greater anger, anxiety, and grief: "We have one that's very angry and has blown up at everybody in this practice. And so that's stressful to us" (New Patient Coordinator Aston Reinhold).

Desperation provokes extreme emotional displays. Dr. Nicole Potter remarked, "They're sometimes even inconsolable in a consult, . . . to the point that they can't stop that and talk." Professionals link this distress and instability to helplessness: "especially the higher achieving women, you've so little control over it" (First Year RE Fellow Dr. Yazmin Kuhn). These patients often can't complete a treatment cycle: "[t]hey're so emotionally distraught that they're not able to proceed through the process" (Psychologist Haylee Randell). "Desperate" patients who prematurely cease treatment contradict the stereotypical patient, who continuously undergoes IVF to the point of personal, social, and financial ruin.

According to providers, "desperate" patients either relinquish control, largely deferring to medical advice, or seize it by the throat, bush-whacking their own paths through treatment. Overly passive patients act as if "I don't want to make any decisions, I want to do everything you tell me to do. If you tell me to stand on my head for the next three days to get pregnant, I'll do it" (Dr. Abbie Walther). A few exceedingly deferential—and therefore vulnerable—patients might even become targets for predatory individuals recommending risky, unhealthy, or futile treatments: "There's some guy somewhere in the country doing pretty cheap tubal reversals, and people will fly down to him and get their $2,000 tubal reversal and then they fly up here. And then six months later they come in because they haven't gotten pregnant. I do an HSG and their tubes are blocked or they only have a centimeter of tube, which there's no way in God's green earth they're ever going to get pregnant" (Dr. Bryant Rowe).

The foil of the fully compliant patient is the distrustful skeptic. "They spend an extraordinary amount of time on the Internet trying to out-doctor the doctor. They try all kinds of complementary and alternative approaches regardless of the evidence base," remarked Psychologist Colin Bulle. Desperate patients might also continuously call their fertility clinics; IVF Coordinator Rosamund Coel recalled one patient who found her cell phone number and called her at home at 9:00 p.m. Other patients develop "tunnel vision": "there's a baby this way, only this way, and it has to happen in this period of time and if it doesn't, there's nothing else in my life" (Dr. Nicole Potter).

"Desperate" patients also have communication difficulties; they hear what they want (or don't want to hear difficult information), and "somehow get to the point where they stop being able to work through issues" (Dr. Nicole Potter). Perhaps a patient might be "unwilling to hear her own chances for success" (Third Party RN Prasad Singh). Providers try to overcome these communication barriers and sometimes must act as gatekeepers, refusing to accommodate harmful or medically futile patient requests.

But gatekeeping is difficult when answers aren't clear-cut, as when patients with infinitesimal odds of conceiving request a "last chance" IVF cycle. Granting this request might allow patients to avoid regret before moving on to donor gametes: "some of them just have to try . . . with their own gametes before they're able to accept it. . . . I feel like they're exercising their right to . . . try it the one time before they move on" (Embryologist Chalise Jones). Using "rights" discourse to describe patients' treatment desires is problematic; patients traditionally have a right to *refuse* treatment, not *demand* elective services. Other providers adamantly oppose such "last chance" cycles, citing medical futility:

> I had one patient who I didn't take through IVF. . . . I felt like her prognosis was so poor it wasn't worth trying. She went out to [a well-known clinic]; they tried three cycles, she failed miserably. She went to [a second clinic] to try cycles; she came back to me and she wanted to try another cycle. And I said, point-blank, "I'm really sorry, but I won't do it. You either have to switch gears to try new donor eggs or seriously think about other options like adoption. If you just keep going down this path trying to retrieve eggs when there are none, the risks outweigh the benefits and I won't put you in that type of situation in my clinic." . . . I think being very definitive and not being wishy-washy and not letting the patient talk you into something [is best]. . . . Maybe I'm a smidge more paternalistic, but I feel like I've the expertise and the wisdom and it's my duty to not put my patients in harm's way. (Dr. Rory Fontaine)

Dr. Fontaine emphasizes that doctors, not patients, have the right to refuse treatment, whether or not patients pay out-of-pocket. But even he considers these refusals somewhat "paternalistic"—too apologetic a word for gatekeeping, which is most often proper medical care.

What special responsibilities should providers have toward patients they consider desperate? Second Year RE Fellow Dr. Peter Gore exercised additional caution in shepherding these patients through treatment:

"Those are the kind of patients that we need to watch out for, in the sense that we need to do a better job in guiding them to more successful treatments and dissuading them from doing futile treatments." Fortunately, providers report that most patients can acknowledge when their chances of conceiving are too low to justify the effort and expense: "if you tell somebody that there's a 5% chance, frequently they'll say, 'Look, that's just too low.' I mean, there's certainly people that say even [at] 1%, 'I want to try,' but I think most people are pretty reasonable" (Dr. Heike Steinmann). Thus, providers often correct misunderstandings through patient education: "often we sit down and I say, 'Well let's just talk. Let's be educated about what really happens in the real world, not something on some sort of TV show or whatever.' . . . It's terrible because the chances of something like [Octomom] happening in a responsible practice like this are almost zero" (Dr. Nicole Potter).

Technological advances and updated standards of practice can clarify ethically cloudy areas and constrain patients' options. Professionals have worked hard on decreasing multiple pregnancies. Head Nurse Melina Draper reflected, "I think in earlier years, patients had more say in the number of embryos to transfer. I think over a longer period . . . there's been greater consideration to that risk of multiple pregnancy, and . . . we're less inclined to allow patients to make decisions that would be irresponsible." Dr. Connor Gibson was gravely concerned about this issue:

> You've patients who say, "I don't care if I get triplets, four, five; I'll take the chance." So the bottom line discussion I have with patients is, "What you want is intact survival." And I feel firmly that I hate putting patients in a position where they may have to make a decision that makes them uncomfortable, . . . where they might be forced to seriously consider selective reduction. . . . I think that someone at least has to say, "Well, these are the possibilities, and do you really want to do this?" . . . It's the same as pregnancy termination. . . . I'm pretty firm about how many embryos I'll put back with IVF because I feel at least somebody has got to call something somewhere and say there ought to be a line drawn because you want people to have a healthy baby.

Providers would rather have uncomfortable conversations in informed-consent-as-ritual rather than risk later harms to patients or fetuses. But outside of IVF, providers have less control over patient behavior and compliance: "If we have somebody who's doing FSH IUI [follicle-stimulating hormone intrauterine insemination], where they're taking injectable medications and they develop eight follicles, [we] certainly can't stop people from having sex at home. But we'll certainly counsel that patient and then tell them, 'We don't want you to take your trigger injection,' . . . and that we aren't going to do an IUI, and we certainly advise that they don't have intercourse, etc." (Head Nurse Melina Draper). When all else fails, providers may need to "fire" patients: "we initially try to explain to them how risky that is . . . and if that doesn't get through to them then we'll actually release them from the practice and we'll give them names of other practitioners that they can contact" (Dr. Gerard Gabler).

CONCLUSION: "THE CATCHER IN THE RYE OF FERTILITY TREATMENT"

I jokingly call myself the "Catcher in the Rye" of fertility treatment, trying to keep people from going off the edge, like "Here, let me save you, let me help you to understand. Don't go down that path that so many have already traveled."

—Fertility Counselor Alivia Warwick

Investigating desperation—the emotion conventionally assumed to undermine decision making—reveals how politicized emotions resonate within patients' treatment experiences. Patients' reflections on desperation demonstrate that most do not fall within pejorative cultural infertility-related stereotypes. Although they can approximate what desperation feels like, these stereotypes vastly overestimate how many patients feel desperate and how extensively desperation influences behavior. As providers note, patients who feel strong emotions are often likely to prematurely discontinue treatment, not pursue futile cycles. Desperation rarely overwhelms a patient's capacities to understand what infertility treatment involves and make authentic, informed treatment decisions. The few who encounter trouble—5 to 10%, according to professionals—are outliers, and they are inappropriate models for stereotypes, let alone crafting policies and regulations.

This case study of desperation illustrates how emotions can help patients integrate knowledge and values and influence complex decision making, and how decisions made under intense emotional pressures may go against patients' settled views or long-term interests. Thus, as with other infertility-related emotions, it's impossible to characterize desperation as entirely "good" or "bad"; instead, it just "is." Desperation can motivate and paralyze and play helpful or harmful roles, and it's often an appropriate response to a tough situation. A motivated patient may zealously undergo IVF cycles, even as a paralyzed patient needs a period of indecision to fully comprehend goings-on, and a patient in temporary denial can use desperation to adjust to unbearable knowledge. But desperation warrants concern when it entraps individuals; it is then that they need a "catcher in the rye" figure, a professional who can help save them from their traumatized selves. This, in turn, entails another question: how do the vast majority of women and men evade desperation and other emotional pitfalls of infertility and find their own coping rhythms?

CHAPTER 3

Conceptive Catch-22s

The Benefits and Burdens of Infertility Emotions

Combing through libraries of articles, books, and Internet sites, hoping to improve her odds of pregnancy, Hannah Sandoval picked up a book entitled *Fully Fertile: A 12-Week Holistic Plan for Optimal Fertility*, promoting "fertility-making" changes like "letting go of the expectations, judgments and negative thoughts we've created around the fertility journey and our own, innate fertility."[1] This advice, simple though it seemed, stumped Hannah: "How are you supposed to think that you're likely to conceive when you're on try number seven?"

Asking people to think about how their emotions affect decision making is one thing; asking them to set unrealistic emotional goals is another. Yet, that is why so much infertility-related advice—including the cliché phrase "just relax"—misses the mark. Infertility is emotional, but emotions often strengthen autonomy and rarely derail competency. But whatever their role, emotions are both an involuntary and unavoidable part of the infertility Expedition. Emotions almost always intensify as fertility attempts progress. Some patients learn to cope with these emotions and even diminish them; others are plunged into negative, counterproductive thinking, which intensifies them.

The operative question is, then, not *whether* infertility is emotional, but what *consequences* emotions have for patients. Are we making unreasonable demands upon individuals negotiating infertility in expecting them to downplay or disengage with their emotional selves? Might we give them too little credit, since most successfully work through this emotionally grueling infertility experience? It stands to reason we can learn much from how these individuals successfully cope with these difficult circumstances.

Emotions alone—even an intense desire to conceive—can't power one through infertility. An individual's determination to complete this journey is like a gas motor. To run, motors need fuel, air, and a spark. The desire for a child undoubtedly provides the spark. But what about the fuel? At first, an individual's eagerness to conceive might provide enough energy to keep the motor running smoothly. But at some point, it sputters with increasing frequency, threatening to stall altogether. Multiple unsuccessful attempts to conceive are huge gas guzzlers, prompting self-doubt and draining motivation. Further attempts require even greater quantities of personal fuel. Moreover, a gas motor needs air; a well-ventilated environment cools the motor and dissipates its fumes. But in infertility, getting air—or airing infertility concerns—isn't as easy as it sounds. The ideal high-octane infertility "fuel" is a cocktail of emotional and physical ingredients: hope, caution, perseverance, humor, and pragmatism, mixed proportionately with time, flexibility, health, and stamina.

Emotions play significant roles in decision making, potentially sowing chaos even as they facilitate choice. In particular, individuals often experience three Catch-22s during their conceptive journeys: the mind-body connection, family and friends, and infertility research. Strangely, these Catch-22s most frequently involve activities that proactive patients use to cope with infertility. Most surveyed patients (58%) observed that Internet resources made them "feel better," along with family and friends (46.4%), seeking medical treatment (45%), support groups and therapists (31%), hobbies (29%), and religious activities (16%).

In the first Catch-22, it's possible that certain negative emotions can decrease odds of pregnancy, although research studies and providers differ as to whether infertility-related emotions can affect treatment outcomes due to a mind-body connection. Yet, these emotions are largely involuntary, leaving patients few options for mitigating their effects.

Meanwhile, when individuals' coping reserves dissipate, they reach outward to friends and family for support. But cultivating support can require sharing intimate details about sore (and sorely private) subjects. Discussing infertility with others can expose individuals to stigma and misunderstanding, including well-meant but hurtful comments like "Just relax!" and "Why don't you adopt?" These hurtful experiences can intensify negative emotions, which, given a possible mind-body connection, can decrease odds of pregnancy. Infertility thus encourages isolation, not sociability, and patients can quickly feel trapped.

At the same time, few patients can resist the temptation to turn to "Dr. Google." Online, treasure troves—or junkyards—of advice, research, forums, and blogs saturated with personal anecdotes and reflections await. This information can assist informed authentic decision making, but it can also blindside readers, describe treatment options that REs may veto, and recommend "stand-on-your-head-while-eating-pineapple" solutions that would've seemed crazy beforehand. Online, it's hard to find accurate answers to important questions. Like attempts to discuss infertility, then, research efforts often intensify infertility-related emotions.

CATCH-22 #1: THE "MIND-BODY" MYSTERY

Trying to get pregnant through fertility treatment can trigger a range of emotions, but some emotions can make it harder to get pregnant.

Emotions can dramatically affect a patient's treatment experience, energizing her or leaving her drained.[2] And, as 92% of providers noted, emotions influence decisions. But can they change a cycle's outcome?

The possibility that emotions could change treatment outcomes raises the possibility of a mind-body connection in infertility. Medical research[3] has not found a clear answer: "There have probably been over 30 studies which have looked at a woman's emotional state before and during IVF cycles. And most of them show that the more distressed she is during the cycle, the less likely she is to get pregnant. Although a couple studies . . . showed that women who were the most distressed *before* she cycled are more likely to get pregnant. So I think there's a complicated relationship" (Psychologist Angela Pierre).

Since scientific studies disagree whether a mind-body connection affects treatment outcomes, fertility professionals are currently the best authorities on whether a connection exists and what consequences it might have. And what providers directly or indirectly communicate to patients about the physical effects of their emotions strongly influences their treatment experiences.

As Figure 6 shows, 68% of reproductive physicians and clinic staff (besides mental health professionals) believed a patient's mental and emotional states *definitely* affected treatment outcomes, and another 23% and 8%, respectively, thought such influence was *likely*. Professionals disagree about the credibility of research on a mind-body connection; two

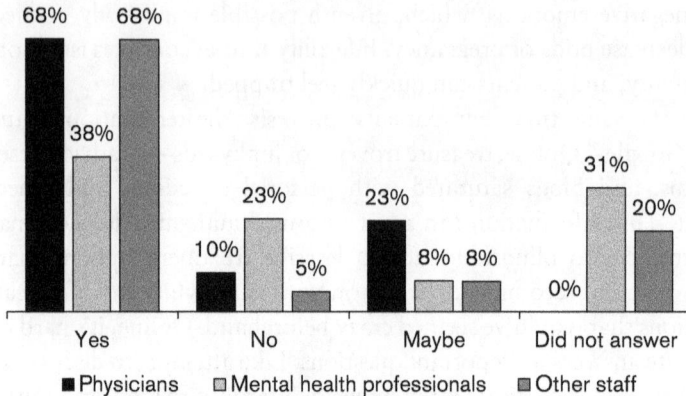

FIGURE 6. Do Fertility Patients' Mental and Emotional States Affect Treatment Success? Source: Jody Lyneé Madeira

contrasting perspectives illustrate extremes on the spectrum of professional opinion:

> Even if they have a study saying that there's no credence in the fact that stress affects whether someone gets pregnant, I think it still probably does play a role in a lot of patients. (Dr. Connor Gibson)
>
> I'm a scientific-type person, too, so I do think that as long as it [stress and emotions] doesn't interfere with them taking their meds properly, I don't think that it probably [has an effect]. I think that it may influence how they cope with it, but I think it's science and it's the bottom line. (IVF Nurse Coordinator Meredith Haynes)

While Dr. Gibson considers other evidentiary sources besides research studies (including experience), Nurse Haynes cites "science" in reaching the opposite conclusion. As these different perspectives illustrate, medical professionals don't always adhere to the rational, clinical Western medicine framework, which conventionally prioritizes scientific research over anecdotal evidence and downplays emotions and a mind-body connection.

Admittedly, it is difficult to research emotions' effects on treatment outcomes. Patients undergoing IVF may downplay stress levels lest providers refuse to treat them, and, as one study reported, "tend more than other patients to give socially desirable answers."[4] Moreover, it would be difficult to identify a baseline stress level; feeling *some* stress is normal and healthy and reflects appropriate coping behaviors.[5] As Dr. Bret Sternberg noted, "I don't think the data is good enough to support one thing or the other. . . . [S]cience is messy. It's rarely black and white, and stuff gets

published of variable quality . . . and it's often pretty hard to clearly demonstrate something which in fact may be very multifactorial." Psychologist
Marcel Park frankly admitted, "I don't think there's any way for us to
access that data. . . . I always wonder about that, especially for people
who . . . have perfect embryos, their lining is absolutely terrific, they've had
stellar cycles and . . . it's still not working. . . . The psyche's pretty strong."
The lack of scientific consensus leaves room for other evidence to fill
research gaps, and professionals may draw on other evidence, like personal
treatment experiences, as proof that patients' mental and emotional states
do play unknown and perhaps undiscoverable roles. For example, Nurse
Arya Mullur linked a recent catastrophic flood to clinic patients' low pregnancy rates: "I don't believe there was but one pregnancy. . . . when it's [a]
bad atmosphere, bad vibes, they're not going to get pregnant."

Providers frequently shared anecdotes about patients' emotions allegedly affecting their pregnancy chances. "One patient recently was just kind
of like *Saturday Night Live*'s Debbie Downer," recalled Lab Director Farran Ibbott. "We finally got her pregnant with [a] frozen transfer; I think
her husband['s] optimism finally overtook her gray cloud. Beautiful
embryos every time. . . . I do think that emotional state can have an effect."
Some are confident that they can gauge a patient's conceptive chances
from observing her demeanor: "the uptight, anxious, overwhelmed
patients . . . we could even look at a patient and it's like, 'She's not gonna
get pregnant because of the way she's acting'" (Nurse Elihu Brant). Many
identify emotional qualities linked to success: "A lot of those people that
come in with less stress, good attitudes, end up being pregnant" (Lab
Director Keane Schultze). Others even offered patients advice on that
basis: "I usually tell them that embryos don't like a stressful uterus. So
whatever it is that they need to do, then they need to do it because it's a lot
of money to waste on stress" (New Patient Coordinator Aston Reinhold).

Other physicians become convinced that a mind-body connection
exists after seeing patients who shouldn't conceive get pregnant following holistic wellness services or exercises. Quipped Dr. Errol Walter,
"[E]very now and then I get a patient I'm sure has got no chance in the
world of getting pregnant, and they'll go see [a PhD-level acupuncturist]
and end up getting pregnant, and I won't understand why." Another
physician explained, "I'm from [the East Coast] originally, so when I
moved out to [the West Coast] and they wanted to do mind-body
classes, I went, 'Oh sure, buddy.' . . . And I was completely amazed at
the differences among people who availed themselves of the opportunity to take these courses. . . . And again, I'm a skeptical scientist."

Proponents of a mind-body connection describe its influence as either physical or psychological. Physically, emotions and stress might produce effects like elevated cortisol levels (Dr. Connor Gibson) or prevent menstruation and ovulation: "somebody that's under so much stress . . . completely shut[s] their periods off; the best example of that is anorexia nervosa. But there are other people in high-stress jobs, like lawyers and doctors, and they just totally shut their periods off and they don't ovulate at all" (Dr. Bryant Rowe).

A mind-body connection seems more plausible if psychological stress causes other physiologic symptoms. "If a patient is so stressed that they're losing weight, they can't sleep, that can cause such a biochemical reaction," observed Dr. Gerard Gabler. "I truly believe that affects fertility." But he was more skeptical as to whether stress alone had a measurable effect on cycle outcome: "Psychological stress without any evidence of significant change in physiology—I don't know how big of an impact that make[s]."

Most professionals are confident that patients' emotions can create "external" barriers to successful cycle outcomes. Mental and emotional states influence whether or not patients continue with fertility treatment in the first place. "[If] you've got a top-quality embryo and a good quality uterine lining, I don't think their mental state makes a difference to whether that embryo's going to implant," explained Dr. Kerry Kushner. "But I think the ability to get to that stage and to persevere with treatment is dependent on their psychological well-being." "Some [patients] will throw in the towel, so to speak, because of the emotional distress, not attempting it the second time when some of those, a great part of those, would've gotten pregnant," said Dr. Sebastian Alfaro. And stress can diminish patient attention and compliance, key elements of a successful IVF cycle: "people who are really, really stressed out make mistakes, and they don't follow directions, and they don't listen, and they fail" (Dr. Heike Steinmann).

Whether or not they find a mind-body connection credible, professionals are concerned about how patients might react to news of its existence. "I think it opens the door to all kinds of stigmatizing and blaming discourses that I don't think are true or helpful," Dr. Bret Sternberg opined. Patients could be blamed for experiencing emotions over which they have little control, or censured for being pessimistic or having conditions like depression. The lack of a scientific consensus provides room for providers to ease patients' minds by counseling them that negative emotions don't have treatment consequences. Psychologist Geoffrey Bourke was reluctant to further burden his patients and shared certain studies that found no emotional effects upon outcomes: "I hate to give people that burden of thinking that you don't have a right to feel sad about it. . . . Usually it's a big relief for me to show people the studies that say, 'Hey, just because you're feeling sad and depressed about this, it doesn't mean it's going to impact how you're going to get pregnant.'" Giving patients a license to worry without consequences might be far more productive: "in my experience, extremely anxious patients seem to get pregnant with the same frequency. . . . I've found that if I tell them to worry as much as they want to, they actually relax more" (Dr. Teagan Shepherd). These assurances keep patients positive—possibly helping them to get pregnant in the bargain.

Finally, a few reproductive professionals (11%) are adamant that a patient's mental or emotional state does *not* affect cycle outcomes. "There's no consistent findings, and if in fact there was [the] relationship people believe there is, we'd be tripping over the evidence," said psychologist Colin Bulle. Others noted that humans have always reproduced under stressful, even traumatizing conditions:

> If our species was so fragile . . . I'm pretty sure that back in the caveman days no one would've had children, because people were constantly being chased by a tiger and trying to figure out when they were going to get their next meal. . . . And women get pregnant in all kinds of adverse circumstances, . . . after incest, and rape, and in prison, and in war, and so I think it's a fallacy to think that only people who are Suzy Sunshine can be successful at a fertility center. (Psychologist Rory Frei)

Regardless of their opinions on a mind-body connection, fertility professionals agree that fostering patients' hope is essential. "Even if a patient won't be successful, I think it's still good to make them feel good about the whole process," remarked Lab Technologist Samuel Hurst. "I think you should do a lot of encouraging . . . that's [] where the doctors come in. I think that, even if they do have a poor prognosis, that the feeling of the team being hopeful makes them deal with everything much better."

This, then, is the Catch-22 that underlies all others—that paradox that, while negative, infertility-related emotions are beyond patients' control, they may make it harder to get pregnant—even if some providers deny it, for fear that these very consequences could occur.

CATCH-22 #2: THE SUPPORT SYSTEM STUMPER

Individuals want and need support from partners, family, and friends, but might have to discuss their infertility to obtain it, which exposes

them to stigma, fears of being misunderstood or rejected, and other neg-
ative experiences. This intensifies the emotional experience and exacer-
bates Catch-22 #1.

While providers can cultivate patients' hope, it can also sprout from
their friendships and family ties. People seek support in diverse ways, at
different times, and from various sources, including partners and friends.
Most find that talking about infertility and treatment is important—
but also unnerving. Deanna Douglas was initially afraid to discuss her
suspicions of infertility with others: "[w]hen we were trying on our
own, I felt very ashamed, embarrassed, like a failure. And we didn't tell
anybody."

Support is so important because isolation is one of infertility's most
common consequences.[6] First Year RE Fellow Dr. Yazmin Kuhn explained,
"We see patients all the time, and you can tell they've been holding it in
for so long because they don't want to talk to their friends about it. . . .
And they get here and they start talking, and it's [a] waterworks 'cause
they just feel so alone."

And popular culture seems to *dis*courage openness about infertility,
just when people are torn between a desire to disclose and a reticence to
risk rejection. Brooklyn Knowles thought that fertility treatment is still
stigmatized, saying that listeners' comments on a recent NPR story
about gamete donation were upsetting because "their listeners are such
informed and educated people, and the comments were so dumb and
narrow-minded. I was just like, 'Oh God, here I'm thinking everybody
gets what we're trying to do, and they're happy for us and think that
we're doing a good thing,' and there are people out there that think
really horrible, negative things about this."

This stigmatization is stronger in some geographic parts of the country than others; as one RE reflected, "this is the Bible Belt—so we do
have a whole bunch of religious [groups] that just don't like IVF, and
the Baptists are sometimes just as staunch about it as the Catholics."
Sylvia Nelson connected this silence to societal discomfort over "sex,
having a baby" and "grief," and Amber Butler related, "[W]e're taught
as very young kids that that's a very private area, your reproductive
[life] is very personal; you don't talk about that." Others felt that this
stigma is ridiculous because infertility has medical causes. "I hate how
fertility is viewed as like breast cancer in the '80s; it's a dirty little secret
and it's taboo and you shouldn't talk about [it]," exclaimed Stella Madison. "Someone has a medical condition; there's medicine that can fix it.
Don't be shy, talk about it."

In the face of such reactions, what does someone negotiating infertility expect to happen when she discusses infertility with friends and family? Of interviewed individuals, 63% discussed their infertility with others, and 15% described themselves as infertility advocates.

Regardless of whether cultural portrayals weigh on their minds, individuals readily acknowledge that openness about infertility and treatments is complex, and they marshal legions of reasons against and for disclosure. Sometimes religious tenets prevent patients from comfortably discussing their treatment: "His family being very staunch Catholics, we couldn't share with them, we couldn't lean on anybody else, we had to keep it all very Q.T. [quiet], and that was, I think, a lot more pressure" (Marie Byrd). Or patients feared their churches or congregation members wouldn't understand; Christine Zimmerman asserted, "even though I think that the church was okay with it, I think there's a stigma. . . . I didn't want people knowing that I did it."

Others prefer keeping such matters private, or feel that it's too painful to continuously give others updates: "I just don't want to get asked at every stage of my treatment, 'Hey did you conceive yet?'; I don't want to have to explain why it doesn't work" (Megan Cooper). Disclosure might expose them to offensive reactions: "[my in-laws'] comment was just that they didn't feel like we should be wasting that kind of money when it might not work. We should just go adopt or something" (Antonia Hughes). And several don't want to worry friends or family: "[I] feel like I'm dragging other people down. . . . I don't want to feel like I'm a burden on my friends" (Patrick Shields).

Often, men are most unwilling to discuss infertility, usually to preserve privacy or avoid the stigmatization of male factor infertility. "I was a little more comfortable with it than my husband, who was very, very reserved about it, and would get pretty upset if people knew the specifics and the details," reflected Brittany Watson. "It was a hit on his manhood and his strength as the husband." Nathaniel Sims didn't think discussing infertility with other men would be helpful: "it's very hard to be able to share that stuff with other men. . . . If you're talking about an issue to a man that knows nothing about that actual problem, then his solution is going to be very resolved: 'Well, it'll work out. My wife and I tried . . . and it's just going to work.'"

But there are also good reasons for disclosure, including gaining support. Most individuals eventually choose to discuss their infertility experiences with at least a few trusted others. Silence can seem painful: "There were times I had to lie to family and friends about where I was going or where I was coming from. Sometimes I wanted to scream, 'Don't you realize there's something wrong!' But they had no reason to know. . . . There was a lack of support, but that was my own choice, because we didn't share information with other people" (Joanne Johnson).

And practically, it can be almost impossible to keep such information secret: "I'm a very open person, and so keeping secrets sometimes is kind of tough. And then having an older son, you need help 'cause you're going to these treatments" (Nicole Bell). Or openness might be the least harmful alternative, especially compared to being fired for missing work due to demanding treatment schedules. Openness can also smooth potentially awkward social interactions: "it does make things a lot easier to not have to come up with excuses for things . . . or to pretend like everything is going great when it's not" (Ashley Carpenter). And openness can ease or redirect stigma, prompting some men to be open about their infertility so that their wives won't be stigmatized: "I went out of my way to share with people what our cause was, [so] that people wouldn't look at her and think that it was her that couldn't do the job" (Luis Torres). Finally, sharing often proves cathartic, as Sheri Lopez discovered when she confided in a friend experiencing infertility: "I was so desperate at the time to talk to someone who was going through it. . . . It was a huge emotional boost."

Putting aside the question of *whether* to disclose, individuals differ as to *what* information they discuss and with whom. "We were very open about going through IVF because I didn't think it really did us any service to not be, and it's good to be open," said Rochelle Rowe. "We weren't that open about donor egg because we [are] kind of still working through those issues around what's fair to the child." Some find it easier to discuss IVF's technological procedures than its emotional impact. "It was difficult to have people connect to the . . . emotional struggle of getting pregnant," Cynthia Gardner reflected. "Short of a very, very select few, . . . they only really ever knew the technical part of it. . . . But the emotional part I held back."

A few become infertility advocates to educate and support others. "I like to call myself loud and proud. I like to advocate for infertility, so when I see an article about this, I'm throwing it up on my Facebook [page] for my 300 friends to see," said May Weiss. "I think it's a shame that it's such a silent disease, and I wish that people would be more open about it." Stella Madison sought to break the cultural silence surrounding infertility, as others had for breast cancer:

[M]y mom . . . had a friend back in the '80s who had breast cancer and it was always *breast cancer*. . . . [N]ow everyone celebrates "ta-ta's," . . . you've baseball players who are wearing pink in honor of breast cancer; . . . it's nothing to be ashamed of. Why should I be ashamed because it took me longer to have a child? . . . I think I made very careful decisions with my life and my career and don't think that I should be judged when it comes to fertility or infertility because of those decisions.

Advocacy can also be therapeutic. "Part of the problem is keeping this gigantic secret. . . . When I was a mess, no one knew why," recounted Simone Henry. "[Now] I'm very, very, publicly vocal about it and very clear with people, . . . that's helped the psychological [effects]." Blogging also can provide a tremendous release, as Cynthia Gardner explained: "It allows me to get out those feelings that I have and put them out there and let them go. . . . It was validating to go through my different cycles and remember, 'Oh yeah, this is what it was like then.' And it was validating to have people say, 'Oh yeah, I hear ya. I feel ya.'"

Finally, openness can introduce individuals to others in similar situations. When old friends disappear, people make new ones. "I've a whole different set of friends now," Jessica Frazier observed. "The friends I had before that were all pregnant and were having kids didn't understand."

Therefore, patients have realized that this Catch-22—reaching out for support from others but risking rejection and stigma—has a built-in escape pod. Patients can find a trusted friend in whom to confide whatever they are comfortable disclosing.

CATCH-22 #3: THE RESEARCH RIDDLE

Individuals try to adjust to infertility through research and information-seeking, but these efforts can intensify difficult emotions like anxiety or helplessness. See Catch-22 #1.

Like other medical patients, individuals negotiating infertility need accurate information as well as emotional support.[7] The vast majority (95% interview, 92% survey) try to get information through research, by consulting others, or from online sources. Internet sites are far and away the most popular research resource (79% interview, 96% survey). Infertility-related Internet sites were consulted most frequently (68% interview, 78% survey), followed by forums (66% survey), blogs (47% survey), infertility medical sites (59% survey), and pregnancy sites (43% survey). Most individuals consulted Internet sources multiple times per day (56%

survey, 12% interview); others visited them daily (15% survey, 22% interview), a few times per week (20% survey, 8% interview), weekly (2% survey, 1% interview), a few times per month (4% survey), monthly (.9% survey, 1% interview), or less frequently (2.3% survey, 2% interview). The most popular non-Internet research resources are medical research articles (62% survey), followed by books (57% survey, 25% interview), newspaper or magazine articles (42% survey, 15% interview), family or friends (40% survey, 14% interview), support groups (31% survey), partners (26% survey), and therapists (21% survey).

Individuals also differ in how much research they conduct and when. Some individuals just have more free time than others. "When I wasn't working, [I was on the Internet] a lot . . . at my worst, five to six times per day," said Heather Stewart. "Now it's getting less and less." Internet research often decreases with time and treatment experience, although especially stressful periods can still intensify research activities. Jenna Moreno recalled, "I would be on more before I went to a doctor . . . just to make sure that, when I had my appointment, I was as thorough as I could be with my questions and possibilities of what could be going on."

Individuals' information-gathering efforts can induce comfort and restore a sense of control, and information itself can educate and empower.[8] Accurate information is a powerful—and readily available—tool. Patients can retrieve online information whenever they need it. "I Googled the hell out of any kind of word I could find . . . from the standpoint of just trying to understand it, embarrassingly feeling like I knew so little about my own body and anatomy," explained Sheri Lopez. "I feel like information is my best friend." Gaining control through research often makes patients stronger advocates. A few surprised their doctors when they shared research findings:

> We've found that a lot of medical professionals don't like when you do research. . . . We ordered that [sperm quality] kit, . . . it told you whether or not . . . there were enough sperm to be normal. But then since it said no, we ordered a second kit that came with a microscope, that you could actually . . . [use to] see how many sperm there are. . . . The urologist couldn't believe that we'd done that. He was just flabbergasted and mortified. He was like, "They were taking things into their own hands," and I was like, "We got the correct result, did we not?" (Samantha Romero)

Patients like Samantha take pride in regaining control—and perhaps also in discomfiting their providers, temporarily upending power relationships.

Moreover, research often brings patients emotional support and reassurance: "most of the time it would just kind of instill a little hope, like

'OK, somebody else has been through infertility, and now they have a child'" (Brianna Tyler). It reduced Jackie Carson's anxiety over her first physician consultation: "I would've been completely out-of-my-element scared with the way he explained [IVF]. But I'd read so much at that point about women who did it, and it worked, or even just women [who] got through it and they didn't lose their minds, that I felt a lot more prepared."

Finally, patients gain a sense of community through research: "I thought it was helpful just to know what other people are going through; it gave me a lot of comfort. . . . all of a sudden it wasn't quite as isolating" (Rochelle Rowe). Even online communities can provide strong support; Monica Hansen consoled a forum friend over the phone whose doctor had turned her away because of a scarred uterus, and a second woman from the same site mailed her leftover fertility medication.

Professionals, too, are quick to concede that Internet research can educate patients, even if a handful don't really want patients seeking their own information: "The Internet, . . . for most of our patients, is good; . . . they come to us with good questions so they're interacting, and you can tell that they're taking their diagnosis or their issues serious[ly]," said Clinical Coordinator Mira Durham. "I feel that our patients come in more educated than they ever were 12 years ago." This shift toward patient self-education facilitates patient autonomy. First Year RE Fellow Dr. Yazmin Kuhn explained, "[P]atients can walk through the door and already understand IVF. They already understand their options."

Patient education in turn promotes healthy and more equal, less paternalistic treatment relationships: "I think it's good for people to be able to get information from more than one place, so that they're not limited by what I might say or someone else might say" (Dr. Shel Kruger). Curious patients use research to take responsibility for their care: "I think they're using it for information, to help make informed choices" (Dr. Oliver Evans). Discussing research findings can even build trust. "I try to validate all the work they've done with their research in the first visit. And I try to understand what they might've garnered from their surfing," asserted Dr. Alexandra Sanford. "I always want them to come to me first and ask me about it." Moreover, patient research can decrease professionals' power. Dr. Bret Sternberg was happy to level these hierarchies: "an educated, assertive patient says, 'I've been reading on the Internet. I've been reading the *New England Journal of Medicine.*' . . . That isn't going to be a problem because that usually will mean that I'll be able to use . . . my medical language, . . . that they'll understand some of it. I mean, sometimes I have to tweak their understanding a little bit. But they're ready to meet me on my terms." Patients' research findings may even prompt REs to consider new options: "they may give me an idea that I hadn't thought of for them. In which case I'll say, 'Oh yeah, that's a great idea, let me think about it'" (Dr. Heike Steinmann).

But fertility professionals have a love-hate relationship with Internet research, because it can also give patients easy access to low-quality information. Many think that there's just too much material out there for patients to absorb. "[T]oo much information without any context isn't helpful, and so part of going to medical school is to create context," emphasized Dr. Nicole Potter. "I've no idea how they can understand all this stuff," Dr. Bryant Rowe quipped.

Most professionals are concerned that information generates more misinformation than education: "[t]here is a lot of junk out there the patients read about. They come here with that information. Again, you have to re-educate them" (First Year RE Fellow Dr. Yazmin Kuhn). For that reason, Dr. Corwin Summers said, "I really do encourage my patients to read, but just be careful of their sources." Patients might have difficulty weeding out irrelevant or inaccurate information, requiring longer appointments: "Patients are always comparing treatment plans as if they're perfectly equivalent, and that ends up wasting so much of all of our time while we respond to all of those queries" (Psychologist Colin Bulle). Providers especially distrust information that isn't evidence-based. "With this black box of reproductive endocrinology that we live in, there [are] a lot of gray areas," noted First Year RE Fellow Dr. Yazmin Kuhn. "There's a lot of experimental treatments, experimental protocols, that patients read about on the Internet. And growth hormone. DHEA. Supplements. And things like that we don't think help and may actually harm your cycle." And providers might feel wounded and confused when well-educated patients try to act on this dubious information instead of REs' advice: "you chose your physician, because you did some research and you saw the credentials . . . what kind of center, what the outcomes are. But then, all of a sudden, you change your decision making based on another source, with credentials you don't know, [at a] center you don't know, you don't know anything."

Problems can arise when patients make research-based requests their providers might hate to refuse. Some patients ask for certain treatments they read about online. "They come in and they announce, 'I want ICSI, or something like that, because I want a baby, I want to do it this way,' and they're not candidates," noted Psychologist Haylee Randell. "I see that [as] partly striving to regain control." When Internet research differs from physicians' advice, patients might place more trust in what they learn online. This often undermines trust and cripples a professional-patient relationship: "if we're not telling them what they think they need, then obviously it presents a problem because . . . in their minds, we don't know what we're doing" (Embryologist Lizbeth Norman). Some patients don't want to listen and "are overly forceful with the Internet data," according to Dr. Oliver Evans. "They've already come in with their treatment plan, and essentially I'm just inhibitory," he explained. "That's [a] more adversarial relationship. . . . they're viewing it more [as if] we're trying to prevent them, [not protect them]."

Nonetheless, these tasks are part of providers' duties: "it's part of the trust thing, that you kind of have to say, 'That isn't correct, and these are the reasons why, and this is what we should be doing,'" explained Dr. Wes Hoffman. Frustratingly, time spent on patient education doesn't always bear fruit:

> [W]ith medicine, people think they can go on the Internet and get a degree. . . . The patient has an absolute right to ask all of those questions, but sometimes . . . it gets a little more challenging than it should. I mean, we very much baby our patients. We hold their hand from beginning to end, and inevitably it's the ones that . . . you have to go ten miles beyond what you'd have to go with anyone else, that they're the ones writing the letter complaining about the service that they got, and that's hard. (Dr. Don West)

Patients' descriptions of their research efforts substantiate many providers' concerns and introduce new ones. Several find what they uncover irrelevant or otherwise unhelpful: "I tried to read a lot of educational journals, medical journals, and I have the thin [body type] variant of PCOS, and there's nothing on it," Brianna Tyler explained. "Usually most of the research they have is on overweight or obese PCOS patients." Joanne Johnson detested the "Ask" websites that "comes up with any one of these things [that] could happen, it's from A to Z, where it says there could be nothing wrong or you could be dying; . . . it was too general." And Margarita Daniels found Internet forums somewhat silly: "they have these rituals, and a lot of words that don't make a lot of sense if you don't know what acronyms mean, and a lot of talk about blessings and cutesy [behavior]."

Often, information is inaccurate. Lily Ellis recounted how distressing Internet research became after her miscarriage: "I went looking for the reason I lost the baby, and then I got some misinformation, and then I freaked myself out." "The Internet is hit and miss. You can always find something ... that tells you everything is going to be just fine, and something on the Internet tells you this is never going to work," emphasized May Weiss. Silvia Spencer thought that some online forums were as accurate as "going to a fortune teller," and David Reid knew that posters are "fairly self-selecting and nonrepresentative." Some are even skeptical of clinic websites, which Marie Byrd found "least helpful. . . . They're a little biased."

At its worst, infertility research can be downright painful or stress-inducing and might even become a compulsion. Sonya Saunders disliked blogs brimming with the negativity that is so prevalent within infertility: "you hear their struggle, their stress and anxiety, and just, ugh." In short, research can aggravate as well as educate, and information can seem emotionally threatening due to negative content or ambiguity.[9] Bethany Brady exclaimed, "Ugh! Bulletin boards! They're a really great source for camaraderie in terms of meeting other women who are going through it at the same time, but they're full of misinformation and people who, because they've gone through IVF once, they think they're some kind of expert at it."

Nevertheless, some patients become overly dependent on the Internet, using it as "an emotional . . . crutch" (Holly Garrett). "At first I was there three times a day, and it felt really almost compulsive," Bethany Brady recalled. "I started to realize it was actually making me feel a little bit worse than better." Or others' virtual negativity might be contagious: "I found a lot of anger in a lot of the women that I was dealing with, and they were talking about how much they hated their friends, and how they were angry with the world. And . . . I would just read those blogs and I would just feel badly about my situation, in a way that I didn't feel badly about it before" (Shannon Ward). On Internet forums, pregnancy narratives are stories-in-the-making, as posts remain unfinished and participants move on. "Once you finally do get pregnant, you don't think to go back to that board and talk about your wonderful experience," Eva Davidson emphasized. "I think there's more negative information than there is positive, and actually after I got pregnant, I went to one of those message boards and put my positive story on there 'cause I felt like nobody did that."

Internet-dependent patients often reach a breaking point where self-preservation requires going offline. "I knew I had to draw a line," recounted Sheri Lopez. "You just start delving so much into [the forum] and getting so scared about your own situation. . . . I just needed to stay off of there and just kind of let go and worry about our own scenario."

Research can even change individuals' personalities. "Everything was, 'How come I'm not getting that medication? How come that dose is different? Why am I not trying that? How come it's working for them?'" Simone Henry explained. "I started making myself a little bit crazy . . . and that's sort of when I pulled back from it." Allison Perkins's friend became trapped in an unhealthy online mentality:

[My friend] just said how she loved the forums, but she did three IVFs, one was unsuccessful, one was a chemical pregnancy [a very early miscarriage], and one she got pregnant with twins and they were born and died a couple of hours later at 20 weeks. And she felt like the forums were very much just [focused on messages like] . . . "Next time is your time," and "This just isn't fair." . . . I would say she's in a much worse place with infertility six years later than I am now, and she actually has two children. . . . I almost [compare] it to somebody who was bigger and lost a lot of weight, and they say that they're like a big person in a skinny body. I say that she has children, but she still has an infertile mind.

Finally, professionals worry that online research makes their patients panicked, stressed, obsessed, confused, and anxious. Research can be a time sink. "Some [patients] are overwhelmed by it. . . . they can get very caught up in needing to know every single thing that's out there, and spend hours and hours and hours on the Internet and read everything that's available," explained Third Year RE Fellow Dr. Wilma Sumner. Dr. Corwin Summers felt it makes patients needlessly scared: "there's other information that, for lack of a better word, just scares the bejesus out of people and actually prevents them from seeking care." Psychologist Rory Frei described online forums as a virtual Wild West that exposes patients to extreme situations and reinforces emotional extremes in turn: "I think some of what comes out online, because it's very infrequently moderated, is the most extreme version . . . the most outlier, worst-case-scenario experiences, which are really scary for a patient. Or [there are] people who have a lot of venom, or [a] deeply hopeless perspective, and there's nobody there to sort of help direct the discussion."

Providers try to weaken the temptations of online research through explanations or, failing that, appealing to patients directly: "There was a patient that we had to give a second beta [pregnancy test]. It didn't rise the way that the first one should. And she was the patient with her notepad at every appointment. . . . [Her husband] called me [and asked], 'How do I handle this?' I said, 'You take her out to dinner. You take her to a movie. You keep her away from the computer'" (IVF Coordinator Rosamund Coel).

Thus, while Internet research can revive individuals' sense of control, level power differences in treatment relationships, and support autonomy, it can also effect real harm when taken to the extreme.

CATCHING ON: MOVING PAST INFERTILITY'S CATCH-22S

Individuals undergoing infertility treatment must navigate a host of involuntary emotions and needs that coincide with commonsense behaviors like seeking support and information. They must walk the thin line between maintaining privacy while building a support network, navigating existing relationships, and undertaking new ones. They turn to books, medical journals, magazines, friends, and the Internet for information about infertility and its treatment, simultaneously regaining some sense of control and encountering further frustration and anxiety. Hopefully, they can escape these Catch-22s, as Deanna Douglas did after she reached a breaking point and couldn't be silent any longer. "I finally came to this realization of, 'What am I ashamed of?'" Deanna recalled. "I couldn't take just holding it all in and having to make excuses as to why I'm not drinking or why I'm not going to the baby shower, so I finally just came out and made this big kind of announcement on Facebook." The result: profound support and relief. "[S]ince then, I felt a lot better, like a weight's been lifted off my shoulder," she observed. "The response was unbelievable. I couldn't believe people came out of the woodwork from everywhere just saying they were going through it."

All of these behaviors are balancing acts. Though beset by strong emotions, individuals gradually realize that seeking support and accurate information can mitigate these emotions' most harmful effects. Support networks combat isolation, and information-gathering is a natural and (within limits) invaluable behavior, especially when patients limit research time and question research sources. Individuals' reflections explain how they find their own coping rhythms and how these strategies change over time. Most tellingly, these comments confirm that the vast majority navigate these Catch-22s effectively, contradicting broad and largely unflattering stereotypes. And activities like building support networks and researching infertility affect how individuals carry out their most effective coping strategy: seeking medical assistance to build a family.

PART TWO

(Re)Productive Treatment Relationships

From Choosing a Provider to Collaborating in Conception

CHAPTER 4

Off to See the Wizard

On the Road to Treatment

You're off to see the Wizard, the Wonderful Wizard of Oz
You'll find he is a Whiz of a Wiz if ever a Wiz there was.
—"Follow the Yellow Brick Road," *The Wizard of Oz* (1939)

By now, patients have embarked upon their infertility Expeditions, negotiating infertility's emotional fallout and using emotions and other information to evaluate various options and decide what to do. But making future forays requires them to put these plans into action. Consulting a medical professional puts women in the ruby red shoes of another famous expeditioner, Dorothy Gale, who was catapulted to a strange land in the classic movie *The Wizard of Oz*. Beginning infertility treatment and consulting with an RE is the reproductive equivalent of journeying to the Emerald City to meet the Wizard—the professional who might help them conceive. But unlike Dorothy, women don't set off on the treatment stage of their Expeditions with a joyous Munchkin serenade, or in the company of jolly traveling companions. Women are far more likely to set off alone, even if they have partners. But their questions and their quest mirror Dorothy's: How do I get from here to where I want to be? How long will my journey take? Where else will it take me? Who will travel with me? Will I find a Wizard? Will I ever be able to "go home" pregnant?

Many dynamics within infertility Expeditions influence how patients begin fertility treatment, make treatment decisions, and select the professionals who will help them. Choosing an RE and a fertility clinic is one of the most important decisions a patient will make. But this choice involves several others, and one of the most important is how to pay for IVF. Payment methods affect treatment experiences and relationships, whether patients pay out-of-pocket or use insurance, or purchase "shared risk" programs (where they pay more up front for a "package" of cycles, with a partial refund if all prove unsuccessful). And many other factors influence treatment decision making; according to providers, the most significant of these are finances (34%), morality or religion (26%), and emotional intensity and energy (6%). Patients experience great pressure to choose well, both internally from themselves and externally from providers and partners, before committing substantial time, money, and emotional investment.

PAYING THE TOLLS ON THE YELLOW BRICK ROAD: FINANCING FERTILITY TREATMENT

Oh God, it [insurance coverage] made all the difference, because
knowing that you're financially sound is the most freeing thing. . . . I
think that's the number one burden on couples. . . . That was a very
heavy weight on my mind, knowing we'd have to somehow borrow
$25K. So just knowing insurance is covering it is like, "Oh my God, I
can never complain about insurance companies again because I feel like
they saved our ass."

—Kelley Bates

Because IVF treatment is expensive, many patients try to make treatment cost-effective. Insurance coverage is the "yellow brick road" that allows patients to reach the Emerald City—a fertility clinic—most painlessly and expeditiously, but few health insurance plans cover IUI or IVF. Only 15 states legally require insurers to provide infertility coverage, but these states have fewer multiple births[1] and give patients the freedom to make treatment decisions based on what's successful rather than what's covered.[2] Thus, most patients cobble together financing for fertility treatment through a number of sources. Most pay out-of-pocket (65% interview, 52% survey); fewer had insurance coverage for their treatments (38% interview, 43% survey). Other means of paying include credit (3% interview, 15% survey), gifts or loans from family or friends (12% interview, 13% survey), and bank loans (2% interview, 4% survey). In general, insurance coverage increases patient autonomy and improves decision making by expanding choices and flexibility.

"It Just Bleeds Money": Financial Pressures and Insurance Coverage

Financial pressures can affect how patients make decisions. Providers and patients must work together to choose the least invasive treatment, while containing costs and maximizing pregnancy changes—potentially contradictory goals: "There'd be times when I would say, 'Why are they still doing IUI? They should be doing IVF.' . . . But a lot of times again that's driven by financial [factors]. . . . And I guess if [this state] was a state that had insurance coverage for IVF, we [might] see a very, very different choice of treatment" (Lab Technologist Samuel Hurst).

To finance IVF, individuals get creative, undergoing dramatic lifestyle changes and accepting alternative financing arrangements. "We did IVF five times. . . . even now, we live in a mobile home because we gave up our house and . . . cars, any kind of vacations, anything to pay for it," explained Patricia Burns. "We took out credit card after credit card to pay for it, just because we were going to give ourselves any possible chance. But it just bleeds money." April Gonzalez obtained money from relatives to pay for IVF cycles before she got unexpected news: "when I was going to stop after my third cycle, I have a cousin in France . . . and she offered to pay for me up to three more cycles. . . . she's had some pregnancy losses and she's quite a bit older than me."

Cost-conscious patients might try to save money by skipping essential parts of an IVF cycle. Dr. Terrence Trumbauer once had a patient who "wasn't going to freeze any embryos because insurance didn't pay for the freezing, and that component of it is fairly inexpensive." These choices might initially seem strange, but individuals negotiating infertility can approach decisions from a unique standpoint: "patients make decisions that seem more logical to them. . . . For them, two plus two equals four and it might seem like it equals five to other folks that aren't in their shoes. . . . I can always see their rationale for decisions they make. They just may not be weighing risks versus benefits from a purely medical standpoint. . . . That's where the discussion has to come in" (Dr. Denzel Burke).

Limited financial resources for fertility treatment means juggling priorities: "you had to balance the risk of multiples versus the risk of having to pay for it all over again" (June Barber). In contrast to other purchases, where money guarantees goods, patients struggle with the unpredictability of IVF outcomes. "It's like if you went to the car lot and they said, 'You're going to give me $10K and then come back here tomorrow, and I might give you a car, but I might not,'" said Rosa Grant; "there are no guarantees here." Even patients with insurance sense opportunity slipping away; as Patrick Shields said, "three [cycle]s [are] the limit, . . . basically three strikes, and you're out, as in out of luck, out of coverage, and out of money." It can even be tempting to overlook IVF expenditures. "I just try not to think about how much we've dumped into it thus far. I just ignore it. I don't want to know," remarked Heather Stewart. Often, women have different opinions on the importance of savings and fiscal responsibility than their partners. "I just kind of threw caution to the wind and said, 'We're gonna do this gung-ho until we're out of money, and then we're gonna figure out how to do it some other way,'" said Bridget James. "But [my husband] . . . handles more of our finances and he worried about it every step of the way."

Many physicians confirm that patients' finances are "the main driver" in treatment decisions (Second Year RE Fellow Dr. Peter Gore). Dr. Stefanie Burgstaller had former patients who returned when offered free cycles: "it's remarkable how many patients are jumping at that opportunity and they'd given up. Now, with this new opportunity, it's, 'By all means, sign me up again.' In some cases we may have just thought, 'Oh well, that patient just dropped out because she was tired of trying,' but I think it's often a financial thing." And these financial pressures are intensified by ticking biological clocks, as Dr. Sebastian Alfaro noted: "Patients say, "You might postpone to have a new house, you might postpone to have a new car, you may postpone to buy what-ever hobby you were looking for, but you can't postpone to have a baby because of the age."

Most patients strongly agree that insurance coverage for fertility treatment would profoundly change their treatment experience. Insur-ance coverage can influence whether patients undergo IVF at all: "If we didn't have the insurance coverage, we wouldn't probably have ever had IVF as an option unless we'd been able to get into some type of clinical trial or some sort of shared risk program. . . . We probably would've tried a couple of IUIs, and we'd have gone to adoption, because I just couldn't have spent $20,000 on a chance of getting pregnant. I would've rather spent the $20,000 on adopting a baby" (Marion Goodwin). So patients struggle to maintain their insurance coverage. "I'm very thank-ful that it covers at least a portion of it, . . . but also anxious, . . . if it doesn't work this time, and we don't end up with any embryos, I would seriously consider getting another job . . . just so it's covered," remarked Brianna Tyler. And those who don't have insurance consider going to great lengths to obtain it. Christopher Franklin, whose insurance didn't cover IVF, noted, "We've actually talked about moving to states that provide coverage. . . . I think that's pretty significant."

Insurance coverage isn't uniform and can cover a range of specific treat-ment options. What is covered (if anything) can determine how patients proceed through treatment. Those with insurance often have to complete three IUIs before moving to IVF, unless they have an infertility diagnosis like male factor infertility. Those without insurance often spend months, even years trying other treatments that are either covered or less expensive than IVF: "if IVF had been covered from the beginning, it probably would've meant we'd have skipped right over artificial insemination and gone straight through" (Tyrone Crider). Sometimes, insurance even affects whether a couple uses their own eggs and sperm or donor gametes. Brooklyn Knowles noted, "if we'd had any kind of significant coverage for IVF, we'd have kept going with our own eggs," whereas Monique Strickland felt her insurance "definitely made it easy to try using my own eggs and to take full chances and not feel so rushed, because I had four IVF cycles." In effect, insurance coverage gives patients a safety net: "[with insurance] you could be a little more selective about your care choices and what you were doing, . . . [having no insurance] compromised the choices you were making because it was basically like trying to get the biggest bang for your buck" (Holly Garrett). Thus, whether or not they had coverage, most feel that insurance increases patient options and autonomy.

It isn't surprising, then, that patients believe insurance coverage aids decision making. "I think it makes you make better decisions when it comes to how many embryos to transfer. I think you end up with much less [multiple pregnancies] because people feel like they have another chance," Rochelle Rowe said. Laura McLaughlin observed that insurance would make things easier overall: "the amount of research that we would've had to do would've been much less. Our stress level would be much less. . . . The focus would really be on the medicine . . . we could be more of patients and less of medical consumers."

Insurance can also weaken IVF's emotional toll. "It wouldn't take the disappointment of it away, but it would take [away] the 'holy crap,'" affirmed Darla Clarke, who lacked insurance coverage. Nicole Bell, who had insurance, said, "That was a huge component of being relaxed about it, because I knew it was covered. I didn't have to worry about the financial end." Insurance helped Jackie Carson to be more optimistic, even after an unsuccessful cycle: "that's a horrible blow to anyone. But it wasn't as bad because . . . we didn't risk everything we saved our whole lives. . . . This is a great doctor; he can do it for me within four retrievals. I know he can."

And insurance coverage for IVF legitimates infertility as a medical condition, supporting patients' perceptions that it isn't elective. Rochelle Rowe saw infertility as a bona fide health need: "[take a] 26-year-old woman who has diminished ovarian reserves. She has a medical condition. And it's so insulting for her personally when it's not covered by insurance and she sees that people who are overweight and smoking and whatever . . . [are] covered." Many patients are angry that infertility isn't covered like other medical issues linked to unhealthy or reckless behaviors. As Adam Woods said, "I see bicyclists on the street with no helmet every day. And their head injury is going to be covered by my insurance, so my rates pay for this unnecessary, incompetent, irresponsible behavior. . . . I don't want to sound like I'm callous, but I feel completely excluded." Accordingly, individuals with coverage often feel different, or find that providers treat them differently. Delores Weber's insurance coverage legitimated her family-building goal: "I saw myself more as a patient." And Miranda Valdez's clinic rolled out the red carpet: "I think that's one of the reasons they were really nice to us, by the way. We had really good insurance. They used to look at our card and go, 'Yes!'"

Clinics help patients to maximize whatever partial insurance coverage they might have. "Insurance paid for . . . some of the ultrasounds and doctor's visits," said Cecelia McBride. "[Clinic workers] were somewhat creative with coding to get as much out of insurance as you could." When insurance coverage isn't an option, providers might discount fees to alleviate financial stress: "My husband and I took out a loan from the bank, and we could only afford to do one cycle. . . . And our doctor was so wonderful that he went well and above and beyond what his normal professional discount is; he gave us almost a 50 percent discount, because he felt so motivated to help us" (Lily Ellis). But for a few patients, insurance coverage makes little or no difference. Perhaps insurance covers everything but IVF—potentially the only viable option. Though Natalia Payne's care was covered under one provider, she chose to obtain care from another she liked better: "since we didn't like the doctors, . . . we decided we'd rather have better care and less money."

Insurance coverage might even make the treatment experience *more* stressful, given its bureaucratic maze of preapprovals and deadlines. "It was a nightmare of paperwork; I definitely think they make you run the red tape in the hope that you'll give up on some of it," Simone Henry complained. Jenna Moreno had to exercise constant vigilance: "It stressed me out because I knew that I had to be on top of things . . . to make sure that we didn't end up with a $20,000 bill. . . . All of the sudden there was a fee for this, there's a fee for that, so I was on the phone a lot with the insurance company." But patients acknowledge such insurance is a precious resource and are overwhelmingly grateful. As Kimberly Harrison said,

> when I picked up the shots, it was like $5,000 worth of medication that I was holding in my hands, and I actually broke down into tears because I felt very lucky that I had a job that provided me with insurance. And I knew that there were people that were out there that couldn't afford the drugs. And I almost felt a little guilty. . . . I donated all my unused drugs back to the clinic because I couldn't in good conscience keep them in my closet in my house and let them sit there and expire.

Thus, insurance coverage is ultimately more of a boon than a burden, expanding access to these family-building options that are difficult or outright impossible for so many to afford and providing the breathing room necessary for circumspect treatment decisions.

Gambling with Gametes: Shared Risk Programs

After patients decide to pay for fertility treatment out-of-pocket through savings or loans or through insurance coverage, another choice often awaits them: whether or not to purchase a "shared risk" IVF program, a discounted package of multiple cycles. If insurance coverage is analogous to the "yellow brick road," shared risk programs are the three heel clicks of Dorothy's ruby red shoes that will supposedly send her safely home. This option allows patients and clinics to "share the risk" that multiple IVF cycles might be needed; couples pay more (sometimes considerably more) than the cost of one cycle up front, but they get a partial refund if all are unsuccessful.[3] Those that purchase shared risk programs are essentially betting on a baby; patients take a financial hit if they conceive on the first cycle, break even if they get lucky on the second, and come out ahead if they get pregnant on the third or can't conceive at all. This option isn't available everywhere; 60% of surveyed patients' clinics offered such programs, and only 32% (and 18% of interviewees) purchased one.

Entering a shared-risk program isn't simple. Couples often have to apply for and be accepted into these programs, and they can be disqualified for poor treatment performance. "That was just an encouraging feeling to have been accepted, so you got this big, 'I got into college' kind of success," recalled Rodney Hodges. Staying in the shared risk program can also be difficult. "We purchased the two IVF cycle package, . . . [but] we were disqualified from the program because . . . they weren't able to retrieve enough eggs," Francis Foster explained. "[T]hey knew they'd probably have to refund the money anyway, and so they kick you out of the program."

Clinics offering shared risk programs have essentially invested in patients' success, and healthy profit margins require that these patients become pregnant as soon as possible. Thus, physicians might reserve the right to exercise more control over treatment decision making. According to Tia Bishop, "they got to make more decisions than they would normally have. So they got to choose how many embryos to put back. . . . whereas if we'd just been doing . . . where you pay each time, then we could've chosen a single embryo transfer, or a two."

Shared risk programs also have a less obvious advantage: eliminating two painful consequences of a failed IVF cycle—the knowledge that a great deal of money has just disappeared, and deciding whether to cycle—and pay—again. These emotional effects are strong; if patients conceive on their first shared risk cycle and thus lose money, they tend to overlook this loss out of joy at being pregnant.[4] For Bethany Brady, shared risk was "a little bit of an emotional decision": "if I did the first one, paid less but then it didn't work, then it would kind of be like a one-two emotional punch. . . . It was going to be really devastating and I would want the comfort of knowing we had one more shot." Sonya Saunders felt that the shared risk program gave her more breathing room: "I didn't feel like it was gonna happen in a try or two . . . we just felt like it was a good financial investment to just go ahead and join that shared risk. . . . At the beginning, . . . that was giving me so much stress because I felt like maybe this is our last one; . . . getting in the shared risk program allows for that space." Because this breathing room alleviates stress, patients hope that it might improve their odds of success, given a potential mind-body connection: "When [my clinic] started doing this whole thing where the second and multiple cycles are free, [the physician] said . . . more people got pregnant faster because they weren't worried about the cost of it all" (Madeline Lowe).

But not every patient is ready to sign on. "The first clinic gave me a sales pitch, kind of like when you go to buy a car, and that really put me off," Lily Ellis recalled. "[I]t just hit me as odd." Moreover, although clinics must control risk to keep shared-risk programs solvent, it seems harsh and even disingenuous to disqualify accepted patients. Racquel Kennedy communicated her distaste: "now I think that I have endometriosis, I don't think I qualify . . . And I hate the idea of you're betting against yourself." Optimism can also dissuade patients from shared risk options. But Dana Harper felt her clinic ran its shared risk program unethically because "we had to lock into something before we even knew how we were going to do":

> When we first met with the doctor, . . . [he] basically told us that he really thought that we had an excellent chance, maybe 70%, [and] that he'd buy the cycle program. . . . So we chose not to do that kind of thing based on his representation . . . and then things went horribly downhill from there. [The cycle] was over $30,000 dollars, and we were totally unsuccessful, with no refund and no frozen embryos, and we have nothing. I think I'm really upset that . . . once they started seeing that I had diminished ovarian reserve and wasn't responding that they didn't switch us to a multi-cycle program.

Finally, others find the idea of shared risk too overwhelming. "I didn't want to do it that many times. I wasn't going to be one of those people where this is my ninth cycle," Christine Zimmerman affirmed.

These reflections illustrate how patients strategize to finance IVF and "game the system" when possible, aided by relatives, providers, and even clinic practices. Confronting these choices encourages them to exercise great initiative even before their first cycle starts.

WANTED—ONE WIZARD: HOW PATIENTS SELECT FERTILITY CLINICS AND PROVIDERS

How do patients navigate the thicket of infertility-related decisions to arrive on the doorstep of a specific RE or clinic? Of surveyed patients, 59% chose an RE first rather than a clinic, and 78% had a choice between clinics. Others' recommendations were the most important factors in choosing both REs (27%) and clinics (33%). Thereafter, patients chose clinics on the basis of statistics (30%), reputation (28%), location (27%), cost (10%), website (10%), and availability (3%). REs were chosen on the basis of reputation (21%), availability (14%), personal interviews (14%), statistics (10%), location (7%), and website (6%).

Patients most often seek particular REs based on others' recommendations. "[My friend is] high maintenance," said Marisa Sims. "If there's a doctor that she recommends for any length of time, they have to have been very good and very patient, because she wouldn't stick around if they weren't." A friend's pregnancy is an especially strong endorsement: "it was proof that he worked for somebody. So I just thought we'd give him a try" (Kendra Figueroa). A few have friends or family members who work with REs they recommend. And the opinions of trusted OB/GYNs or other medical professionals carry special weight:

I made an appointment with the [first] doctor . . . because he had only a week wait to get an appointment. . . . And then I had an appointment with my OB, who said, "I really suggest our RE here," . . . so I called back and I said, "I'd like to switch my appointment . . . and they said "Oh, okay, . . . the quickest we can get you in would be the end of January." . . . And I thought about it for a second, and I said, "Okay, let's do it, let's make the appointment." Infertility isn't one of those things where you wanna go with a second-rate doctor; you want to go with the best. (Sasha Goodman)

But patients can rely too heavily on referrals. Sonya Saunders didn't like her RE, who was "recommended by an OB/GYN who I adore," but relied on the referral because "we really felt so overwhelmed and confused." Others aren't aware they should be researching REs, or they don't know how. Monica Hansen learned this lesson the hard way:

I chose the doctor based on my husband's urologist. He said, "He's good." . . . I didn't [research]. . . . And then by the second failed cycle I felt like something wasn't right. And that's when I really started to research him, and I saw that he had a very low success rates. And I went to another clinic. . . . [The doctor] asked me, . . . "Did Dr. So-and-So refer you to this doctor?" And I said, "Yeah." "Well," [he said], "they have something [like a kickback] going on together."

Early or late in the process, many patients investigate potential providers through diverse methods and with varying levels of effort. Philip Barnett said, "[M]y wife is definitely a researcher, so . . . every step we took it definitely was looked at and analyzed." But Natalia Payne took a more relaxed attitude: "at first I just went on [the basis of] the recommendation, and then, after our first visit, I did a little bit of checking on them, but not much, because I just saw glowing reviews, and I loved them." Patients frequently peruse clinic websites and read online patient reviews of certain providers. "There was a comment about that specific doctor, how he didn't really have a good bedside manner and was kind of mean," recalled Kathryn Patton. "I decided, 'Well, I'm not gonna go to that place.'"

The Centers for Disease Control (CDC) website, which provides statistics on individual clinics' pregnancy rates, is the most influential resource for selecting providers—if patients even know such data exists. "I didn't know about that until I joined an online forum," remarked Megan Cooper. But some find these statistics too general. "I was more interested in what *my* percentages are going to be like, taking into account my personal factors," asserted Rosa Grant. Others don't trust this data, believing clinics fudge their numbers. "I've known enough people that got turned away from [a local clinic] because they don't want hard cases there," said Rochelle Rowe. "I just always felt that those numbers could be easily manipulated, so I wasn't driven by them as much." Some patients interview potential REs, feeling interaction reveals something more—or more valuable—than online reviews or statistics. As Rosa Grant commented, "We ended up deciding that we'd make an appointment for consultation, . . . [since] bedside manner is also important to us. . . . For me, getting pregnant wasn't just a medical procedure; it was the whole experience. Like the office was really nice and bright and technical; they had all the latest equipment as far as I could tell, and very modern-looking. And yes, I'm spending a lot of money, but look at the facilities I'm at!"

Of course other factors are important as well, including (as real estate agents say) location, location, location. Clinics' whereabouts are crucial given IVF's rigorous and compressed schedule of office visits, ultrasounds, lab work, and procedures: "it was super-duper-duper close to work so I knew it would be very easy for me to go to appointments and stuff like that" (Phoebe Paul). Location may be less important to patients with treatment experience. Lily Ellis initially chose a closer satellite branch of a larger clinic 60 miles away: "because of the employer that I had, and because he was so worried that I was going to get pregnant and spend so much time away from his office, . . . against my OB/ GYN's opinion, I went with this guy rather than the original guy that she recommended. . . . I was trying to please everybody and I should've just been pleasing myself. . . . I realized he was a jerk and I left, but in those four months I saw him for a total of maybe ten minutes." Like so many other aspects of fertility treatment, then, choosing the right provider is a learning process—and the more effort patients put into the process, the happier they generally are with the results.

By this time, patients have received an infertility diagnosis, decided what to do, and followed friends' recommendations, provider referrals, online research, and statistical trails to the offices of their chosen providers. They have also surmounted several daunting barriers—coping with suspicions something was wrong, confronting infertility, deciding to begin treatment, and following through. Becoming patients, however, raises new, daunting queries. What will I think of my doctor and her staff? How will it feel when I learn to give myself shots? What will treatment procedures involve? What impact will treatment have on my friends, family, and finances? Most importantly, will it work?

WHEN IN OZ: PATIENT EXPECTATIONS ABOUT
TREATMENT PROCEDURES AND RELATIONSHIPS

Most patients enter fertility treatment with no real expectations as to how extensive or invasive it will ultimately become. Julia Norton ended up needing more extensive treatment than she anticipated: "I went in kind of thinking, 'Oh God, maybe we need to do an IUI,' but I didn't ever anticipate I would end up doing five IVFs, [as well as] different protocols and all of the things we tried."

In contrast, most patients do have concrete expectations about what the treatment experience will be like, including office visits, procedures, asking questions, fears about diagnoses, and providers' bedside manner. While 54% of interviewed patients had no expectations, others had certain ideas about doctors or procedures, including learning why they were infertile (12%) or conceiving quickly (15%). Surveyed patients were hopeful that REs would be honest (57%), understanding (56%), polite (54%), friendly (54%), compassionate (52%), respectful (51%), competent (49%), patient (45%), businesslike (30%), and warm (29%). Conversely, few believed they would be arrogant or condescending (2%), cold (2%), curt (3%), or hurried (6%). These expectations held up fairly well in practice; patient descriptions of providers either were fairly close (as for friendliness, 50%), or were lower by 9 to 16 percentage points. Patients underestimated negative characteristics by smaller margins (arrogant (10%), rude (7%), curt (7%), misleading (7%), or cold (9%)). Though subject to psychological biases,[5] these expectations affect how patient-provider relationships evolve, for better or worse. Lana Houghton expected to see her RE much more often: "I thought that the doctors would be more present than they actually are. In reality it's the nurses that you really interact with more."

Similarly, patients have diverse and contradictory expectations about treatment procedures. A few think IVF will be daunting: "I was scared to death. I mean, I don't know how I'm going to get over needle things" (Patricia Burns). In actuality, most have a pretty accurate perception of what cycling will be like. "I figured it was going to be extremely regimented," recalled Aaron Schneider. Patients' expectations are most inaccurate with respect to the side effects of tests, surgeries, medications, and other interventions, which most find easier than anticipated: "It ended up being a lot . . . better than I thought it would be. I was really apprehensive about the shots, I was pretty apprehensive about the hormones, about how would I feel" (Shannon Ward).

In keeping with conventional assumptions that doctors know all, patients also expect to learn conclusively what is causing their infertility. Racquel Kennedy remarked, "I figured they were just going to have the answer." Having these expectations dashed is discouraging; it challenges, and in some cases decreases, patients' faith in medicine: "I thought more highly of medicine when I first started this whole thing" (Monica Hansen).

Patients who expect a conclusive infertility diagnosis often believe they will conceive quickly with the right intervention: "I thought when we got to the clinic, she was going to have some magic pill, that I was going to be pregnant that next month. And that was four years ago" (Lauren Mack). May Weiss, who suffered from secondary infertility, thought it would only take one cycle: "I really thought that we'd do one round of in vitro and I would be pregnant. . . . I have three children; there's nothing wrong with me. This is going to work, this is going to work fast, and the doctors really kind of felt that way too."

A resounding 93% of interviewed patients were optimistic when they began treatment. Optimistic patients like Lauren and May might initially experience less emotional distress, only to become more disappointed later: "we were kind of destroyed when it didn't work, 'cause we thought it was going to work. She [our doctor] said it was going to work. So we kind of went into it originally . . . pretty naïve" (Antonia Hughes). In the end, patients must confront the uncomfortable truths that medicine is as much an art as a science, much of fertility is a black box, and infertility diagnoses might be "unexplained."

In the end, the accuracy of patients' original expectations matters quite a bit. More realistic expectations facilitate trust and partnership, while less accurate ones mean unpleasant learning curves, for which patients might blame themselves or providers. "Crash courses" are rarely enjoyable or productive, and patients might feel stupid depending on how providers communicate new information. Many patient expectations in fact relate to how they will respond in treatment situations— often guided by trying to become ideal patients or avoid becoming difficult ones.

SUNNY, OR SO OVER THE RAINBOW?: IDEAL AND DIFFICULT PATIENT ARCHETYPES

Once patients choose a provider, what happens next depends on whether they have effective support networks, if they've researched infertility, how infertility has changed relationships and self-conceptions, and how easy it has been to muster resources like time, energy, and money. Consulting an RE begins a new stage in family-building, forming treatment teams who may guide patients the rest of the way.

But as women and men prepare to meet their care teams, two patient archetypes hove into view: the "ideal" patient, which real patients hope to emulate, and the "difficult" patient, which patients try to avoid becoming. "Ideal" and "difficult" refer not so much to specific behaviors as to a patient's ability to effectively participate in a treatment team that includes her partner, physician, nurses, and other clinic personnel. Personal qualities that enhance participation make for an "ideal" patient; those that undermine it make one "difficult." These categories are well known throughout medicine.

Because these two categories are mirror opposites, defining one entails defining the other. Ideal patients are positive, realistic, cooperative, communicative, flexible, inquisitive, patient, responsible and responsive, well-informed, and respectful of expert knowledge. Ideal patients make things easier for both providers and themselves. Difficult patients have too much or too little of every good quality. They're pessimistic, unrealistic, uncooperative, dogmatic, impatient, overconfident in their expertise, noncompliant, domineering, inordinately inquisitive, angry, rude, emotionally unstable, and either distant or overdependent.

It's important to note that the difficult archetype *doesn't* apply to patients who ask many questions, cry in office visits, or discuss decisions with providers; it applies to those at the margins who can't function in care relationships and whose treatment *breaks down* because of a chronic inability to cope and behaviors like extreme skepticism, ceaseless crying, and noncompliance. Interestingly, the difficult patient archetype matches popular stereotypes of how women experiencing infertility behave, including the demanding, aggressive career woman who relentlessly charges through treatment, or the overemotional woman who melts into tears at the slightest provocation.

Together, the ideal-difficult dichotomy establishes an interesting trend. On the one hand, patients emphasize that *confidence in self-competence* comes before healthy, trusting treatment partnerships. Most patients believe, then, that they enter relationships fully capable of agency and autonomy. On the other hand, providers emphasize patients' *trust* in their treatment teams, implying that trust precedes and facilitates patient agency and self-competence. From this perspective, patients gain agency and autonomy through the treatment partnership.

Patients' remarks about "ideal" patient qualities reveal great enthusiasm for collaboration with providers; as Adam Woods remarked,

> I'm very comfortable with all the technical information you can give me, I maintain my own records; when we were getting semen analysis, I actually had my own spreadsheet with my numbers. . . . As a patient I try to be a partner with my physician. I seek out physicians that appear talented, bright, conscientious, but also just workable within reason. I comply with medication as much as possible, probably better than most people. I'm probably a slightly high-maintenance patient on the information side and on the interaction side, but . . . I don't seek emotional counseling from my doctor. I go and I try to get that from my family or from my own personal spiritual study or from the psychologist.

Adam appears to be the very genesis of the ideal archetype. His sunny outlook makes him a pleasant (and proactive) treatment partner, and even his "high-maintenance" characteristics, seeking information and interaction, are assets.

Most fertility professionals (62%) agree the vast majority of patients are, like Adam, "pretty ideal" (Nurse Tamela Isaacson); providers named several ideal characteristics, including being open-minded (37%), not obsessed with the Internet (10%), trusting (8%), intelligent or able to follow explanations (8%), well-informed (7%), friendly or positive (5%), and having a remediable diagnosis (10%). "Like any other type of human relationship, there's some people you're just attracted to in terms of their personality. And they're easy to get along with, and they follow directions, and they're upbeat, and they're just more fun than others that are more stressed out," explained Lab Director Keane Schultze. Dr. Corwin Summers agreed: "I would say about 90% of my patients, I look forward to seeing them. . . . most patients are absolutely lovely."

Although most patients approximate the "ideal" patient archetype, a few don't, with memorable consequences. Difficult patients make up an extremely small subset of clinics' patient populations. "You get an extremely irrational 1%. They may be abusive, they may be excessively narcissistic and demanding," Dr. Kerry Kushner said. "[W]e see 8,000 new patients a year in our practice; we have 23 doctors. And we probably will ask five or ten patients a year to seek care elsewhere." Dr. Corwin Summers described these patients slightly differently: "[T]here's that small 10% or so that are either very angry about the fact that they have to be at a fertility center, or you feel like they're really rushing through this decision-making process despite your best efforts to slow them down. It makes you a little bit uncomfortable."

Difficult patients tend to occupy opposing ends on the spectrum of patient agency: overly deferential and overly domineering. Each category was mentioned by 15% of professionals. Dr. Kerry Kushner outlined this dichotomy: "the two extremes I'm unhappy with are someone who doesn't understand a thing [about] what's going on and just wants to be told what to do [and] someone who spends their life surfing the Internet to look for every nuance, [who] is going to come up with lots of issues and questions and uncertainties about whether to follow the recommendations."

Providers can find patients challenging for any number of reasons, but most fit within these two categories. Some don't listen (19% of providers), others become jaded from prior treatment experiences, and a few are just plain negative, angry (37% of providers), high-strung, needy, distrustful, decision-adverse, or demanding. Perhaps a challenging patient "just doesn't follow your recommendations" (Dr. Gerard Gabler) or is "that resistant patient that refuses to be guided" (New Patient Coordinator Aston Reinhold). But working with challenging patients is inevitably part of medical practice. "[P]eople just react to that stress differently, and you have to expect that. Some are going to be easy and some are going to be difficult. It's part of the business" (Lab Director Keane Schultze).

Complex reasons for so-called difficult behaviors often lurk beneath patients' belligerent or boneless exteriors, including distrust in medical providers, grief and frustration over failed treatments, helplessness over an inability to change treatment outcomes, and anger at the unfairness of it all. Most professionals feel a responsibility to work through these complications. "The difficult patients . . . are guarded for whatever reasons," said Senior Embryologist Lizbeth Norman, "and then it becomes a process of knocking down that wall slowly, brick by brick, to get them to a point where I feel that they're much more trusting and confident in your abilities." Professionals empathize (to a point) with difficult patients whose hostility is rooted in emotional pain: "sometimes they're mad at the world when they can't have a baby and they're looking for somebody to blame. . . . We're here to help them" (Nurse Practitioner Michi Glover).

How do professionals handle difficult patients? While 25% of providers provide explanations to patients, others try to be understanding (12%), refuse patient requests outright (6%), or give patients time (4%). To encourage patients to make independent decisions, providers outline options and discuss the pros and cons of each (25%), remind patients the decision is theirs to make (25%), and give them research information

(22%). Thus, the ideal and difficult patient archetypes are mapped onto real behaviors that then become identified with these labels, which patients learn to avoid and providers learn to anticipate, with sometimes grave consequences for treatment:

> When we call patients and families "good," or at least spare them the "difficult" label, we are noting and rewarding acquiescence. Too often, this "good" means you agree with me and you don't bother me and you let me be in charge of what happens and when. Such a definition runs counter to what we know about truly good care as a collaborative process. . . . Culturally, we could benefit from a lens shift toward seeing more vocal patients and families as actively engaged in their health care, presenting new, potentially important information, and expressing unmet care needs.[6]

HEARTS, BRAINS, AND COURAGE: LOOKING TOWARD TREATMENT RELATIONSHIPS

Once patients are confidently underway on their Expeditions, these ideal and difficult patient archetypes inform reproductive care relationships and motivate patients to exercise vigilance and model positive patient behaviors. When they reach a clinic—the fertility equivalent of the Emerald City—their goal is to find their wizards, obtain professional help, and return "home" pregnant as expeditiously as possible.

Patients and physicians need one another. Without physicians, patients' health care needs go unfulfilled; without patients, physicians can't satisfy their desires to help others, deepen knowledge and skills, design treatment innovations, or make a living. These complementary interests provide strong partnership incentives. Sometimes these partnerships are successful; sometimes they break down. Much of their success depends upon how patients and physicians see themselves in relation to medicine and to one another.

Reproductive medicine professionals are merely human; they do their best to care for all patients, but can become exasperated with those unable or unwilling to cooperate. "Ideal" patient qualities map onto what works best with professionals' personalities, routines, and clinical norms, making it easier or harder to practice medicine. These "ideal" qualities also usually translate into closer, more productive treatment relationships; providers must devote excessive time and attention to break through the personality traits or past experiences underlying "difficult" behaviors. This, then, is the bargain reproductive medical professionals look to strike with patients: if patients look to providers for emotional support, providers expect compliance in return so they can provide support to as many patients as possible. For both patients and providers, then, it is the quality of time spent together, not its quantity, which makes for a productive and personally enjoyable partnership.

Here, too, *The Wizard of Oz* provides a wonderful metaphor. Like Dorothy, many patients are at first intimidated by their fertility providers, who seem more like the Great Oz than ordinary mortals—only to find for one reason or another that this wizard is actually quite human. Fortunately most patients find providers who, unlike the actual Oz, are forthright, highly competent, and likeable. So much of what happens next depends on the personalities of both patients and providers. Will a provider choose to direct affairs from behind a curtain, remaining a majestic yet invisible presence? Will a patient insist on piercing that veil, demanding access to her physician? Most importantly, how will a patient and provider allocate power, share information, and work with each other in their interpersonal relationships?

CHAPTER 5

Being Patient

Patients' Perspectives on Treatment
Relationships

A patient's interpersonal relationship with a medical professional can either sweeten her treatment experience—like that spoonful of sugar that helps the medicine go down—or be a bitter pill to swallow. These extremes are illustrated in the treatment experiences of patients Cecelia McBride and Sasha Goodman.

While many patients describe deep provider relationships that ease traumatic outcomes like miscarriages, a few feel mistreated. Cecelia McBride's physician berated her, angered that staff interrupted his vacation to ask him about her misdiagnosed ectopic pregnancy:

> My [first] hCG [blood pregnancy test] came back a nine, and so they told me, "Oh it's a chemical pregnancy; you'll start your period very soon," and it never did. . . . And they tested it [again], and it had gone up. . . . The nurse called me and said, "Congratulations, this is great news, you're pregnant." And then they called back . . . [and said] that, "Sorry, we shouldn't have told you that; the doctor suspects it's ectopic because of the way the numbers look." . . . When the doctor returned to town, he came into an exam room with my husband and I and proceeded to curse at us; . . . he got in my face and pointed his finger, and told me that I ruined his "fucking" vacation.

But Sasha Goodman's RE was "very caring" and helped ease the trauma of her first miscarriage. After Sasha learned her fetus no longer had a heartbeat, clinic staff initially said they couldn't schedule a D&C[1] "for a while." After she objected—"I can't walk around with that dead baby inside of me"—the clinic scheduled the procedure with another doctor. But Sasha's RE rescheduled other appointments to perform the procedure himself. Sasha said, "I'm tearing up just thinking about it. . . . I really wanted him there."

These anecdotes signal what is at stake in treatment relationships. But even in more commonplace treatment situations, infertility-related emotions encourage patients to turn to fertility professionals for emotional support as well as medical care—and motivate them to ensure these relationships succeed. Ideal and difficult patient archetypes outline how patients "should" behave within these relationships. Once treatment begins, cycle outcomes generate new emotions that strengthen or weaken these interpersonal connections. Tragic outcomes test treatment relationships, and it matters enormously whether providers handle these calamities in traumatizing or tender ways. Moreover, patients' trust in their providers strongly influences how they react to informed consent interactions and aids. Greater trust makes patients more receptive, while less trust makes for angry patients who scrutinize every document and challenge many provider recommendations.

Patients' relationships with fertility clinic personnel are atypical in modern medical practice. They are unusually extensive, can entail great emotional and physical intimacy, potentially last for months or years, and unfold in office settings more often than exam rooms. The most popular physicians, nurses, and clinic staff members usually put extra "care" into their roles as care providers, lest patients be emotionally devastated. Moreover, the doctor-patient relationship itself significantly shapes treatment decision making. Providers believe that most patients follow their advice regardless of what outside research reveals: "if they can afford to do it, I think most people are going to do what their doctor tells them to do" (Dr. Don West). For instance, one RE polled his patients as to their top decision-making influences: "when I've asked [about] family, friends, books, Internet, social media, that kind of stuff, [I've found] that . . . discussions with physicians and health care providers comes out on top" (Dr. Denzel Burke). Fortunately, providers want to build sound treatment relationships with good communication (30%), trust (23%), and mutual understanding and respect (11%).

The provider-patient relationship thus lies at the heart of the fertility treatment experience. Patients turn to clinics for help conceiving, but they often hope providers will become partners on this journey, providing reassurance, compassion, support, and empathy. Do—or can— providers live up to these demands? How do patients negotiate these uniquely intimate and influential provider relationships? Taken together, patients' assertiveness, attempts to create positive impressions, and the perceptions of "good' and "bad" bedside manners are both the building blocks they use to construct successful treatment relationships based on trust and the tools they use to work through treatment and decide when to seek care elsewhere.

A PATIENT ATTITUDE: UNDERSTANDING PATIENTS' TREATMENT PERSONALITIES

Interviewer: How would you describe your patient personality?
Patient: Probably annoying. We'll say inquisitive.
—Allison Perkins

Just as every medical professional has a "bedside manner," each patient has a "treatment personality"—the unique combination of qualities that determine how she responds to providers and treatment situations. For example, surveyed participants described themselves as educated (66%), nervous (50%), assertive (35%), trusting (33%), understanding (29%), calm (28%), skeptical (18%), impatient (17%), confident (15%), demanding (11%), passive (5.2%), and uneducated (2%). Treatment personalities are constantly in flux and can change markedly over time.

A patient's assertiveness is central to her treatment personality. Assertiveness, in turn, consists of fixed and changing qualities, like introversion or extroversion, educational background, and inquisitiveness. The vast majority of patients considered themselves assertive overall (75.3% interview, 82% survey), as well as when obtaining other medical care (78% interview, 87% survey), and particularly when obtaining fertility care (83% interview, 91% survey). Patients are naturally more passive or assertive, but fertility treatment has different stakes and unique incentives that often compel patients to become more assertive than usual. "I think [I was more assertive] because I'd done so much research on my own for that," Joanne Johnson said, "whereas if I'm just going to the doctor for an ailment, I don't look into it as much." And patients are literally invested in treatment outcomes: "we're paying them a lot of money. There's a lot at stake; one little mistake can blow an entire cycle" (Lana Houghton).

Patients regard assertiveness as a personality trait, not a passing attitude. Christopher Franklin described how assertiveness improves treatment relationships:

if we're defining assertive in the sense of, "I'm not afraid to [speak] up, I'm not afraid to ask questions, I'm not afraid to explain what I would like to see, and why." . . . I treated my physician as a consultant. Now, that said, I was respectful; I was professional. . . . You catch more flies with sugar, so you don't want to treat people that are taking care of you in a disrespectful manner regardless of what happens. . . . So that's why I would describe it as assertive, not aggressive.

Patients often link their assertiveness to curiosity, especially asking questions, and contrast it to collaboration without questioning, which they consider overcompliance. Most patients experience tension between being collaborative and agreeable, on the one hand, and being assertive and informed, on the other. While Nicole Bell described herself as "definitely compliant . . . [I would] stand on my head naked and whatever," Rochelle Rowe conditioned her collaboration on trust: "There [has] to be a baseline trust, and, if I find that, I kind of trust that person to make that decision with me." But most surveyed patients didn't hesitate to disagree with their physicians (55.7%) and to discuss their concerns with treatment teams (63%).

Collaboration doesn't necessarily entail passivity; patients can be both collaborative and assertive. Patients use collaboration to fulfill their treatment responsibilities, like following protocols: "I'm the kind of patient that does everything they tell me to do meticulously. . . . I have a log book, to the point I make myself a little crazy taking care of things" (Joanne Johnson). It can become a point of pride: "[I'm] eager to please the doctor, I guess. I was very good at following the doctor's instructions, just like kind of the perfect patient" (Kendra Figueroa). And collaboration allows patients to efficiently accomplish treatment goals: "I try to expedite things as quickly as possible, and that means being prepared for appointments or taking all my medications when prescribed and how it's prescribed" (Josephine Palmer).

But when patients begin to collaborate without question, the patient-provider relationship might break down. For instance, Jackie Carson confessed she "struggle[d] with being assertive with doctors. I'll come in with a list of ten questions, and then I just feel so rushed that I only ask three of them." This conduct leaves patients vulnerable to providers who are predatory, unreasonably cautious, or wrong, allowing them to control the relationship, destroying patient trust and even inflicting harm. Unsuccessful treatments and relationships end up making patients more assertive in uncollaborative ways. Patients often resolve the tension between collaboration and inquisitiveness by learning to ask questions, and these "street smarts" can change their treatment personalities. Most patients (83% interview, 93% survey) were comfortable asking questions.

Some individuals become more assertive over their treatment careers. "I started out being a passive, 'Whatever the doctor says' . . . type of person," said Danielle Greene. "I've changed definitely into being more proactive . . . in terms of really being much more vocal early on. . . . Now, I don't have trouble bothering the doctor." Experienced patients develop more informed expectations about what makes treatment relationships work and realize that assertiveness can be a productive collaboration strategy:

> I expect the doctors to explain things to me, I expect them to listen to me and at least . . . let me know why or why not what I was thinking is the way that we should go. But I definitely expect a more involved relationship with [the] medical world. . . . I think there was a sense of empowerment as I researched and learned that I should research, and should find out how my body worked and what I could do for myself, and that realization that the doctor isn't the god, and they're just human. (Cynthia Gardner)

But this evolution might also follow unsuccessful cycles and relationships:

> I think I put the doctor on a pedestal, kind of, and then . . . after I've been going through my first two IVF cycles . . . I began to really question the doctors . . . and I began to have less trust in the doctor, and I began to feel like I needed to be more in the driver's seat. . . . I feel like I have to think independently. I can't rely on a doctor anymore, . . . because they don't care as much as I do about getting pregnant. (Monica Hansen)

This assertiveness can be counterproductive; these patients might find it harder to trust, undermining treatment relationships.

Others find being assertive harder for several reasons. Jackie Carson felt inundated with emotion: "There are just so many emotions that I would just get so overwhelmed and talk myself out of advocating for myself. It got better as I went further along." June Barber wasn't used to the patient role: "I haven't really been that sick otherwise, so I haven't had the experience. I just get things like sinus infections." Others feel insecure or ignorant; while Sonya Saunders "felt scared that I would offend them," Kay Elliot felt "there's so much I just don't know about." More passive behavior, then, can indicate unpreparedness or feelings of disempowerment—dangerous qualities, if patients have the wrong RE.

Finally, many patients regard assertiveness as counterproductive because they lack control over treatment outcomes. Assertiveness can

seem risky or more difficult, and compliance becomes the safer and easier route. "At that point, you're not in control, . . . you can assert yourself all that you want, but there's really nothing you can do" (Victoria
Santos). Nicole Bell felt altogether helpless: "I think the state of mind I
was in was, 'Please just take care of me, and I'll do whatever you say,
and make this happen.'" Here, far from being weakness, patients regard
passivity as a strength, lubrication for treatment interactions.

Ideally, patients' assertiveness dissipates when their treatment needs
are met: "I think that we were pretty much handled with respect, and
we were asked our opinions, and I think we were listened to; I don't
know that I really needed to be assertive" (Ian Johnston). Some patients
even warn their REs that negative experiences elsewhere make them
more cautious and assertive: "I tried to explain to my doctor . . . about
my experiences with previous doctors that I've had. . . . And she said,
'Fair enough'" (Monica Hansen). Instead of identifying assertiveness or
passivity with particular treatment roles, like physician/patient or ideal/
difficult, these perspectives imply that these qualities are actually cycli-
cally related.

Assertive behavior has its benefits. It enables patients to clarify which
information is necessary to complete IVF cycles: "I definitely was seeking out what I could and ask questions whenever I was confused about
something" (Inez Griffith). It can protect personal values and ethical
boundaries: "for us, preserving life was one of the most important
things when we went into it, and so we were very cautious about it"
(Kyle Vargas). It encourages patients to take more proactive treatment
roles, strengthening partnerships: "with fertility, like with any chronic
illness when you're repeatedly seeing the doctor, you get to recognize
the terms and the typical cycles of treatment. . . . then you're in a better
position to say, 'That didn't work last time, so what can we do this time
differently?'" (Penny Hill).

More importantly, assertiveness prompts patients to learn more
about infertility and treatment options, facilitating healthier, more equal
provider relationships. David Reid educated himself about infertility to
become more self-reliant and realistic: "I want to really understand
what's happening, so that I can set my expectations of what's going to
happen as a result of some treatment possibility." Most patients consider themselves informed—which can affect treatment relationships,
depending on professionals' preferences. Diane Barrett said, "I'm a very
knowledgeable patient, so if you're the kind . . . that likes a knowledgeable patient, then you'll love me, but if you're the kind of person who

just wants a patient that would do whatever you say, you're gonna hate me." Several patients who considered themselves informed also conceded providers could find them "annoying": "I bugged [my doctor] to death and asked him tons of questions . . . I was a very, very active participant in my own treatment" (Jessica Frazier). Assertive self-education can strengthen patients' sense of control: "I do a lot of reading, and I work really hard to be my own advocate, because I feel like nobody knows your body as well as you do, and nobody is going to stand up for you like you're going to stand up for yourself" (Racquel Kennedy). Sadly, patients sometimes feel more informed than their REs: "a lot of times [I know] more than the dufus who happened to see me that day. . . . there are times when . . . people hadn't even looked at my chart before they came in" (Juanita Poole).

In summary, patients regard assertiveness as productive when it is appropriately balanced—neither too inquisitive or aggressive, nor too timid and naïve. Rightly or wrongly, patients believe physicians dislike "difficult" behaviors, like asking "too many" questions. Lena Coleman unapologetically described herself as "[p]robably one of the doctors' worst nightmares": "if anything was kind of off, I was calling. . . . I listened to them, sure, and I followed their directions and advice, yes, but . . . I was an advocate for myself." But there *are* friendly ways of being assertive. "My second RE . . . called me 'endearingly controlling,'" Anne Kelley said. "I wanted to know what was going on and why they were doing it but I tried to do it in the sweetest-type way so they'd answer my questions." Thus, assertive patients tried to identify and stay within certain behavioral boundaries, avoiding the "difficult" patient archetype.

SPIN DOCTORS: HOW PATIENTS BEHAVE IN TREATMENT SITUATIONS

Most patients have strong intuitions about how they should interact with their REs and how REs should respond, and they are very conscious of what fertility professionals might think of them. "I'd love to hear how they'd describe me; who knows what's been written all over my charts" (Juanita Poole). While 63% of patients interviewed didn't try to adjust their behavior, the remaining 37% tried not to get emotional (20%) and to seem proactive (13%), professional (11%), and honest (6%), and avoid being domineering (11%)—in short, behaving like the ideal patient archetype. Lena Coleman attempted to mirror her

provider's behavior: "REs are very analytical. . . . If you want to connect with a person, and you want to get the most out of that relationship, you kind of have to be a chameleon and change your behavior to
kind of match that person's behavior." Changing personal behavior
exemplifies both passivity as subordination and strength as self-control,
making temporary changes to achieve a cherished goal.

While 63% of patients interviewed felt comfortable displaying emotion in front of their physicians, they felt that it was important not to let
these displays get out of hand. Thus, patients often try to regulate and
subdue emotionality, particularly crying, which they think reinforces
popular stereotypes of women with infertility. As Shannon Ward said,

> I tried to be upbeat and positive when I was meeting with [my doctor]; I tried
> to not seem crazy, and I tried to not seem too emotional with him. . . . I was
> very aware of the perception that we're all so desperate and we're all so
> emotional and we're all just willing to do whatever. And I wanted to just
> come in and be positive and upbeat and not question and just kind of go
> with the program. . . . [to] be a good patient and . . . sort of counteract the
> anxious, crazy person.

To these ends, Sonya Saunders prepared herself before appointments:
"you gotta act like you're okay, so get ready. Like, brace yourself, don't
cry." These behaviors are strategic, designed to improve treatment outcomes either by increasing patients' knowledge or incentivizing REs to
do their best. Such efforts might make treatment relationships stressful,
not supportive.

Men also try to regulate and conceal their emotions in office visits:[2]
"I kind of still believe in that clinic cleanliness, the white coats, so to
speak. . . . We want to stay focused; I don't want to distract them from
exactly what we're here to do" (Adam Woods). Adam felt emotional
displays were effeminate and irrelevant: "I was raised that men deal with
the situation at hand and go cry at home later. And you cry alone. . . .
I didn't feel it was remotely relevant to burden them with how I was
feeling. [My wife] didn't feel that way though." Men's reactions reveal
the gendered norms surrounding emotional display; if men are strong
and unemotional, then women often felt they had to mirror that same
strength—an impression likely reinforced by most clinic environments.

An upbeat manner smooths patients' interactions with providers,
and patients can deploy cheerfulness strategically:

> I connect with the nurses very well. . . . Anyone from the front desk people
> to the people who take my blood to the financial people, I think that they'd
> know my name. . . . I could tell you all of them, their family, their friends,

their boyfriend; . . . I'm personable. I think it's really important to have a relationship with people. I'm not super emotional in front of the doctors and staff; . . . I want them to take me seriously and I want to try and keep as calm as I can to really hear what they're telling me and remember and process what they're saying. There are points in the process where I've lost it in a consult or something but that's pretty rare. . . . I kind of want them to get the impression that I have my shit together. (Sonya Saunders)

Sheri Lopez was proud that her provider had literally taken note of her optimism: "I got my medical file from our first try . . . and the doctor's note said, 'Really positive affect.'" Patients feel that cheerfulness makes provider relationships more productive: "I was excited! I was looking forward to every appointment because I knew that was just bringing me one step closer to getting pregnant. I had good rapport with all the nurses and the doctor. . . . I looked forward to going there because I knew they were helping me" (Marion Goodwin).

Suppressing emotion might literally improve treatment outcomes by improving communication. Many patients are afraid emotionality prevents them from understanding information, complying with treatment protocols, and ultimately having successful cycles. "[I was] really making sure that I wasn't letting my emotions hear things that they weren't really trying to tell me" (Brittany Watson). Others are afraid excessive emotionality will alarm providers, who might require them to see a mental health professional before treatment, or turn them away altogether. Ethan Reeves concealed his wife's distress from their physician: "I, at [my wife]'s request, refrained from telling them how truly upset and disabled she was from the emotional aspect of this."

Others feel the clinic environment—at least at first—isn't conducive to emotional displays. "[You behave] kind of like if you were meeting with an IRS auditor," Sean Gray said. "You're very careful, very on your guard, not quite sure what to say." Several patients believe their physicians are too busy for such things, or don't want to burden them. "I know he's a very busy man. If I have to let out my feelings, I should go to a counselor," Nicole Bell said. But if patients like Nicole don't discuss their emotions with providers, they might deny themselves access to an important support resource.

Along these lines, several patients try to suppress their emotions to appear professional: "I tried to be professional [before the doctor], where[as] with the nurses, I was probably more myself" (Nicole Bell). This might mean dressing nicely and putting more effort into personal appearance. While Christine Zimmerman will be "in my pajamas and

I'll get dressed for an appointment . . . because I want them to have a higher opinion of me," Cynthia Gardner took an extra step: "I shaved my legs before I went. . . . I don't think that my OB got the same treatment." But professionalism goes beyond appearance to behavior. Lena Coleman's behavior was businesslike: "I kind of treated it as if I were in an interview or in a meeting at work. . . . I tried not to get too emotional." Professionalism also means appearing informed, engaged, and committed to treatment. "I didn't want to feel like I did something wrong. I didn't want to feel uninformed. I didn't want them to think I was stupid about this and that's why it wasn't working," Simone Henry emphasized. Here, professionalism acquires masculine and unemotional overtones.

Many patients are entirely comfortable displaying emotion. Lena Coleman regarded emotions as natural: "Even if I did cry or get slightly upset, I didn't feel weak by any stretch. I mean, we're hopped up on hormones at a level that no one should be on for a normal situation." Displaying emotion also allows patients to gauge providers' compassion: "if they're ignoring me at this stage when I'm actually a lot more emotional about something, I don't want to be around you again" (Tyrone Crider). Moreover, emotional behavior can demonstrate trust in providers, strengthening treatment relationships: "especially towards the end, because you develop a relationship, I was fine showing emotion towards [my doctor]" (Juanita Poole). Significantly, these uses of emotional displays aren't passive, but strong, strategic, and even defiant conduct.

And not everyone is able—or even interested—in changing their behavior. Sometimes patients just can't repress emotions. Recalling the moment when he learned he and his wife had conceived triplets, Aaron Schneider explained, "I think I was actually crying. . . . [My wife] was sitting there, going like, 'Holy crap, how are we going to afford this,' and I'm sitting there going like, 'Oh my God, I'm going to be a father.'" Juanita Poole felt she lacked self-control: "if you're at an emotional point in a cycle, you can't really control it. I definitely cried once or twice there. . . . I didn't really have that much control over myself at the time." Some don't even try: "I'm kind of who I am, and especially when I'm stressed, the not nice parts usually come out and there's not much I can do about it."

Ultimately, what matters is not whether patients are able to control their behavior, but their keen awareness of what effects this conduct has on treatment. Patients' willingness to be themselves reflects their self-confidence and how they see their own status vis-à-vis providers.

"BETWEEN A CACTUS AND A GOD":
THE IMPORTANCE OF BEDSIDE MANNER

[My doctor] was very personable, had a great bedside manner, he answered all of my questions, and . . . he had great statistics and, and everything, so I trusted that it would work.

—Keira Wilkinson

A provider's "bedside manner"—the equivalent of a patient's treatment personality—is vital to creating healthy provider-patient relationships, retaining patients, communicating important treatment information, and even seeming competent. The vast majority of surveyed patients ranked bedside manner as "very" (42%) or "quite" important (29%); another 23% said it was of average importance, and only 6% considered it "not very" or not at all important. Many patients even regarded bedside manner as important as medical expertise (53% survey). Thus, liking one's provider is important, and patients generally do; 95% of surveyed patients rated their RE's personality as at least "likeable"; 52% liked their RE's personality "very much," 27% liked it "quite a bit," and 16% thought it was "average."

Personability is particularly important within reproductive medicine given this field's lengthy treatment relationships and intimate bodily access. Marisa Sims said, "I needed . . . more of a doctor with [a] good bedside manner, because I did kind of feel emotionally and physically fragile." In fertility care, then, a "bad" bedside manner is more conspicuous than in other medical fields, where limited patient access often creates a buffer. A good bedside manner can ease treatment uncertainty and make it less traumatic when textbook cycles go awry, beautiful embryos fail to implant, and chromosomes get confused.

What provider attributes do patients desire? Preferences vary wildly; some seek a nurturing personality, while others prioritize less empathic qualities. Above all, interviewed patients valued a doctor who was sincere, caring, and supportive (34%); beyond that, they desired a provider who would be a good partner, who would give options and help them to evaluate information (33%), and attend to their emotional needs (23%). Other valued qualities were taking time with patients (17%), a warm and personable demeanor (16%), making patients comfortable (16%), honesty (13%), and familiarity with patients' individual cases (7%).

To most, then, a "good" bedside manner means the doctor "was just really, very nice and he wasn't condescending . . . it's almost like he knew what I was going through, and so he was very sensitive to that" (Keira Wilkinson). A physician's bedside manner might literally be on display in her waiting room. Seeing how highly other patients regarded his physician impressed Aaron Schneider: "You sort of felt like you were entering like a family, . . . we'd be sitting in the office waiting . . . they have all the books, and here's all these personal letters of people saying like, 'Oh my God, you were amazing, I couldn't have done this without you'; . . . that's like, 'Wow!' And I think this is the guy that we really need to talk with." Showcasing such heartfelt patient testimonies are perhaps one of clinics' most subtle—and effective—marketing strategies, simply because of the genuine gratitude these messages contain.

As providers have to be virtually "in the bedroom" with their patients, a certain human touch is appreciated. But this isn't always what patients get: "there are some IVF clinics that are almost like a McDonald's, where . . . they go so quick, they don't make those connections with the doctors or the nurses just because . . . they don't have that time" (Sasha Goodman). Contrasting her provider with less personable ones, Penny Hill said, "this one woman, she was just very brusque and really all-business, and I didn't like her because it felt cold." Patients might find it particularly jarring when female REs have a clinical demeanor instead of exhibiting feminine norms like warmth and patience—although many female patients purposely adopt more "professional" personas in treatment environments.

Nonetheless, a more abrupt bedside manner suits many patients just fine, so long as they receive thorough information and quality treatment—and hopefully leave with a baby. "[My doctor's] not a very warm and fuzzy doctor, but I think that's what makes her so good at what she does. She's very knowledgeable . . . she's very smart, does her research, she's very current, and I don't need someone to hold my hand and give that hug" (Kimberly Harrison). Patients recognize that clinical competence is no guarantee of personality: "someone that's an excellent clinician isn't necessarily a hand holder. . . . You wouldn't have him over for a cocktail party. He was very business, all business, didn't really make eye contact. . . . I don't care, I have two babies [because he treated me], so whatever" (Tia Bishop).

Others also prioritize expertise over emotional availability; Bethany Brady noted, "coming home to my husband or talking with my family or friends is where I'm going to seek that emotional warmth. And from the doctor, I just want him to be intelligent and listen to me and know what he's doing." In fact, patients are willing to tolerate a great deal—

even excessive paternalism—from competent physicians. Jessica Frazier's doctor was domineering and forthright, but very skilled: "He'll basically let you know that he's the expert, and while he appreciates that you've done some research. . . . What he wants to do is what's going to happen, and if you're not okay with that you can go somewhere else. . . . The way he's looking at it is that I need him a lot more than he needs me."

Bedside manner's significance varies according to treatment stage; providers' emotional support might be more important early on. Monique Strickland wanted a different bedside manner while deciding whether to undergo one final IUI cycle than when beginning a donor egg cycle: "[my RE] was against [the IUI], but he said, "I can understand psychologically why you'd want to do it, but medically it's not warranted." Which we like, because [we] finally had somebody who . . . was very cut-throat. . . . I started crying and he didn't really pamper me. . . . When I did my egg donation, I requested a different doctor that I wanted to be a little nicer to me because I felt like I could use a cushioning." Bedside manner's importance can wane after patients are committed to a particular clinic—and when they likely have more treatment experience as well: "I definitely didn't like her personality . . . but I think because I was already there, I was already established, and we had a treatment plan. . . . I basically didn't care by that point in time, because I already knew what was going on" (Kathryn Patton).

Several provider traits, particularly immutable ones like age, sex, perceived eccentricities, and religious background, affect patients' perceptions of bedside manner. Older and younger REs each have distinct advantages. Dora Adkins appreciated her doctor's more advanced age: "[h]e was like a grandfather, he listened to your concerns, and he didn't dismiss you, which a lot of the other doctors tended to." Ida Olson, on the other hand, found her RE's youth energizing: "I like her just because she's younger and she has fresh ideas."

A doctor's sex is more important to most patients than age. "I always try to seek out female doctors; I throw my support towards women," affirmed Stella Madison. "I'd rather give them my dollar, and I think that there's most of the time a different level of care that you get from a female doctor." Female doctors are often better at making patients more physically comfortable: "this guy didn't warm up his instruments . . . I was like, 'Hey, P.S., doc, next time you probably want to warn a girl or warm up the instruments.'" Male physicians could seem unsympathetic: "I had an OBGYN for years . . . but I felt like when we started going through these tests . . . he constant[ly said]—this drives me bananas— the 'Just relax.' Like, 'just relax' is a medical diagnosis? . . . It really started to bother me, and I said to my husband. . . . I want to see a female gynecologist who can understand that . . . my feeling for a need for treatment is coming from a place of panic" (Simone Henry).

Or women might feel less comfortable displaying emotion before a male RE: "I tried not to cry like a baby, even though I always wanted to . . . because I just didn't want to look like a fool. . . . If he was a woman, I probably wouldn't have minded crying in front of him, but I tried to tough it out" (Jackie Carson). But many women are entirely satisfied with their male providers: "He was genuine and, as much as a man can, [he] underst[ood] what a woman in our position is going through" (Brooklyn Knowles). Predictably, patients' reflections largely reinforce gender norms, such as that female providers are more emotionally intelligent.

Like indifference, provider eccentricities can unnerve patients. When Brooklyn Knowles's doctor was performing an ultrasound, he asked her, "Do you know how many states start and end with the letter 'A'?" "I thought, 'That's not my big priority right now, to play this game with you,'" she said. But when she had a D&C for her second miscarriage, she recalled, "I remember him holding my hand as I fell asleep under the anesthesia." "He's a very kind person, but he has a sometimes loopy personality," she concluded. "Depending on where you are in your cycle and how you're feeling emotionally . . . it can hit you at the wrong time."

Finally, a few felt providers' religious beliefs helped or harmed treatment relationships. "I felt kind of led, like I should be going to this doctor. . . . He was Christian, which I really loved," Maggie Copeland explained. "He said that he prayed for his patients, which was important to me." But the spiritual stars didn't always align so neatly, as Sean Gray learned: "I brought up . . . that I had some hesitancy [with treatment details] because I was Catholic, and he didn't seem to like that at all. And so . . . I wouldn't say that I liked him on a personal level." If religion drives patients and providers apart, the fallout likely seems more personal, and more painful, than if discord stems from other reasons, like personality.

"Dr. Feelgood": A "Good" Bedside Manner in Practice

In treatment, a good bedside manner is healing in itself; personable providers seem compassionate and honest, and they make patients comfortable, transforming treatment relationships into partnerships. "I really like to work with my doctor, I really like to talk with my doctor, I really want my doctor to view me as somebody that they can talk through options with," affirmed Shannon Ward. This partnership needn't be particularly warm and fuzzy to feel like a relationship between equals. "I have a biology background, so I want answers and I want explanations, and I want you to discuss them with me as you would your colleague," noted Heather Stewart. "I don't need to have this personal relationship with my doctor. I just want him or her to get me pregnant."

Setting patients at ease requires more than procuring comfortable clinic office furniture. It requires coherently explaining treatment history and protocols, incorporating spouses into conversations, anticipating questions, and simply being there: "When you first meet with them, they sit you down in their office, not in the exam room. . . . She was also able to speak to my husband. . . . [It was as if she said], 'Here's all the information that you need and probably a lot of questions that you've had leading up to this point, and I'm just going to answer them for you' without us really having to ask. It just felt good" (Victoria Santos). Similarly, Anne Kelley felt more at ease with her doctor's casual demeanor: "the major selling point to him was that he'd use the 'F word' during our consultation, and that delighted me because it just made me feel real and human and not so doctorly."

A good bedside manner also means discussing infertility and its treatment at a level appropriate for each patient: "they were very able to vary what they were telling us based on what they knew about us, as far as we were college educated and we were fairly good medical researchers . . . so they didn't dumb things down for us" (Marisa Sims). It might even mean that providers share their own experiences:

> [My doctor] was somewhat impersonal, and that was a complaint that a lot of people had about him. However, when I had my second miscarriage . . . my impression of him totally changed. . . . He shared his personal experience with me and said, "I'm so sorry. My wife and I experienced a very similar loss." And I could tell it really pained him, and I'd never felt that connection prior to that. So . . . we plan to go back and use him again. That really impressed me, that he was willing to share his personal experience with us. (Bridget James)

Thus, personability is essential to a good bedside manner. Penny Hill described her physician as "very down to earth, very funny" and appreciated that "he really made you feel at home. . . . It was just very, very low-key and very welcoming." These qualities make doctors less god-like, more human, and more relatable.

A friendly, open provider demeanor engaged patients as partners in fertility care. Rochelle Rowe's relationship was conversational and collaborative: "He asks what you're about, what your fears are, what your concerns are. . . . He's very good at explaining what's about to happen and why he chose a protocol for you. . . . He had a lot of those qualities that [are] more of a partnership; . . . he wasn't dictatorial." These partnerships are, in Allison Perkins's words, a "good balance of being compassionate, which I think is unique in a specialized field like infertility, as well as kind of shooting it straight to us." She was impressed when her physician put her medical needs ahead of his commercial interests, advising her to undergo IVF since "IUI is just giv[ing] me, the doctor, money."

Balancing honesty and encouragement is hard; patients want both optimism and realistic assessments of their reproductive odds. Ideally, providers use their experience to make things more transparent for patients. "He laid everything out, like I'm sure he had 5,000 times before that, but he knew every question we were going to ask and had every answer. And [he] was extremely candid," recalled Brooklyn Knowles. Thus, many patients wanted a provider who, like Jake Collins's RE, "doesn't sugarcoat it."

Providers with a good bedside manner also involve spouses within treatment. "My husband was so comfortable at [our clinic]; I hadn't in two years heard him talk so much about infertility, and what he felt like, and what his concerns were," Simone Henry enthused. "I think that moment of knowing that we were both in it, . . . also helped [me] pick this doctor." Inclusion was particularly crucial for male factor infertility patients. "[My provider] made my husband feel . . . that this was going to work, it was a possibility, where the other doctor I guess had given him . . . anxiety," said Abigail Ramsey.

Moreover, a doctor with a good bedside manner takes time to really be there for patients. Despite a long-distance treatment relationship, Brittany Watson's provider still felt close: "Even though he was four to five time zones away from us, he was accessible; . . . he treated me as not just a patient." Few things impress patients more than a doctor's willingness to be there whenever her patients need her, even on weekends and holidays. "[My doctor] attributes his success rates to the one-on-one interaction he has with his patients," Stella Madison said. Recalling Sundays and holidays when she had appointments, she continued, "I was like, 'What are you doing here?' And he was like, 'Honey, I'm your doctor, and you're paying a lot of money for this. The very least I can do is show up on a Sunday or a holiday for you.'" Such remarks blend market rhetoric with an interpersonal care ethic, illustrating the hybrid nature of reproductive medicine treatment relationships. REs themselves also benefit from healthy communication. Marie Byrd's physician would call her from home and converse for over an hour: "He actually said the one time, 'Well, I save calling you back [until] when I'm actually doing my laundry.' He said, 'I can lock myself in the basement and have a nice long conversation with you, and we both feel better in the end.'"

Doctors who convey their sympathy or enthusiasm at treatment outcomes melt patients' hearts. Sergei Bennett bonded with his physician at embryo transfer: "when they put up on the screen the cells, and we could see our baby, we were in tears, and [our RE] was in near tears, and afterward, in recovery, I just remember her being emotional. And she was in it with us." Patients find such personal involvement very encouraging. One of the most heartwarming accounts was how Stella Madison's doctor told her she was pregnant: "he had everyone, his whole staff, on speaker [phone] and they all congratulated me; . . . they were all cheering and excited, and it was nice." Patients are devoted to these providers; as Sasha Goodman gushed, "[my doctor] is one of those people I put on a pedestal as one of the greatest human beings that ever walked the face of the planet. Not just because he got me pregnant . . . but he's just so incredibly caring and wonderful and great and an amazing human being." Paradoxically, then, the bedside manner that makes providers seem more relatable makes patients revere them all the more.

"Bad Medicine": A "Bad" Bedside Manner in Practice

He just had this very odd bedside manner that was kind of a cross
between a cactus and a god; he just lacked empathy.

—Anne Kelley

If a good bedside manner can forge camaraderie and trust, a poor bedside manner might make it hellish. Poor bedside manners often include arrogance, sugarcoating, and indifference.

Patients generally don't like arrogant or condescending providers, but they will tolerate competent ones. Before her IUI, Antonia asked her RE why she had prescribed a medication with warnings not to take it during pregnancy. In response, the RE became defensive, making Antonia feel ashamed and angry: "I thought that was a legitimate question. . . . I feel like a patient should just be able to ask your doctor questions without being made to look stupid." Sometimes, arrogance just comes with the territory: "what he does works, so he can be arrogant," Phoebe Paul said. Cecelia McBride felt she had to accommodate her provider's arrogant and domineering personality: "he'd always make comments about me being an attorney; . . . he didn't like to be challenged. So I would always tell my husband, 'Don't ask him any questions; he doesn't like us, and we need him to like us.' So I felt like he wanted a more submissive patient." Such reactions undermine treatment relationships; patients feel penalized for conduct conventionally regarded as useful.

A lack of empathy or indifference also taints bedside manner. Marie Byrd's RE was dismissive of her violent vomiting following egg retrieval: "he was just like, 'That's nothing, it should be fine.'" Other providers don't even talk to their patients during procedures: "I met [my doctor] only on the day of the implant [embryo transfer]; . . . he spoke to the nurse," Stella Madison recalled. "He was like, 'Her bladder's not full enough [for the ultrasound]; she needs to drink more water.' Well I'm right here, you could tell me that!" Or providers can seem suddenly distant after unexpected treatment results, when patients need them most: "when I conceived the triplets, I think he was as shocked as I was. And I kind of got the brush-off from him at that point, which was hurtful" (Marie Byrd). *Too much* empathy also makes for a bad bedside manner. Ethan Reeves and his wife hoped an IVF pregnancy would provide hormonal relief for her endometriosis and resented staff assumptions that a baby was IVF's only legitimate outcome: "we weren't thrilled with the diagnosis, weren't thrilled about having a baby, and not thrilled to be there. And the people who were particularly cheerful and optimistic and happy and 'baby-baby-baby' made things worse. We felt like we were [a] highly abnormal type of patient couple. . . . We did IVF because it was the least offensive treatment for endometriosis that we were offered. Not because we wanted a baby." Most often, providers could improve bedside manner simply by heeding patients' cues, exhibiting concern or sympathy at appropriate times, or simply listening.

Bad bedside manner often surfaces when providers deliver bad news—timing it in ways that might prompt patients to evaluate it more negatively, or not delivering it without being prompted. Rochelle Rowe felt shunted aside when she asked her RE why she began bleeding after her first IUI: "I didn't understand that I was going to get my period . . . and I met with a very unsympathetic doctor . . . who was annoyed at me for bothering her." Rochelle later helped to reform her clinic's policy for delivering bad news: "They have a policy at my clinic that they don't say they're sorry. And I found that out and I said, 'That's ridiculous, you're not making widgets.' This is somebody's high-stakes family, this is their whole life, this isn't [the same as] 'Sorry, we don't have that vacuum in stock.' . . . When you call someone to say this didn't work, you say, 'I'm sorry.' You say something empathetic."

Patients often scrutinize providers' words and gestures and might think they detect ongoing blame. Cycle progress reports can seem like hostile declarations, as Isabella Glazier discovered: "it was our first round of IVF and the clinic called, and the nurse said that 'I'm putting you on notice that we may have to cancel this because you don't have enough follicles,' and it was like she was scolding me or that it was my fault." Dismissiveness makes a devastating event almost unbearable. Philip Barnett's RE reacted in an unsympathetic and inappropriate manner after his first IVF cycle resulted in a Down syndrome pregnancy: "he was like, 'Well, that's a risk of doing infertility,' not like, 'I'm so sorry that happened.' . . . [Our nurses] were both like, 'Oh my God, I can't believe that happened to you guys.' . . . So you would hope for an emotional response. . . . A half-hour later, he ended up calling me, like 'Oh, I guess you could be upset by that happening,' like an afterthought: 'Maybe I could be a human.'"

Or an unemotional reaction may suggest that providers don't take patients' concerns seriously. April Gonzalez felt her provider dismissed her chromosomally abnormal pregnancy: "he was very sort of flippant about, 'Well, those things happen. It's very common,'" she recalled. "That wasn't good enough for me. I wanted to do genetic testing. . . . And he wasn't very receptive to my requests."

Distraught patients might even interpret apparent indifference as abuse. Tim Ballard's wife felt attacked when she unknowingly interrupted her RE's golf game to discuss disturbing test results: "She called him and he was on the golf course. . . . Just before he went to play golf, he called and left a message from the blood tests. He said, 'Well, it looks like you're going to have a miscarriage,' . . . and he was upset because she interrupted his golf game." At these times, a bad bedside manner is especially egregious—these are the very worst situations patients can imagine, and a little compassion goes a long way.

One of the worst bedside manners belongs to physicians that seem eternally unavailable. "Dr. Invisibles"—routinely inaccessible physicians—are a persistent thorn in patients' sides. Lola Lewis didn't meet her physician until her embryo transfer: "The staff is real nice and everything, but a lot of the time they can't really answer stuff that should be answered by the doctor." Doctors who aren't there for many treatment phases—or any—are even worse: "he never did one ultrasound. He didn't even do the egg retrieval or the transfer. In the end he did nothing" (Dana Harper). Human contact was especially important when telling patients whether they were pregnant: "The final straw for me was, . . . you have to call a phone number, and a voicemail message is left for you to tell you if you're pregnant or not" (Antonia Hughes).

Of course, providers, like patients, are human. Patients know that their physicians and nurses deal with others like them every day and can become desensitized to questions, concerns, and complaints. But patients are clear that the monotony of workaday routines doesn't excuse providers from performing their jobs well. "[Providers should] not be annoyed when somebody calls you with a question, because you may have done it a million, trillion times, and they may be doing it the first time, and they need a little hand holding," affirmed Rochelle Rowe. Providers who don't try to show interest and compassion, communicate well, maintain transparency, and convey information might seem to be in reproductive medicine for the profits, not their patients: "[My clinic] was like a factory—get 'em in, get 'em out, stick 'em on the table. They didn't know you even though they saw you every week. It was just like money, money, money" (Krista Carrillo). These failures destroy the most critical element of treatment relationships: trust.

TAKING IT ON TRUST: WHEN PATIENTS HAVE CONFIDENCE IN PROVIDERS

Trust is the glue that makes treatment relationships safe, stable, and effective, even if patients don't conceive. Most interviewed patients (86%) trusted their physicians. "I think the more trust I gave to the doctor, the more willing I was to be agreeable and understand anything," Brittany Watson observed. Conversely, when patients feel their needs for communication, information, and support aren't being met, they're much less likely to trust their providers. Cecelia McBride described the many factors enhancing patient trust:

> whether I feel like I'm being viewed as an individual, as opposed to just another patient. Like whether my history, and my test results, and symptoms, and prior courses of treatment are being viewed individually and being reassessed often. And how much time you feel like they're giving you. How often you see the doctor as opposed to just the nurse, or a practitioner. And just general honesty; . . . I appreciated that he was always [honest that] . . . it might not work the first time, that there's only so much that's in their control.

Patients assess trustworthiness through provider interactions: "[it's] their professional demeanor that inspires my confidence in the level of technical skills" (Adam Woods). Several factors could decrease patients' trust in providers, including bedside manner (78%), knowledge or competence (32%), and treatment personalization (24%). A provider's bedside manner provides clues as to whether patients chose their provider wisely. Other influential dynamics include whether providers seem motivated by profits or a passion for patient care, honesty, communication skills, accessibility, and competence and professional credentials. A final factor has nothing to do with providers and everything to do with patients—whether patients have endured medical mistreatment, especially from other fertility providers.

Money, Accessibility, and Treatment Customization

The sense that physicians cared more about patients' wallets than their wombs withers trust's fragile bloom. Patients warily acknowledge that reproductive medicine has a different profit structure than other medical fields: "I have a lot of concerns about there being a lot of financial incentives for my treatment. I feel like the fertility arena is somewhat similar to cosmetic surgery and that it has . . . a lot of potential for financial gain, where it may not always be 100% in the best interest of the patient. So I could easily lose trust if I felt like decisions were being made that were a little bit more for financial gain for the doctor or the clinic than for me" (Sonya Saunders).

Distrustful patients often question whether providers really want their cycles to succeed, because failure can be more profitable. As Tia Bishop said, "I think there's always a little bit of cynicism. . . . Do they not want it to work, because if it doesn't work, then now I'm going to come back and give them twenty grand for IVF." A negative experience with one apparently money-hungry provider made Aaron Schneider worry, "[A]re they all just going to be like, 'Okay, give us our money so that we can drive around in our expensive cars and everything?'" Fortunately, he found a provider who prioritized patient care: "the way he explained it, the way he'd talk about his family; he didn't give you that sort of like, 'I'm just the guy here for the paycheck' type feeling."

Some patients even question whether certain procedures are medically or monetarily necessary. Monique Strickland felt cheated when her clinic converted an IVF cycle to an IUI instead of cancelling it because she had too few eggs: "[My doctor] said, 'Yeah, you shouldn't be doing this. You don't even have any good eggs.' And I said . . . 'You're trying to make money off . . . me.' . . . He was obviously not doing what was good for me. He's putting me through a procedure just to put me through a procedure for the money."

Repeat testing and seemingly random charges also raise patients' suspicions. Antonia Hughes was angered at getting a high bill for a cursory and unproductive initial consultation: "my OB/GYN did a lot of tests already. . . . The very first time I met her [the RE], she charged me $300 to walk in her office. I was in there for 15 minutes, and she basically just handed me a folder about her business and said, 'Well, we're going to do some more tests.' I mean, she didn't even have the information from the OB/GYN."

Rachael Wilkerson had a sort of checklist for how patients could evaluate providers' motives: "do they seem to value me as a person, or are they going to take that phone call about getting their car waxed, or about their stock options . . . when they should be thinking about our chart? Do they seem to value their patients; do they seem to have a calling? . . . And if they're just there to make money, I don't want anything to do with them. If they really value their craft and they value their patients as people, I can tell they'll execute their craft in an outstanding fashion." These factors simply require that REs be present for their patients.

High patient volume and short appointments also signal profit seeking to some patients. Busy clinics can feel like fertility factories, where patients are herded through office visits: "it's just not taking the time with me, trying to rush through exams . . . you're more like just a number, or you're a dollar figure coming in and out of the door or whatever, so I think that's the main thing [for trust] is the time spent" (Kendra Figueroa). Or clinics might seem impersonal and overcrowded—the very opposite of conceiving a child in love and privacy:

> it felt like a business, and you felt like cattle. Especially at some of these bigger places. [The doctor] had his little nurse following him around telling him the patients' names. So I heard her tell him our name, and he walked in and was like, "Hey." And I know he sees so many patients, and so that doesn't bother me so much, but you do get that feeling like you're just dollar signs. . . . And you don't want to feel this way because it's about having a child, [but] you can't conceive a child in a regular, loving way. . . . The environment for creating this child has become so sterile. I don't know [how] you try to find a way to make it less sterile. Little cushions in the petri dish or something. (Heather Stewart)

But it only takes a human touch to stop the production line. "When they're really busy and you just had to wait, . . . you were being processed and there wasn't a ton of personal interaction," Phoebe Paul explained, "but . . . everybody that I encountered was really nice, and by the time I left . . . a couple of the people . . . have come up and hugged me and said, 'Congratulations.'" Patients like Phoebe might have a million reasons to leave a practice, but earnestly look for that one good reason why they should stay—human contact.

Uncommunicative, inaccessible, and therefore untrustworthy providers make patients feel overlooked. Monique Strickland repeatedly tried to corner her provider: "I sat down with my doctor . . . and I said . . . 'I need better access to you.' It was very leery. He [said] 'Email me. Email me directly.' Well, we tried to email; we tried six different variations of emails and we never got to him. And when we called the office to ask him his email address, they didn't have it. And it got to the point that we couldn't access this doctor."

Kay Elliott and her husband faced even bigger problems when their clinic closed early in their gestational surrogacy cycle: "we received a two weeks' notice that that doctor's office was closing and that we had two weeks to get our frozen embryos out. . . . We were told that our money would be refunded back to us, but that ended up not being the case." Such stories are nightmarish, implicating stereotypes of greedy and unethical providers who exploit the vulnerable.

Likewise, because trust requires individualized care, April Gonzalez began to have doubts about her physician: "I started to feel like he had a lot of patients, and I started feeling like he wasn't really even paying close attention to the individual specifics of my case." Personal care doesn't necessarily require much effort, so it's frustrating when even minimal standards are dropped. For Victoria Santos, trust could be diminished by "petty, minor things like not remembering my name, or where we are in the cycle, or something like that, because they didn't look at the chart before they came in the door." Providers' inattention to such minor details could signal more serious forms of neglect.

Honesty, Realistic Optimism, and Other Communication Skills

But even accessibility and personalized care aren't enough to build a trusting relationship; effective communication is also important—beginning with honesty: "I trusted our doctor from the beginning . . . she just told it as it was" (Sergei Bennett). But honesty and optimism are in delicate balance: "the doctor giving hope without giving false hope is a very, very, fine line to walk" (Rodney Hughes).

One hallmark of honesty is a realistic assessment of pregnancy odds. Monique Strickland ditched a doctor who couldn't "bag his pep talk" after her cycle appeared perfect, but still failed. "He was still being so positive. . . . 'You're going to get pregnant. There's no way this isn't gonna work,'" she recalled, "I don't want a pep talk. . . . I felt like I didn't have any trust in the medical advice that was being given." And some providers seem to cultivate hope as a cash crop, creating unreasonable expectations that leave patients feeling swindled or even victimized.[3] As Marie Byrd said, "[T]hey hold that shiny gold star out in front of you that at the end of this you'll have a baby. You just want to believe." Unfortunately, this makes things difficult for providers trying to convey genuine, well-founded optimism about patients' reproductive chances.

Conversely, it's easy to distrust providers whose estimates of conception seem unfounded or suddenly change. "[Our doctor] was optimistic when we first saw her; she gave us a 20% success rate. But then after we failed, she said that the IUI only has a 1% success rate, so I was doubtful with her credibility at that point," said Megan Cooper. Or dubious estimates could be "one-size-fits-all." April Gonzalez questioned why her doctor gave a 42-year-old friend with six unsuccessful IVF cycles the same odds of conceiving—10%—that he had quoted her, "at 32, with only three failed cycles." Impressive credentials are great, but patients would rather have the straight dope: "I'd much rather have somebody speak candidly that . . . I guess figuratively had a B– average in medical school than that A+ doctor that can make a mistake on a bad day and not even acknowledge it" (Nathaniel Sims). Thus, trust is fluid across treatment relationships, ebbing and flowing with interactions and outcomes.

Competence and Credentials

Trust without professional competence is dangerous; patients want to know that their providers make "good clinical decisions" (Shannon Ward). A resounding 98% of surveyed patients believed their doctor is at least competent; 67% described their RE as "very" competent, 25% as "quite" competent, and only 6% as of average competence. Professional accomplishments and credentials are enormously influential: "I trusted her. I mean, she has the credentials" (Holly Garrett). Patients can lose trust if their reproductive endocrinologists lack important achievements, like board certification: "[M]y OBGYN was like, 'Why would you go to that woman? She's not board certified,' so at this point I would say trust [in the RE] was diminished" (Stella Madison). Besides credentials, several deem CDC statistics the gold standard for measuring provider competence: "if their clinic has successful results, then that says more to me than anything else" (Philip Barnett). And most patients want evidence-based treatment plans. Deanna Douglas was irate when her physician recommended a novel and perhaps experimental protocol: "I was just angry about him putting me on a Menopur-only protocol when the nurse . . . flat-out t[old] me, 'I don't know why he has you on that, 'cause it's never worked for anybody.' [This] made me feel like I'm the guinea pig. . . . [it's like the doctor said], '[She]'s only 33. We'll just have her waste her time and money and try this thing and see if it works.'" Patients, then, are keenly aware of their vulnerability and lack of knowledge vis-à-vis physicians—an unsettling prospect if they don't trust their providers.

Of course, medical errors—and their correction—also significantly affect trust, with misdiagnoses undermining it, even as correct diagnoses enhance it. Patients are impressed when physicians correct prior errors, either of their own or others' making: "[T]he first thing that made me trust him more was that he clearly showed that the initial diagnosis I got was wrong" (Jessica Frazier). And patients' trust vaporizes when medical errors inflict physical harm, regardless of bedside manner and other relational dynamics.

Reviewing the many qualities that affect patients' trust in providers, it is striking how little effort many of them require. It's entirely reasonable for patients to expect that their chosen providers will attend them at key treatment stages (barring advance notice to the contrary), and to anticipate that they will be treated with compassion and respect, even if warmth and empathy aren't in a physician's toolkit.

CLINICAL DISPOSITIONS: WORKING
WITH TREATMENT TEAM MEMBERS

The staff at the [first] clinic . . . were just awful. They were bitter and nasty and they were the kind of people where you're like, "Oh, you hate your job!" The nurses were very nice. But if you had to call the answering service or something, you dreaded it because you knew they were going to be mean to you. You knew that you were going to have to call them three or four times before the doctor would call

you back. Then at the other clinic, everybody was so friendly. . . .
The office staff was involved in my case, and they cried when I got
pregnant and they were happy.

—May Weiss

The vast majority of patients have very positive experiences with clinic
employees who aren't REs, including receptionists, administrative assistants, insurance coordinators, lab personnel, and nurses. Patients expect
different types of interactions with clinic staff than with physicians, but
value many of the same qualities. Of surveyed patients, 67% felt their
clinic staff was friendly, and many patients also considered their staff
polite (53%), respectful (46%), compassionate (46%), patient (38%),
businesslike (35%), understanding (43%), warm (35%), competent
(32%), and honest (32%). Very few patients evaluated staff members
negatively, as rude (11%), curt (11%), misleading (7%), condescending
(7%), or disrespectful (7%).

Friendliness is most important; ideally, staff merit Darla Clarke's
glowing description: "everyone was super welcoming, and when you
call, it's never like you're bothering them. . . . Even . . . the secretaries at
the front desk were in tears when it didn't work, so we feel like they've
always cared for us and been rooting for us." Relationships with clinic
staff can last even after couples cease treatment: "I still send updates of
the girls. It was . . . like a family, and that's the approach they take"
(Brittany Watson).

Emotional investment is just as welcome from staff members as from
REs themselves: "It was all very professional and caring when things
didn't work out or they had to give you bad news. You could tell that
it was hard on them too" (Marion Goodwin). Some clinics adopt
empathic practices, like asking patients not to bring children. As Lily
Ellis explained, "They don't schedule your appointment when you aren't
pregnant when they have patients coming in who are already pregnant
for their tests during the first trimester. . . . It's really hard to sit in a
room with women who are pregnant and have kids" (Lily Ellis). Or clinics might give patients information and training preemptively, making
allowances for inexperience and confusion: "the first office [I visited]
charged you to teach you to do your medicine, like $100, $150, and
they didn't teach you anything. This office, they spent three hours with
me; they actually took my husband into an exam room and had him
practice putting a needle in me a few times. . . . You didn't pay for their
instruction, and it was so much more thorough and caring" (Monique
Strickland).

Patients are grateful when staff members get to know them, even if such familiarity was bred of technology, not memory: "they took your picture, so that every time you came in, it was like they knew who you were. They did that so that you felt like you were at home. . . . I felt like I was the only patient in their office" (Keira Wilkinson). And because IVF appointments are so frequent, it's hard for some patients *not* to genuinely get to know staff members: "eventually you become like part of the woodwork there; . . . they all knew me, they all knew my story. I knew the nurses in the back, I knew the nurses in the front, I knew the front desk staff" (Sasha Goodman).

Like familiarity, staff availability helps build effective and empathic relationships. Patients rave when staff members return calls promptly. "If we called in to the nursing line, we got a call back usually within the hour at some point, usually quicker than that," enthused Victoria Santos. Monique Strickland experienced vast differences in staff accessibility at her two clinics; in the first office, "it was the rigidity of it, when you have access to certain people. . . . Meanwhile at the other office, you can have any doctor at any day; you saw a doctor during your ultrasound." Sometimes an especially empathic staff member provides extra support outside clinic walls and operating hours. "[After] our first miscarriage, one of the nurses called my wife and talked to her for probably three or four hours . . . that evening because she just felt so bad and knew that we were going to be experiencing a lot of things," Timothy Ballard recalled.

Very few patients have a wholly negative experience with clinic staff—but these rare episodes can taint the entire treatment experience. As Francis Foster said, "[W]hen you get there and the staff could just give a rat's ass that you're there or not, you really don't feel all that great." Rochele Rowe described her nurses as "emotionally flat-lined": "I think the nurse staff was pretty abominable when it came to interpersonal dynamics. I thought they thought that questions were bothersome; . . . delivering bad news was just . . . too rote for them; they'd become too desensitized to it and what it really meant for people. . . . These clinic staff nurses to me were just in a factory kind of mentality about this stuff, and didn't understand that you were doing it for the first time." Cecelia McBride's clinic staff "were in horrible violation of HIPAA.[4] I mean, they'd call your name out, and what you were there for." One clinic employee gave Andre Baker "some pretty bad information about insurance that ended up costing us our insurance coverage for . . . both of the IVF cycles." Consequences of poor care can range from embarrassment and discomfort to loss of privacy to thousands of dollars out-of-pocket.

Patients are far more likely to dislike just one or two staff members, and even the best clinics have their curmudgeons or incompetents. "There was one nurse in this particular group who said . . . really horrible things to me," recalled Joanne Johnson. "I would walk in, and if a door opened, I would look to see if she was there, and if she was, my heart would immediately start palpitating." Sometimes, staff members made critical errors; Silvia Spencer learned during her *second* ultrasound that her twins were really triplets: "another nurse, who hadn't done our initial ultrasound, said, 'Now how many were you having again?' And I kind of freaked out because I thought something was wrong. . . . I said, 'Twins,' and she said, 'Uh, there's three.' . . . We were like, 'Oh my gosh . . . how did the person before not catch this?' And the person that did the ultrasound before . . . got fired."

Patient priorities and staff routines might also conflict; Dianna Lee's IVF coordinator got angry when they found a cheaper source for IVF medication than her clinic: "when we told her . . . you can get them from Canada or the UK, and it is the same exact manufacturer, she just blew up all over us." And patients' efforts to see nurses that they like can cause friction among clinic staff: "It got to the point where I actually called and I would ask what nurse is on, and then we'd schedule appointments around nurses. One of the doctors called me up; he says, 'Look, you can't do that. . . . They have feelings too, and it hurts their feelings to know that you won't work with them.' Well, it hurts my feelings and it hurts my wife that we do have to work with them" (Timothy Ballard). Here, patients' efforts to retain and build upon treatment relationships— conduct that's usually encouraged—turns out to be disruptive to clinic functioning and makes these patients seem "difficult."

Although patients put intense time and effort into selecting and forming relationships with physicians, it's their relationships with clinic staff, particularly nurses, that often turn out to be more influential in care experiences. Doctors might come and go, but staff members remain a constant presence—at the front desk checking patients in, in the lab drawing their blood, in offices discussing financing or informed consent matters. Ultimately, most patients form treatment relationships with providers and staff members they like and respect. A patient's assertiveness and other qualities often evolve with increased treatment experience, as does her knowledge of what she desires in a provider. But sometimes satisfying these needs mean switching to a different provider in the same clinic, or changing practices altogether.

IS THERE (ANOTHER) DOCTOR IN THE HOUSE?: SWITCHING PROVIDERS

When they choose a fertility provider, the last thing patients are thinking about is leaving—but things change in unexpected ways. Even after being confronted with their providers' errors, patients can still feel conflicted. Though patients can't change a provider's personality or clinic policies, they can choose another one, even if they have to travel farther or pay more. And many, if not most, patients (44% survey, 42% interview) took advantage of that opportunity once (56% survey 28% interview). Some switched providers multiple times, including twice (7% survey, 6% clinic) or three (4% survey, 4% interview), four (.7% survey, .8% interview), five (.4% survey, 1.6% interview), or more times (.8% interview).

Fertility patients generally don't hesitate to switch providers, whether they transfer to another in the same practice or in an altogether different facility. As Dr. Errol Walter observed, "[P]robably 20 to 40 percent of my patients are coming to me from [another] reproductive endocrinologist, where they've left ... for a dozen reasons, including cost, the reproductive endocrinologist really has a vested interest in doing IVF on the entire world, their personality problems, all those other things that people get rid of doctors for."

Sometimes patients switch providers voluntarily; other times, circumstances made it impossible for them to continue in their current practice. Predictably, patients' reactions to switching providers differs greatly depending on why they're leaving. Over half of patients (53% interview) obtained a second opinion. The most common reasons for leaving were seeing if another provider would be more successful (20% survey, 6% interview), bedside manner or physical availability (15% survey, 16% interview), obtaining services current providers didn't offer or lacked experience offering (9% interview), financial reasons (8% interview), disliking a particular clinic experience (9% survey, 6% interview), disagreeing with REs' decisions (12% survey, 3.3% interview), having an RE who wasn't aggressive enough (9%), patients' moves (5.8%), doctors who moved or closed (6% survey, 3% interview), clinic success rates (5% interview), and when REs refuse continued treatment (12% interview).

Patients who voluntarily switch providers often blame failed relationships or diminished trust. Abigail Ramsey fired her current provider because he was demeaning: "he just made me feel dumb, and I couldn't

[ask] questions without feeling dumb." Monica Hansen ditched her provider for not being more forthcoming with important information, as she learned when she checked her medical records: "I began to find out that he had all kinds of observations about me he wasn't sharing with me. It was crazy! And I went to support groups, and when I would mention my first doctor's name to different people . . . they'd say, 'Well, he only says things on a need-to-know basis.'" Sometimes a patient isn't sure exactly why she dislikes a provider enough to switch: "I just didn't care for him. I don't know; I couldn't really pinpoint [it]. He had a big flash[y] gold bracelet on and . . . he just didn't fit well personally with me" (Amber Butler).

Other patients switch because physicians are unavailable. "He was trying to be too many places at once. He'd schedule an appointment with me and then call me [and cancel] the day before," said Lily Ellis. "I felt like I was being jerked around big time by everybody." Other clinic practices irritate patients enough to leave. Megan Cooper's clinic chronically procrastinated in obtaining insurance authorization for each cycle: "at my first clinic, they kept putting it off until the day of, when I got my cycle. So it was too late. And I just decided not to go there anymore." Patients are used to completing treatment responsibilities promptly, and they expect their providers to do the same.

Patients might also switch clinics because they disagree with providers' treatment decisions. May Weiss and her husband discovered their clinic had made a momentous and likely unethical decision without consulting them: "they mixed my husband's sperm and the donor sperm so we don't even know, biologically, what embryos we put back in that cycle. When that happened I was like, 'I could've had twins, one being a donor and one being my husband's.' . . . There's just no way this is okay." This admittedly extreme example nonetheless demonstrates the informed consent project's continued importance throughout the IVF cycle.

Patients also switch providers to accommodate life circumstances. Patients move, insurance changes, and current providers might not offer particular treatments. Sara Harper had to locate an out-of-state practice when none in her state offered natural IVF. Similarly, Patricia Burns changed doctors because she received a nonprofit grant to pay for another IVF cycle, Lola Lewis transferred to use donor eggs, and Julia Norton sought care from a more experienced clinic: "I think they had under 20 patients a year, so we just wanted to go with someone who did a lot more."

Or patients outright distrust providers' treatment decisions, like persistently following unsuccessful treatment protocols. Nathaniel Sims said, "[W]e switched because the protocol that failed wasn't going to change. Our doctor was convinced that it was still the right protocol." Or providers aren't aggressive enough: "It wasn't that we didn't trust [our first doctor]; it was that he wasn't going to go to another level and we weren't pregnant, so therefore we needed to make a change" (Darla Clarke). Sometimes a physician ends a treatment relationship, usually because of medical futility; Rachael Wilkerson observed, "[T]he doctor that we were with basically told us there was nothing more she could do for us. So we had to find somebody else who thought differently." When patients use such disagreement as a springboard into new or more aggressive treatment relationships, it can prompt concern, since providers likely have sound reasons for declining particular protocols or refusing treatment altogether.

But perhaps the most serious reason for switching providers is medical error—not surprising, given how provider mistakes vaporize trust. Josephine Palmer suffered through a number of unnecessary tests and a surgery because of a misdiagnosis: "after my 3rd IUI failed . . . [I thought], 'I'm not going to put my body through any more.' . . . [Another doctor] did the right blood test, and he was the one that found that I had [an] autoimmune problem." Switching providers is especially painful when patients feel genuinely connected to them. Anne Kelley's provider had undergone infertility treatment approximately "20 to 25 years ago," which made her "very empathetic, she was very caring, she was very nurturing." But that physician later transferred two embryos, violating Anne's consent; only one embryo could be safely transferred. "She put in two, and we ended up with triplets somehow. . . . Even after the horribleness she caused, she'd still cry with us, and that was huge," Anne recalled. "In half of my brain, I hated her guts, and [in] the other half, I want to be hugged." Nonetheless, this was a death knell for that treatment relationship; Anne took advantage of free cycles, but transferred after "[w]e just lost trust and respect for her."

Consistent with their enthusiastic participation in treatment decisions, several patients obtain a second opinion before switching providers: "they couldn't really give me any answers. . . . [but] for my own peace of mind, I needed to have a second opinion" (Lauren Mack). Usually, this consultation is comforting: "we needed the reassurance that I was doing everything that I could." Patients may lack control over many aspects of IVF, but at least they can confirm that their providers are recommending sound protocols.

In summary, patients view switching providers as a form of assertive behavior that protects one of the few matters within their control—the freedom to choose who treats them. This freedom is a key ingredient of successful patient-provider relationships; it motivates providers to work for and with patients, lest unhappy patients seek other professionals. Moreover, this freedom allows many patients to find a provider they like and respect, laying the foundation for what will likely become an intimate, lengthy relationship.

CONCLUSION: HEALTHY RELATIONSHIPS—NOT JUST WHAT THE DOCTOR ORDERED

Doctor-patient relationships provide endless opportunities for patients to both take and cede control. *Taking* control can allow patients to become more engaged in treatment, partner with physicians, form positive connections with clinic staff, and switch providers when necessary. *Ceding* control can mean relying on trusted providers for emotional support and knowledge, and acknowledging professionals' expertise— but also risking manipulation by unscrupulous professionals. Fortunately, the same dynamics that improve patient comprehension also enhance patient agency; promote emotional, psychological and physical well-being; improve treatment experiences; and thereby increase chances of conceiving.

Above all else, patients prioritize trust and bedside manner as they reflect on their treatment personalities, preferences, and experiences. Thick trust and a warm, efficacious, respectful, communicative, and empathic provider relationship encourage patients to lower their guards. This suggests that many or even most patients form supportive relationships with their care providers—and demonstrates how easily an unscrupulous provider can manipulate a patient who is, by definition, vulnerable. This is when informed-consent-as-ritual can and should step into the breach, because informed-consent-as-relationship has failed.

But reforming effective informed consent doesn't mean undermining healthy treatment relationships. Genuine empathy and a good bedside manner shouldn't be discouraged just because false empathy and an ingenuous bedside manner can be manipulative tools. It's far more important to foster the conditions for successful treatment relationships than to undermine them by hobbling trust or imposing greater interpersonal distance. Paradoxically, patients who enjoy empathic treatment relationships might be more understanding about the need for consent documents, but view forms themselves as less important. But these patients still receive necessary consent protections, just in different and unanticipated ways for which medical and legal bureaucracies rarely make allowances.

Moreover, these men and women don't sound like the desperate, helpless, bitter, angry, or obsessive creatures inhabiting popular infertility stereotypes. Rather, these patients realize that they have choices, expend great effort to make the best decisions they can, and consciously exercise their agency in the process.

Finally, patients are quite savvy about the various incentives within reproductive medicine. They know that the close interpersonal relationships they forge with providers are embedded in two worlds, with goals, norms, and methods that are often contradictory: the realm of medical standards and ethics, and a commodified market system including clinics, financiers, and insurance companies.

Though they acknowledge that fertility clinics are businesses and that profits matter, most patients choose to ground their treatment experience within interpersonal relationships, not the commodified medical marketplace. Indeed, patients guard these relationships carefully against market intrusions, rejecting fertility "factories" and other overly commodified, depersonalized care practices. Patients believe that most providers have priorities other than collecting paychecks, including solving medical mysteries and assisting others to improve their health and achieve life goals. Thus, acknowledging that fertility care, like other forms of medical practice, is commodified doesn't compel patients to surrender to that reality, or condemn them to distanced provider relationships and contracted care. Nor does it prove that they are ignorant; discounting commodification is not the same as denying it.

Patients' reflections on treatment relationships, and especially on the importance of trust and communication, raise the question of how *providers* experience their relationships with patients, how they negotiate the fine line between profit motive and patient-centered care, and whether, in fact, these two can be compatible.

CHAPTER 6

Doctoring Hope

Providers' Perspectives on Treatment
Relationships

There are eight doctors in my family. I like to joke I was 35
before they told me I actually could've done something else.
In fact, it's a privilege to be a physician, particularly in this
country at this time in this society, and I see it as that and
I never try to lose sight of that, and I try to be respectful
of that. I also take a lot of personal pride in trying to be a
good physician.

—Dr. Bret Sternberg

Because patients look to reproductive medicine professionals for both
medical care and emotional support, these individuals fulfill many other
roles in family-building. They are translators, explaining complex biological processes and medical procedures. They are counselors, listening
and encouraging patients in need of a trusted, supportive expert. They
are mentors, who must teach patients that medicine is an art as well as
a science, that facts and knowledge can be fallible, and that what appears
black and white to patients might actually be gray. They are gatekeepers, who must apply ethical and professional standards in deciding
whether or not to treat a patient, and how aggressively. And they must
switch roles at the drop of a hat; in one appointment, a provider might
congratulate a couple trying to conceive for years on their new pregnancy, but in the next have to explain to a confused, frustrated, and
perhaps irate patient why refusing care is in her best interests.

In filling these roles, professionals, like patients, focus on issues like
trust, bedside manner, and availability. But they also consider other,
equally important factors: the substantive elements of medical practice,

its market realities, the need to make a living, and the obligation to follow legal and ethical guidelines, including informed consent. All of these concerns might be in tension with one another, particularly when standards and practices are established by diverse groups with different priorities, to achieve different purposes. A physician's desire to spend time with a patient could be at odds with bureaucratic record-keeping demands and keeping up with a busy practice's patient volume. There can be friction between efficiency and interpersonal communication, between emotional desires and medical standards of care, between care incentives and profit motives, between what's best for patients and what's best for business. When are these dynamics in tension, and when do they come together to improve treatment relationships and experiences? How do professionals develop trust in the face of impersonal policies and skeptical patients?

"TRUST ME, I'M A DOCTOR?": DEVELOPING PATIENT CONFIDENCE

IVF isn't without harm. There's a lot of complications that can happen with IVF. So there's a lot of trust involved in letting this physician give you these medications and tell you, well, this is how we're going to get you pregnant. And, if the patient doesn't trust you, they may still go ahead with treatment. And we've got some patients . . . that question every single treatment we give them. But, I think trust has a huge, huge role to play, in not only how well a patient sort of accepts your treatment decisions, but how satisfied they are with your care.

—First Year RE Fellow Dr. Yazmin Kuhn

Professionals unanimously agree that trust lays the foundation for the provider-patient relationship. "I hope that most patients, if they don't trust a doctor, would get out of his office really quickly" (Dr. Errol Walter). It can enable other qualities of a healthy treatment relationship: "with trust you have a question of honesty; if you don't trust me, will you be honest with me? And if you're not honest with me, how can there be a good decision-making process?" said Nurse Gabi Simpson. Trust also ensures that providers and patients are working toward the same goals: "we have such great relationships with our patients; . . . they trust that we're looking out for their best interest, and that we're here to help them, and that we want to give them a baby as much as they want it" (Nurse Iola Lowry). It therefore facilitates cooperation, enabling patient and provider to proceed with no regrets: "you want them to trust you so that you've [got] that good rapport back and forth, and make sure they're feeling okay with the decisions they're making and that you're making for them" (Nurse Tamela Isaacson).

In reproductive medicine, trust is especially important, because a patient's relationship with her treatment team can be lengthy, often lasting through extensive testing and multiple treatment cycles. "The longer [the relationship] has to last to be successful, the more important [trust] is. Like if you have a heart problem and you need your valve replaced, you don't really need to like the guy because you're going to have a one-episode interaction and it's over," said Dr. Roselle Suarez. "But for some of what we do, it lasts many months, and they don't get to the finish line if they're distrustful." Distrustful patients are more likely to discontinue treatment, and they have often endured poor treatment at the hands of other providers: "they've had people take care of them that were doing things that were suboptimal and who are ... downright inappropriate. And those that realize that they've been poorly managed or taken advantage of are perhaps the most challenging to take care of because they then go overboard and are questioning everything you do" (Dr. Sachie Keefe).

In legal, bureaucratic, and commercial contexts, trust might be governed by documents or contracts that regulate arms-length transactions. Documents themselves have distinct trust rules that favor fair provisions, transparency, sufficient time to read and agree to terms, and so on. But interpersonal relationships, including doctor-patient conversations, also have norms, unwritten expectations for how participants will behave toward one another in trusting situations, like positive body language: head-nodding, smiling, attentiveness, and eye contact. And these norms apply even when these relationships have both commercial and social (and medical) goals and consequences. At times, rules from different contexts, like law and social interaction, can clash, with distressing effects; patients might expect to have a relaxed conversation about treatment information, but instead receive impersonal consent forms. Dashed expectations alert individuals that their relationships might not be what they thought.

Professionals believe that patients instinctively trust them: "I think most patients innately have some trust in their doctor; it's where they kind of start getting to crossroads [when making treatment choices] that they're like, 'Oh, did I make the right decision?' And that's where it gets scary for them." This trust usually extends to nurses and other clinic personnel. "The nurses here are more of their lifelines; we're who they talk to," Nurse Tricia Peters said. "They know that through us they get to the other areas, like to the doctors or to the labs or whatever it is that they need to do. So they've [got] to be able to trust us or they wouldn't come to us."

Although patient trust is (for the most part) instinctive, professionals must work to sustain it, especially as treatment progresses. For this reason, Dr. Sachie Keefe viewed trust as reciprocal: "I can't just say, 'Trust me, I'm a doctor.' . . . You have to gain their trust and they have to gain yours." Because other dynamics of the treatment relationship, like power imbalances, can be in tension with and erode trust, astute providers constantly need to monitor trust and, if necessary, work to rebuild it. To these ends, Dr. Cary Priestley described a careful strategy of reassurance: "I can . . . have a certain demeanor; that makes them understand that I'm going to work at their pace, that I'm understanding their issues, that I'm willing to work with them in everything that's rea- sonable and healthy and safe for them, and that I can provide them with the best information that's available to me."

Trust should never be "blind trust": "The patient should also always question things that their doctor says if it doesn't sound right or they're concerned it's not right" (Dr. Gerard Gabler). And earning trust is a skill that might take time to develop for junior physicians:

> There's something magic that happens when you're in your fourth or fifth year after medical school, where all of a sudden you realize that you can recall all of what you know without having to look within your pockets for notes. . . . I tell them that once that happens, that then their job is to constantly be monitoring the patient's reactions to what's going on. . . . I may just say, "Would you feel comfortable telling me how you're feeling now?" . . . If you look for it, patients will give you clues, and then all you have to generally do is gently ask about it. (Dr. Bret Sternberg)

Thus, trust can be threatened by both medicine's professional aspects—short appointment times and other practices—and its scien- tific, substantive elements—like superior knowledge, power imbalances, and treatment outcomes. To retain and strengthen trust, providers advise "try[ing] to make [patients] active participants . . . in the deci- sions" (Dr. Jie Hue), answering patients' questions so they "feel that they can call and talk to you about anything" (Nurse Tricia Peters), and even asking them "some open-ended questions to make sure that you aren't just putting your own thoughts into the interaction" (Dr. Stefanie Burgstaller). And this process continues for the duration of the treat- ment relationship: "that starts right at the beginning of the relationship, with listening to them, . . . when you have your first consult and listen to what their needs are. . . . I think trust comes from the patient, who's feeling like I know them and I know what their medical history is, and where they've been and where they'd like to go. And, so I sort of [have to] do my homework before I meet with them. Let them know I've reviewed their case and records" (Dr. Jaxon Arnaudo).

It's also important for providers to communicate confidence in their own abilities, in treatment protocols, and in patients themselves: "Anything unsure—'I feel nervous'—you never say that. You have to go in there with 'I've done this five million times; I've got to make you believe that I have and I'm going to do a great job for you today'" (Nurse Arya Muller).

Here again, patients' trust is sustained or undermined by bedside manner—a supportive, respectful professional demeanor suggests to patients it's safe to rely on a provider, be honest with her, and give one's self over into her care. And because REs and nurses might have different approaches to bedside manner, they also might have different ways of gaining and retaining trust. "Making a diagnosis and prescribing a treatment is just very different than the nursing role in general, [which involves] how you're going to help your patients get through testing, get through treatment, get through that emotional part of dealing with not having treatment that's successful," Melina Draper said. "Just having somebody that they can bounce those thoughts off of and that emotion off of, I think, makes a difference."

PATIENTS ARE A VIRTUE: WORKING WITH INDIVIDUALS' TREATMENT PERSONALITIES

Patients have many qualities that enhance trust and smooth treatment interactions, including being inquisitive, kind, optimistic, informed, level-headed, and realistic. But providers realize that undergoing treatment can throw many of these qualities out of balance, and that treatment relationships can either help to restore equilibrium or make things even more off-kilter.

Fertility professionals are thankful when patients are friendly and have a positive outlook. "Patients who are even-tempered are easier to work with than those who might jump to conclusions or be easily angry," asserted Head Nurse Melina Draper. Others like the challenges more intense patients bring: "I like to work with those patients the most that are a little bit anxious but willing to do what it takes. I'm okay with tears, I'm okay with anxiety, [and] I'm okay with high-strung" (Nurse Gabi Simpson). Such providers want patients to be themselves, rather than trying to become "ideal" patients.

Professionals like curious patients. "[I enjoy] the ones that are the most open-minded as far as they want as much information as we have to give them," asserted Nurse Melanie Simons, "and they're . . . kind of fresh as far as they haven't done a lot of Internet searching, where they've stressed themselves out to the point that they just can't even hear what you're trying to tell them." Inquisitiveness can be in tension with flexibility and compliance; the easiest patients for Nurse Iola Lowry were "probably ready to listen, ready to learn, ready to be educated and follow our instructions." Patients should also be responsible: "we also have to make them accountable for their side of things as well. . . . Not necessarily saying that 'I'm going to do every single thing for you.'" (IVF Coordinator Maggie Roy). Patients can use inquisitiveness to more effectively exercise their treatment responsibilities.

Curiosity goes hand-in-hand with being well-informed. "I actually kind of like when patients come in with a little bit of knowledge. . . . They're informed, they're open to other ideas. They're very up front about what their expectations are," said Dr. Abbie Walther. Some REs try to confront their biases as to which patients they consider well-informed. As Dr. Bret Sternberg confessed, "Unfortunately, the more culturally they're similar to me, [the more] that they can understand at . . . almost an intuitive level what I'm talking about and how I'm talking about it." But even the most well-informed patients don't know everything, and professionals hope people will ask questions to fill in their gaps in knowledge. Nurse Practitioner Michi Glover appreciated "somebody that asks questions, answers questions easily. They're not timid, they're not shy. They're very open with their medical history. They're respectful of our time." Ironically, many patients fear that questions are burdensome to care providers and hesitate to ask very many. "I feel like a lot of them don't ask enough questions," said Nurse Jaylen Abbott.

Emotional equanimity also fosters learning; Dr. Stefanie Burgstaller remarked, "in an ideal situation . . . [someone] isn't overly emotional about the situation, but can think things through and make good, rational decisions based on the information they have." Emotions aren't problematic unless they consume a patient's attention and govern her conduct. Calmness facilitates communication. "We get a lot of patients that are very angry about their diagnosis even before they see you, and that hostility adds into the relationship, so that they're not really asking a lot of good questions," said Dr. Corwin Summers. "[O]ccasionally you get patients where they're so anxious to get started they don't even ask any questions." These traits also align with so-called desperate patient behaviors.

Finally, professionals enjoy working with realistic patients—or ones with realistic odds of conceiving. For Third Year RE Fellow Dr. Wilma Sumner, "younger patients [are easier], because there's more likelihood for success. . . . I think the most difficult ones are the ones with diminished ovarian reserve, where there's not as many options as far as using their own eggs that you can offer them." Not all patients want to hear what providers have to say about such issues. "There are occasionally patients who really don't want to engage with the medical issues, the scientific issues, even the emotional issues. They just want me to fix it, and . . . it becomes more difficult because it's not reality-based," noted Dr. Bret Sternberg. Being "realistic," then, means accepting the limits of medical technology and personal physiology—including one's odds of getting pregnant. Dr. Denzel Burke admitted that, although "it can be more gratifying to handle a difficult problem . . . it is nice to have that quick gratification to be able to handle a simple problem." Providers don't like it when they can't help their patients: "It's frustrating when there's so much pathology that there's nothing you can do" (Dr. Kerry Kushner).

There is a fine line between many "ideal" qualities like being curious, well-informed, emotionally stable, and realistic, on the one hand, and being demanding, know-it-all, too needy, or detached and cynical, on the other. All of these characteristics fit within two overarching behavioral categories, assertiveness and aggression, that best illustrate the fine line between exercising agency and undermining providers' authority and expertise, between a steady patient and stable treatment relationship and a hot-tempered patient and volatile care connection. Trust is precariously related to such qualities, illustrating how norms of medical practice overlap with trust and bedside manner, and when the two are in tension or in concert.

Dynamics of assertiveness and aggression are undeniably complicated by certain biases that explain why women and people of color are routinely understood as more aggressive when they speak up in the same manner as white men. Social norms encourage women to be warm and nurturing and minorities to be silent and subservient; those who violate these norms are often socially penalized. For instance, women

are often punished for direct, explicit forms of assertiveness, like negotiating for higher salaries, as compared to men who made the same
requests.[1] It's imperative to keep these biases in mind when patients are
described as "assertive" and "aggressive."

Several professionals place assertive and aggressive patients on a
spectrum; at the low and mid points, such behavior is to be welcomed,
but at the high ends, it becomes difficult. IVF Coordinator Meredith
Haynes said, "I think there's an appropriate way to be assertive and an
inappropriate way to be assertive. . . . [when patients question every-
thing] it does make our job a little harder sometimes, to feel like you
have to justify in a nice way what their physician has ordered." Or
patients attempt to accelerate treatment in unsafe ways: "It's like, 'I've
been waiting long enough, I don't want to wait any longer, how fast can
we get this done?'" (Nurse Nylah Chen). Nurse Devan Neville described
a recent phone call with an assertive female patient: "I was . . . recommending to her the testing that we need to do, and she's like, 'Nope,
I don't wanna do that; I wanna jump into this.'" Neville quipped,
"[T]hey're just gonna take the next step without taking the necessary
step." Providers have varying perspectives on when assertiveness
becomes difficult: "there's a point, and it'll be different for different
physicians, at which stage you'll find it frustrating. . . . I expect patients
to be a little more respectful of 20 years of experience and knowing that
I have their best interests at heart. But it's an important balancing act"
(Dr. Kerry Kushner).

Assertive patients are often easy to trust: "I think you have to be
assertive to walk in the door and seek help. . . . I think infertility patients
overall are pretty assertive and motivated and compliant" (Dr. Wes
Hoffman). And they can be wonderful partners "when they're rational,
within the difficulty of being rational in a situation like this" (Dr. Cary
Priestley) (note the privileging of rationality). Assertive patients often
"are just trying to get information" (Psychologist Robbie Leavitt), and
"when they get the appropriate information, they're very cooperative"
(Dr. Cary Priestley). Assertiveness can help "drive [patients] to get to a
certain point where they're comfortable and successful with everything"
(Nurse Elihu Brant).

Different patients take different roads to assertiveness. According to
Third Party RN Prasad Singh, this behavior is often related to patients'
pasts: "Some of them are assertive because they're women who waited
to have children, and they've learned through their own careers that
they have to be assertive to get what they want out of life. And others

are assertive because there's been so much failure along in the process that they feel very scared, and they have to ask so many questions along the way. . . . So assertive just kind of depends on what the woman has been through before, I guess, and her own life experiences." Indeed, assertiveness often evolves over the course of treatment: "if they don't get pregnant, then they try to put their fingers in the pot a little more" (First Year RE Fellow Dr. Yazmin Kuhn).

Assertiveness allows patients to own their treatment decisions and be involved, educated, and in control to the extent possible. Assertive patients are organized and vocal: "I think they come in and they have at least a semistructured agenda per visit. They want to fully inform you about their history and let you know about their desires and their specific questions and their desired outcome, and they make sure they have a voice" (Dr. Denzel Burke). Psychologist Rory Frei described these relationships as collaborative and more egalitarian: "An assertive patient is interested in partnering with their physician. They're not sort of in the 1950s model of 'he tells me, and thus I do.' . . . They want to understand what's going on, they want to sort of sit at the table and discuss what their options are, and how successful an option is likely to be, and how expensive it's likely to be, so they really want to form that kind of a relationship with their RE."

Assertive patients also have many more "ideal" qualities; they seem more informed, in part because they ask questions: "they've made it to us kind of having a good knowledge base or at least read a lot. . . . They make it clear what their needs are, and they're not afraid to tell you" (Dr. Teagan Shepherd). They also take the initiative to educate themselves and "do research on their own, bring different things that we may not have presented" (Dr. Shel Kruger). Assertiveness makes sense: "it's their body, it is their money, it is their time, it is decisions they make that affect them for the rest of their life" (Dr. Terrence Trumbauer). For these reasons, assertiveness can make treatment relationships productive: "I can take their forward-moving energy and say, 'Great, you want to go forward, let's make a strategy today'" (Dr. Bret Sternberg).

Geography influences what social norms patients use, as well as professionals' estimates as to how many of their patients are assertive. One lab director in the Midwest thought that assertive patient populations are largely concentrated on the East or West coasts: "There's . . . maybe not as much trust, and . . . certainly more centers and availability for treatment. So there's that threat of 'I can go down the street,' and that's the way business gets done" (Lab Director Farran Ibbot). Dr. Errol

Walter, practicing in the South, found his patients less directive: "in the South, assertive is, 'Don't you think this would be a good idea?' But it's not, 'Bozo, get this done.' . . . If I were still up in the North, it would be, 'Bozo, get this done.' So I'm used to both."

And certain patient groups—most often professionals—are generally more assertive; Dr. Sachie Keefe stated, "a lot of . . . professional patients are very used to getting what they want." Attorneys and other physicians are frequently pegged as assertive, usually not in positive ways. "Can you say J.D. [juris doctorate, a law degree]? They'll cross-examine us. They'll try and argue their point. They'll practice splitting [up the doctor and nurse] very often, and they often will miss the big picture," said Dr. Alexandra Sanford. Certain professions might also prompt women to delay childbearing in addition to attracting determined individuals; to Dr. Connor Gibson, the "most assertive are the professional women, especially attorneys and medical professionals, who have come to fertility treatment late in life, because they think, 'I can do this any time I want,' and then they find out they can't."

But when patient assertiveness becomes aggression, triggering provider distrust, it might not be so much *where* patients come from or *what* they say, but *who* they are and *how* they say it, raising the possibility of provider biases and microaggression. Hallmarks of aggressive patients include angry and disruptive behaviors like cursing, exhibiting rage, making negative comments or abusing clinic staff, making demands, and exhibiting extreme stress, anxiety, or frustration.

According to providers, aggressive patients express themselves verbally and physically in more intense, confrontational ways. "Instead of coming in and saying, 'Can you help me understand how this fits in to what you were saying?'" Dr. Roselle Suarez said, "they come in and say, 'I think you're wrong and let me show you why.' It's with an attitude." Donor Coordinator Assistant Louis Whitaker described an aggressive patient's demeanor: "the tone of voice is very forceful. . . . They're face-to-face with you, you can see it and, just the expression. And then you can just feel the body language. It's just closed down and 'I want what I want.'" Dr. Kerry Kushner recalled a "really funny story" about a colleague who was pushed too far by a patient:

[A] friend of mine is a very world-renowned physician. . . . And he had a patient who'd done six IVF cycles elsewhere and came in with two inches of records and the husband's this hot-shot Wall Street guy. [This doctor] . . . goes through all the information, and he gives a very brilliant analysis of everything and spends the time and explains it. And the husband looks unimpressed. And he says, "Well, I was online last night and I was looking at some stuff and I think you're wrong. And here's what you really need to be saying." So [the doctor] started getting annoyed, and he said to the guy, . . . "Tell me what you do." So he says, "Well, I'm an investment banker and I'm in trade in these exotic derivatives and that sort of thing." He said, "I'll tell you what." He says, "Tonight, I'm going to go online, I'm going to spend an hour reading about your field, and tomorrow I'll call you and tell you how to do your job." . . . The husband ended up respecting him, too. But I'm always amused at that.

Aggression, then, implies that patients disrespect providers and their training. For instance, Senior Embryologist Lizbeth Norton encountered a patient who was "thinking he knew more than I did." Fortunately, it occurs "on rare occasion" (Dr. Jie Hue) and warrants empathy and understanding.

It's hard to feel trust and empathy for an aggressive, disruptive, or even abusive patient: "They're the ones who kind of more view [us] as [an] adversary instead of a fellow team person. They're calling and they're yelling at you because they didn't get pregnant," said Nurse Tricia Peters. To Dr. Shel Kruger, anger is a distraction within the treatment relationship: "you're a lot of times focusing on dealing with the anger portion of it instead of focusing on their different treatments and that sort of thing." Aggressive patients also commonly require clinics to reallocate resources and may even change clinic practices, either because they demand certain accommodations or because clinics must protect employees. Even scheduling aggressive patients requires more effort: "we're all starting to walk on eggshells to try and take care of that person as best as you can, to make their experience better. Suddenly there are providers they can't see, and there are stenographers they can't see, and they don't want to talk to someone on the phone" (Physician's Assistant Nora Stanton). These accommodations no doubt increase professionals' frustration with these patients.

Staff members, not doctors, are usually the first targets of aggressive patient pressure or abuse. "Patients are more than happy to beat up on the staff [in ways] that they wouldn't do to the docs," Dr. Bret Sternberg remarked. Nurse Nylah Chen described what it was like to be on the receiving end of such an interaction: "I try to answer their questions as they're talking and screaming at me on the phone. . . . The only time I absolutely disconnect from a patient is if they start swearing at me. Then I normally go back to them and say, 'I'm sorry, but you don't need to speak with me like that. I'm more than happy to answer your questions, but I don't feel I need to tolerate language like that.' And if they continue, I usually hang up, which is what we're usually told to do."

Usually staff members confronting aggressive patients will fetch a physician. Dissatisfied aggressive patients might even threaten legal action, which "starts to bring in certainly that trust issue as well" (Head Nurse Melina Draper). Unfortunately, these individuals can even affect other patients. "We've never had to call the police, which is wonderful," Draper explained, "but I've had to tell patients that their behavior, the volume of their talking, or [their] language is disruptive." But even as they celebrate assertiveness and bemoan aggression, providers know *why* patients adopt such behaviors—stress, loss of control, nervousness—and try to help them manage these feelings. "They come across as being very abrasive. But I don't think that they're masking desperation. I think that they're masking uncertainty. They're masking fear" (Senior Embryologist Lizbeth Norton).

Nonetheless, aggression can inject wariness and emotional distance into treatment relationships: "I go into "cautious" mode in that it becomes more of a business rather than an information-sharing [relationship]— you just have to be very careful what you say because you don't know [how] it's going to be interpreted" (Nurse Gabi Simpson). Treatment relationships feel more commercialized when they lack trust. Demanding patients also require more time and can be "totally inflexible with time restraints that we all have to work with as a team. . . . Those patients are a little frustrating because you just don't feel like you can ever make them happy or meet their needs" (IVF Nurse Coordinator Meredith Haynes).

On the other side of the spectrum from aggression, overly deferential patient behavior also poses real problems for trust and treatment relationships. More than half (61%) of providers stated that patients try to defer to them—particularly about whether they should continue treatment or implant a certain number of embryos. Like aggressive or defiant patients, extreme deference illustrates how dynamics in the patient-provider relationship can create tension between maintaining trust and fulfilling professional responsibilities and ethical norms. Under conventional definitions of autonomy, patients, not physicians, make treatment decisions. But for some patients, that's untenable.[2] Deference can be healthy if it reflects trust, not helplessness and desperation. But it's counterproductive if patients can't or don't trust themselves to make decisions.

Extreme deference is very different from seeking a provider's approval. Patients understandably want professional guidance for any number of reasons; fertility professionals become Sherpas, guides through the dizzying array of choices and procedures that comprise the infertility Expedition. But, as Dr. Errol Walter noted, excessively deferential patients want much more; they "come to me as a god [and] want me to tell them exactly what to do [or] . . . want me to be their patriarch," as opposed to "patients who think I'm just an information source." Deference might be situational; staff members note that the same patient can morph from defiant to overly compliant when a physician appears: "We'll get the comments and the dirty looks and the shortness of attitude. But when the physician walks in, everything is rainbows and glitter" (IVF Coordinator Rosamund Coel).

Heightened deference also exacerbates patient ignorance if they don't ask questions or try to understand reproduction and fertility procedures. Extremely underinformed patients might not even know how their bodies function. Working with such patients requires providers to overcome serious communication barriers and quell their own biases toward patients whose deference is hard to understand. Dr. Bret Sternberg observed, "[I]f there's no science education whatsoever [it's a problem]. . . . When I'm presenting information to a patient who doesn't understand the menstrual cycle, a woman who had no idea . . . what her ovaries, her eggs, her tubes, her uterus . . . were there for—that's difficult, because then it really boils down to all I have to offer them is magic."

In addition to aggression and overly deferential behavior, providers are concerned about patient dishonesty, chronic insecurity, magical thinking, and extreme emotional intensity. Here, providers worry that their patients could potentially compromise care. Dr. Bret Sternberg cautioned medical residents about certain patient behaviors: "Be careful of the patient who comes in praising you to the skies . . . because this is a patient that wants magic from you and is thinking that if she can only win you over, then you'll give her the magic. . . . Also be careful of the patient who starts off the interview complaining about the last infertility doctor that she saw, because you may be tempted to think, 'Well, I'm going to be different. I'm going to be better.'"

These patients can pose legal as well as medical challenges. "There are extremes of behavior where you're like, 'I don't even feel safe providing care for you,'" emphasized Dr. Corwin Summers. "It usually means that they don't listen, or they're shopping around for someone to tell them what they want to hear," said Dr. Heike Steinmann. Such patients might even imperil professional relationships with other providers.

"[Patients] may actually say, 'I can't believe Dr. So-and-so didn't check my TSH [to ascertain thyroid functioning]. . . . Can you believe that they missed that?'" First Year RE Fellow Dr. Yazmin Kuhn said. "As a physician, those are your peers, and you have to be very, very careful with those patients and not say, 'Oh, I can't believe . . . that,'" she continued. "You say, 'Well, everybody does some things a little differently. This is what we do here.'"

Finally, providers find it hard to work with insensitive patients who regard gamete donors, surrogates, and other reproductive partners as mere functionaries whom they're paying to perform a mechanical task. "When you're doing donor egg cycles, something that always raises a huge red flag for me is when they seem so concerned about starting that they're not really concerned about the well-being of their donor," Dr. Corwin Summers said. Psychologist Janine Dedrick recalled, "[T]he most alarming situation that I could think of with an intended parent was some difficulty understanding that the gestational carrier was a person."

Professionals agree that issues in treatment relationships should be resolved directly and as early as possible, ideally through empathic conversation, not hostile confrontation. "We try to address it directly with them and say, "Is there anything else going on, how else can we help you?" (Dr. Ronnie Avery). It's usually far more productive to work through potential issues with creativity, empathy, and innovation than to make patients defensive. Dr. Cary Priestley said, "[a]s long as I see they aren't becoming a danger to themselves or they're not jeopardizing the treatment dangerously . . . it is better to work a little harder trying to help them." Professionals like Dr. Ronnie Avery "bring up the therapist with almost all of my patients . . . a lot of people have found benefit with regular meetings with a therapist, or even a one-time meeting."

Overly deferential patients need encouragement to make independent decisions. Dr. Jaylen Abbott remarked, "I try to medically put it into perspective: 'That may be personally what I would do, but in a perfect world, medically, this is what I would recommend.'" Or providers avoid directly stating what *they* would do and instead discuss options with patients, share information on research and outcomes, and guide them through decision making:

> I offer them the choices and then to help them with the decision making, I have a little acronym I've used: TEAM. Time, emotional energy, attitude, and money. And I walk them through how they can think about these choices. Time can mean how old they are, how long have they been trying,

how long they envision continuing trying. Emotional energy would imply how much emotional energy do they feel they have to go through this process. The "A" can be attitude, but it can also be aggressiveness. Do they like the technology? . . . And money is how much do these things cost. (Dr. Bret Sternberg)

Aggressive patients in particular might be too hot for many providers to comfortably handle. Providers tend to follow several steps: acknowledge, communicate, adapt, stay calm, be firm, and let patients know that continued aggression will cause treatment delays or denials. But each aggressive patient is also unique. "There's so many other possible causes for this; each of them has to be handled in a specific way," said Dr. Cary Priestley. "And people who've had bad experiences before, I think it's fair to ask them, 'Please give me a chance, press the reset button.'" Dr. Teagan Shepherd advocated openly discussing the conflict: "You have to be extremely direct with them, extremely honest, just very open with them, and acknowledge . . . that, 'Look, it seems like you don't trust what I say.' . . . Maybe if you look at it as part of their disease process [it makes more sense]. If you don't address it . . . it's sort of this elephant in the room, and you've missed an opportunity . . . something that would help you treat them better, or understand them better, or even bring you closer together."

First and foremost, providers must keep their cool—not easy in the face of defiance and disrespect. "I stop and count to ten quite a bit," said Dr. Abbie Walther. Once patients are calm, professionals can try to discuss specific concerns and identify what is prompting aggression: "A lot of times you have to let them just say their piece. . . . And then I try to very carefully sort of pick apart the argument . . . and as we continue to talk, ultimately, we typically get to a point where we agree. . . . In my experience, antagonistic patients want to be acknowledged that there probably is something true in what they're saying, and they need to be validated that they're smart and get it" (Dr. Nicole Potter).

Providers tell patients that aggressive behavior can't continue: "I would . . . say to them, 'You may not behave like that. You may not treat other employees like that. If you wish to be treated here, you'll treat people with respect.' . . . We set very clear boundaries. . . . That's partly about how you take care of your team, it's partly how each of us individually should be respectful to ourselves" (Psychologist Colin Bulle). Thus, professionals wear several hats simultaneously in treatment relationships: reproductive expert, therapist, cheerleader, teacher, and referee. Patients' support needs come in all shapes and sizes. Some are sugarcoated; others are downright sour. Hopefully, trust and communication are enough to find resolutions palatable to all. But other factors in clinical practice and patients' personal lives threaten to undermine trust.

TRUST IN TROUBLE: MAINTAINING PATIENTS' CONFIDENCE IN CHALLENGING SITUATIONS

In *Star Trek*, the doctor has a little scanner . . . [and] just kind of scans somebody and reads something off, just like mechanics do when you bring your car in. I see nothing wrong with that on the one hand. On the other hand, it goes against . . . the importance of human interaction and all that implies between a doctor and a patient. So, although it'd be nice perhaps for a doctor to be able to scan somebody and say, "OK, you have lymphoma, and it's spread to here," . . . [o]n the other hand, there's the whole business of the personal relationship.

—Dr. Alexandra Sanford

Medical practice demands both social skills and technical expertise—and these competencies are intertwined. Several dynamics can either make treatment relationships healthy and rewarding or threaten the trust that bonds patient to provider: clinical practices, requests to pursue medically inadvisable treatments, other patient health conditions, domestic conflicts between patients and their partners, and factors like cultural differences and language barriers. Medical customs and policies are largely beyond parties' control, but they threaten to undermine patient trust.

Patients' other physical and mental health needs also influence and potentially complicate treatment relationships. REs work with other physicians to stabilize and treat uncontrolled diabetes or heart conditions, obesity, mental illness, suicidal tendencies, substance use problems, or poor self-care. Domestic conflict between patients and partners often gets worse when stress, emotions, and treatment teams are added to the mix; relationships can be unstable or abusive, and partners might have different treatment goals or be uncommitted, dominate interactions, or even dishonest. Finally, a host of other characteristics—race, religion, socioeconomic status, cultural gaps, and language barriers—influence nascent treatment relationships. The IVF experience is embedded in sociocultural webs seething with stereotypes, values, norms, and judgments that, though "external" to any individual patient, influence treatment relationships writ large. Providers must engage these issues directly and can't eliminate the human dimension of medical practice by hiding behind technology.

Clinical Practices, Medical Norms, and Patient Trust

Professionals don't merely practice *on* bodies who have trouble conceiving; they practice *with* people. The personal relationship between patient and provider is essential to diagnosis and treatment, and most practice as much for the pleasure of the patient relationship as the medical challenges. As Lab Technologist Samuel Hurst said, "It's not just a job, it's not just my work. It's something that I feel very strongly, that I was given a skill that I can do this for people, and now I want to let them know that it's very important to me. And I do think about those embryos in the incubator when I go home at night, and I always tease the patients that I'm their first babysitter."

It's true that a few providers view their patients as conglomerates of reproductive statistics—sperm count and egg quality, AMH and FSH, age and diagnoses—but most recognize fertility is linked to emotional, physical, and psychological well-being and try to infuse treatment with respect, compassion, dignity, humility, and humor. Empathic providers know they're the elephants in the "bedroom" and realize how uncomfortable this process can be for patients.

Fertility professionals say that they often bond with patients. "It's more than just a doctor's office and a nurse. We're very close to our patients because we see them so frequently; they become more of an extended family member," emphasized Sonographer Lalita Pond. This rapport helps patients discuss potentially embarrassing subjects: "people don't like to talk about their sexual relationship or . . . about any sort of dysfunction . . . you have to open up the doors and invite that intimate relationship in order to be able to help them overcome those things" (IVF Coordinator Rosamund Coel). Thus, interpersonal bonds actually further diagnostic processes.

Many providers feel that the best treatment relationships become partnerships. Partnerships are more egalitarian; as Dr. Denzel Burke said, "each of the members of the partnership brings different things to the table. The physician brings more expertise in the area, and the patient brings their own personal needs and background experiences." Even when professionals have to refuse patients' requests for particular treatments, they want patients to know this decision stems from concern and isn't an arbitrary exercise of power: "we have to say to them,

'We're in this together. I know that I said no to you, but it wasn't because I wanted to say no'" (Nurse Tricia Peters). REs might form partnerships more naturally with patients who are similar to them:

> The high socioeconomic status patients in my private practice . . . could be lawyers or psychologists or whatever, and [in] pretty short order they'd have a working knowledge of infertility that was better than the medical students I was lecturing, and many of them would be able to identify where the weaknesses in our knowledge were and point them out. And honestly that was never a problem for me at all. . . . Then I could have more of a collegial conversation with them, and . . . we'd kind of compare notes on what they knew and what I knew, and to me that's an easy patient because . . . the more equal the relationship, the better. (Dr. Bret Sternberg)

Power imbalances can't be entirely eliminated; providers always possess both the bulk of substantive medical knowledge and the ability to act on it. "There's never completely parity in that relationship, because generally . . . you're seeing patients that are coming to you for a service which you offer" (Dr. Terrence Trumbauer). But these differentials can be mitigated. Some providers, like Dr. Connor Gibson, try to minimize them: "I'm older and was trained in an era where people tended to address patients by their first name and you were 'Doctor So-and-So.' And I thought that was degrading to patients. A lot of people and I are on a first name basis." Other providers try particularly hard to involve partners who aren't actively undergoing treatment, usually men: "What I'm trying to do is sensitize them to the needs of their partner . . . but they've a very important role to play in terms of support" (Dr. Bret Sternberg).

But tensions between efficient mechanical diagnostic procedures and time-intensive interpersonal communication and relationship maintenance are higher when emotions run hot and precious resources like time and patience are short or altogether exhausted on one or both sides. Time is a scarce commodity for both patients and professionals; patients want a baby as soon as possible and often have busy schedules, while providers usually have packed calendars and must work within brief appointments. These restrictions make it hard to communicate complex information, assess comprehension, and deepen trust. Ideally, "I think that's one of the biggest challenges for patients and physicians: trying to get the amount of information down into an amount that they can comprehend in the time space that we have," said Dr. Don West. But spending too much time with patients can disrupt patient flow: "you spend as much time with [patients] as you possibly can without

disrupting anything else that's going on in the unit or getting repri-
manded for it" (Nurse Arya Mullur). Time constraints thus make it
difficult to build trust—especially with wary patients with whom "relationships take a longer time to build" (Senior Embryologist Lizbeth
Norman). Thus, efforts to reduce power disparities may have to fit
within and bend to clinic needs.

Finally, informed consent and other ethical duties require that providers give honest assessments of whether a treatment is viable and its odds
of success. How professionals describe patients' chances of conceiving is
critical. "They want to hear . . . 'You've a great chance of getting pregnant,' but when they hear that and they don't get pregnant, that really
destroys their trust in you," Dr. Abbie Walther explained. Thus, well-
meaning physicians can easily undermine trust if they aren't careful.
Dr. Gerard Gabler advised providers to "not [try] to overestimate success rates, [and] not [try] to underestimate complication rates."

Over time, good communication practices reassure patients that providers care about them and not just profits: "I think the more we have
contact with each patient, they're able to feel . . . why we're there. They
see that we're here for their best interest . . . nobody here's just trying to
make a buck, and they're part of our family" (Embryologist Chalise
Jones). Thus, paradoxically, tensions between medical practice and
trust can prompt providers to consciously think about developing and
maintaining trust in ways that comport with clinical norms, improving
treatment relationships.

Patient Requests to Pursue Medically Inadvisable Treatment

Patients who persistently try to pursue medically inadvisable goals or otherwise take risks endanger providers' ability to trust them, like seeking
unnecessary medications or procedures (3% of providers), or transferring
back more than two embryos (10% of providers) when ASRM guidelines
dictate transferring one embryo for women under 35, and at most two.[3]
Often, these requests are motivated by lack of knowledge, financial concerns, obtaining outside information, values and beliefs, or a willingness
to try every option. Slightly over half of providers (51%) believed that
patients tried to make such decisions. Professionals disagreed about how
often this occurs; estimates ranged from "all the time" (Dr. Alexandra
Sanford) and "many, many times" (Dr. Cary Priestley) to "I don't think it
happens many times" (Clinical Coordinator Mira Durham) and "rarely"
(Nurse Emilee Powell).

Trust can encourage patients to heed REs' warnings that certain options are inherently risky. Nonetheless, some would still gamble their health to get pregnant: "We also have a few patients, a Turners [Syndrome] patient, and there's a 2% chance that [she could have] an aortic rupture and die . . . or [patients] have had a previous history of cancer and they want to have frozen embryos transferred back, and they may die within the next year" (Physician's Assistant Nora Stanton). Or patients might unknowingly risk others' health, including their children's or grandchildren's well-being. One troubling request is becoming more common: older adults desiring grandchildren are bringing their single children with autism or mental health issues to a clinic. Dr. Abbie Walther recalled one mother who visited a clinic, her 42-year-old single daughter in tow, to inquire about conceiving a grandchild although her daughter had a "long diagnosis of bipolar disease and schizophrenia." These would-be grandparents are caught in a sorrowful double-bind: they "have missed the opportunity to have the child they wanted and they've missed having grandchildren." And these would-be patients trail baggage trains of ethical issues; one autistic son was particularly uninformed, to the point where Psychologist Haylee Randell felt he "wasn't capable of giving informed consent, hadn't [had] even a friendship level of sexual relationship, ha[d] no interest in having a baby, and was requiring supervised reading . . . himself."

Unusual requests can seem odd to providers but make perfect sense to patients. Dr. Corwin Summers exclaimed, "[A] lot of times the strangest requests aren't even biologically possible!" He recalled one especially memorable experience: "We had a lesbian couple a couple of years ago who, after her partner became pregnant, she said, 'Okay, well now, can you take the fetus out and put my genetic material back in for where the sperm donor was?' . . . They didn't completely understand the biology of reproduction." Unsound ideas may also come from well-meaning friends and relatives: "They get ideas from nonmedical folks. . . . Her sister says she ought to be on X drug and that'll get her pregnant" (Dr. Gerard Gabler). Others ask to meet their egg donor. Although this request is legally and medically problematic, IVF Coordinator David Winther understands patients' reasoning: "We think, 'No, this is a private thing.' But as the new mom or a new dad, [they ask] 'Can't we just [meet and say] 'Nice to meet you; this is possibly what my child might look like?' . . . I get why they may want to make that contact." It's easier for providers to empathically refuse such requests when they understand patients' motivations for making them.

Finally, a few patients take risks just because they think they know better, or want to bypass resistant providers. Sonographer Lalita Pond recalled one patient, a nurse, who tried to "manipulate the system": "[With progesterone,] she wanted to switch back and forth; one day the shot, one day the suppository . . . [that] wasn't the current protocol that we use. . . . The nurse spoke to the doctor, and [he said], 'No, you can't.' [She'd] go to another nurse and say, 'I was told I could do it; could you call in the prescription?' And unfortunately, the first nurse didn't make a note and that prescription was called in and she switched back and forth." Such conduct is exceptionally frustrating to providers, who can't effectively perform their jobs and safeguard patients' interests in the face of such dishonesty.

Perhaps the toughest patient requests concern medically futile cycles and embryo transfers—gray areas, where certain answers might be better or worse, not right or wrong. Requests to cycle with minimal or unrealistic chances of success can come from patients' belief that the truth—and a cure—is out there somewhere: "For those of us who understand that we just are never going to have all the answers, that, to me, is irrational. But not everybody understands that" (Dr. Errol Walter).

Inadvisable or dangerous patient requests force providers to decide how far they're willing to bend. Sometimes lines in the sand are easy to draw: "If you've had a tubal ligation or you have an HSG that shows blockage and you refuse for me to do a laparoscopy, I'm not going to do IUI. That's stupid; that's unethical" (Dr. Don West). But it's more difficult to identify ethical grounds for refusing a last-ditch IVF cycle, particularly when a couple desires a genetically related child and doesn't want to use donor gametes:

> If you have to do IVF and [you have] an FSH of 40 and you understand that [you have] a less than 1% chance of success, I'll let you try it once. After that, I'm probably not, unless you just had some miraculous [result]. I had a patient [whose] . . . husband has zero motile sperm. And we went through a cycle and they had a biochemical pregnancy. I was like, "Okay, we can try it again." They still understand that I was skeptical as to whether it was going to be successful, but within their culture, they won't use donor [sperm] . . . as long as they understand the risks and benefits, and I don't think I'm doing something wrong, [I'll go ahead]. There's a lot of gray areas in what we do. (Dr. Don West)

In this respect, reproductive medicine might be unique. Dr. Shel Kruger believed patients in other medical fields probably wouldn't undergo procedures with such low odds of success, but "there's just something about that chance":

> If you look at some other kind of medical procedure, and you say this has a less than 1% chance of working, most people wouldn't do it. But when you say that to someone and it's fertility . . . there are a lot of people that are willing to take that chance. . . . If you were a cardiologist and you told someone it was a 1% chance or less than 1% chance of this working, then you probably wouldn't do it; you'd probably choose the treatment option that had the 70% chance of working—to correlate [that with] a donor egg type of thing.

Thus, professionals empathize with and are finally willing to accommodate patients' need for closure.

Paradoxically, granting requests for medically futile cycles might help some patients realize their choices are unreasonable, encouraging them to consider donor gametes or adoption. Dr. Oliver Evans argued that, for a hypothetical 46-year-old woman with at most a 3% chance of conceiving, a "last chance" cycle might be worthwhile: "there's still value in that. . . . They usually won't complete the whole treatment. They'll get partway into it, and then they'll find that her ovaries aren't responding; she's not making eggs. But she has closure now." This also explains why patients' low odds of success seem less damning in reproductive medicine than those in other fields: saying "no" to treatment might mean saying "no" to biological children.

Another ethically ambiguous issue is transferring high numbers of embryos. "One of the big issues is how many embryos do we put back in, and ASRM, which is sort of our governing body, has guidelines, but those aren't black and white," First Year RE Fellow Dr. Yazmin Kuhn said. "So you've [got] patients who say, 'I just want you to put them all back in' because they just want to get pregnant so badly they don't care if they have quintuplets." Despite the lack of firm governance, providers acknowledge the importance of transferring fewer embryos: "over the years we've cut down regularly on the maximum number of embryos that we transfer from six to five to four to three, but it's this move from two to one that people are really more resistant about. . . . I think part of it is the desire for some patients for multiples, the feeling that twins are all cute and all do well, when the reality is [that's] not the case and we know we're negatively changing the chances of preterm delivery across the county" (Dr. Denzel Berke).

Transferring multiple embryos can harm patients and their offspring: "[a] lot of people will say, 'Well, I'll get the two-for-one deal,' but . . .

[t]hey haven't seen the babies in the NICU that can barely make it" (Psychologist Geoffrey Bourke). Thus, Dr. Ronnie Avery emphasized, "our goal is one healthy baby at a time and . . . if twins happens, that's a side effect of the treatments, but we'd never look for that." This is precisely where many physicians, like Dr. Connor Gibson, draw their lines in the sand: "I won't put back five embryos, I don't care what you want." But others might still consider granting these requests, consequences be damned: "[it] is up to the physician's discretion, because that physician can say, 'I'm refusing treatment because I'm not going to transfer three [embryos].' Whereas another physician will say, 'OK. You want three? I'll give you three. But you're going to sign that that was against my medical advice.' . . . I think when you get numbers above three embryos, you're going to get more physicians that [are] going to say, 'Sorry, I'm not going to do that'" (Senior Embryologist Lizbeth Norman).

Finally, other medically unsound requests might have lower stakes, but still waste patients' and clinics' resources. A good example is freezing all remaining embryos regardless of their chances of surviving freeze and thaw:

> The patient . . . may say that, . . . they'd like them all frozen . . . even if that's going to cost another $5,000. . . . And then for them to emotionally go through a whole extra prep cycle . . . it just doesn't make medical sense at all. But for that patient, you can understand where they're coming from. . . . And then as a health care provider, you just have to decide what's putting us at risk, or is it a resource thing, or are we using limited space in our freezer to do this, or [are there] other reasons we just can't offer it at all, or is it just because we don't think it makes sense. (Dr. Denzel Burke)

Identifying problematic areas is one thing; knowing how to negotiate them is another. Nurses and other clinic staff often prefer that doctors resolve these issues: "I relay the information to the physician, and the physician takes it from there" (Sonographer Lalita Pond). REs handle medically unsound requests in many ways. First, they can acquiesce, largely to protect patient autonomy: "you try and treat patients like autonomous beings, so if it's not too irrational, I usually go along with it. . . . There have been very few instances where a patient has been absolutely irrational and I've said, 'Absolutely not'" (Physician's Assistant Nora Stanton). Dr. Cary Priestley provides treatment only after carefully weighing factors like patient intractability and potential harm: "When I see there's no way to get them out of where they are, I would consider whether that [choice] would be appropriate for them to emotionally come to peace with the idea that they do have to take the next step. And [when] the treatment won't damage them, basically nor financially or emotionally or in any other way that I can think of, then I would provide it to them." Approving patient requests is appealing because, as Dr. Gerard Gabbler puts it, "any time you go against what a patient wants, then you're setting up conflicts, and you've gotta make sure that the conflict is warranted." Providers can also consult their colleagues when making such decisions: "sometimes we'll bring it to the group and get other people's opinions" (Dr. Nicole Potter).

Providers can also try to educate patients about why a decision is deficient. In these difficult conversations, Psychologist Haylee Randell relies on "sympathy, empathy, truth, and very careful, slow, active listening." Fortunately, after discussing why certain options are unsound or risky, most patients comply with professionals' recommendations: "once I could explain this information to the patient, she was receptive to understanding that" (Head Nurse Melina Draper). Dr. Jie Hu observed that these conversations help patients gain foresight: "probably half of my job is being a psychiatrist sometimes, and trying to explain to them why I think their decision isn't a good one and try to give them evidence. . . . You have to try and take them out of the moment and let them see long term." After all, patients stand to gain (or lose) a lot each cycle: "people really want these cycles to be successful; they're investing so much in them, and they often really believe that if they're not happy or doing well, the cycle won't work. And so, I think it's more a decision that they reach with my encouragement . . . instead of what I'm imposing upon them" (Psychologist Rory Frei).

Ultimately, when providers capitalize on their gatekeeper role and decline problematic requests, these refusals are healthy, not paternalistic: "I think part of a good relationship with a physician is for the physician to say, 'Well, I'm not willing to let you make that choice. I'm not going to do it.'" Dr. Abbie Walther puts it more directly—"My role is to say 'no': . . . what I usually tell people is that 'I'm not willing to make you sick. I'm not willing to hurt you and I'm not willing to harm you, and that won't be a good situation for you.'" In so doing, professionals keep their oath to "first, do no harm."

Patients' Mental and Physical Health Issues

Providers' attempts to improve patients' health status or conditions beyond infertility can also threaten the development of trust. Among the hardest physiological factors are traits over which patients have little or no control, like age and obesity. All are highly sensitive, subject to social norms like politeness, and require uncomfortable patient-provider discussions.

Some patients don't react well to learning that their infertility is age-related. "The people that I think sometimes struggle the most are the women that are, let's say, 38 to 42, that have delayed childbearing and now have poor ovarian reserve," Dr. Terrence Trumbauer said. "[T]hey eat healthy, they exercise, they don't smoke, they don't drink; . . . every other thing in their life has worked and now why isn't this working." This cause of infertility is extremely common. "We only have three problems: age, age, and age. . . . Fertility starts declining significantly around age 33, and then the numbers start to get pretty ugly around age 40, and extremely ugly over age 43," Dr. Bret Sternberg quipped. "Our colleagues love to use the old 'diminished ovarian reserve,' which is a made-up word that I think we use because we didn't want to use the word 'age.'" This is especially frustrating for well-intentioned parents, who may have waited to start families until they had established careers and financial security.

Professionals must also initiate tough obesity-related discussions with patients, which can be especially difficult because some patients and experts frame obesity as a political as well as a medical issue. Advising patients to lose weight threatens their self-esteem and entails treatment delays. "If I need for them to lose 10% of their body weight, which is the minimum target that you can shoot for, I['ve] got to sell them on the idea of taking at least six months to lose some weight," Dr. Bret Sternberg explained. "I try to sell them on the idea of the healthy pregnancy and the healthy baby . . . and I often use a training kind of idiom . . . we're training for pregnancy just like they would if they were training for a race." But treatment delays can further reduce older patients' chances of conceiving.

Some patients may have ignored other serious health conditions, and poor self-care can raise questions about how patients will fare in IVF cycles. "[When] a patient comes and you can tell that they aren't taking care of themselves, you worry about them taking care of a child," said Nurse Practitioner Michi Glover. "I also have patients that are unhealthy medically . . . for example, uncontrolled diabetes [and] extreme cases, like women that have congestive heart failure [who] have been told that they should never get pregnant," related Physician's Assistant Nora Stanton. Providers might even refuse to treat patients for whom pregnancy would be life-threatening.

Substance abuse or overindulgence might also warrant postponing or refusing treatment. Often, patients don't know the drawbacks of heavy drinking: "I had a patient earlier that her alcohol intake was fair," Dr. Don West said. "His alcohol intake was way higher than what it should be, and both of them were blown away that I didn't think it was appropriate for him to be having ten beers a day." First Year RE Fellow Dr. Yazmin Kuhn saw a patient who "was very honest" about her heavy drinking: "the idea of actively getting her pregnant, knowing that she was drinking, saying that 'As soon as I get pregnant, I'm going to stop,' . . . was probably the most uncomfortable situation that I could think of." Smoking, too, suggests a patient "doesn't take care of their health": "[smoking] cigarettes . . . doesn't seem to me committed and engaged in . . . doing everything they can to get pregnant" (Dr. Jaxon Arnaudo). Physicians take a firmer stance against illegal drug use: "drug dependency is a bigger one where I've said that I'm not willing to provide treatment" (Physician's Assistant Nora Stanton). These lifestyle habits force providers to differentiate between objectionable patient conduct and that which is truly incompatible with further treatment.

Mental health issues attract the most professional concern; it can be hard to discern whether mental distress is a temporary state or a more permanent pathology. Providers are particularly concerned about patients who are seemingly at their breaking point, who can't handle bad news, and who cry excessively. Nurse Tricia Peters said: "I've had some patients where you'll even go to [the RE] and say, 'I'm really concerned about her; if I had to tell her one more time that she has a negative pregnancy test, I might send her over the edge. She needs help.' [They may] sob so hard that you can't even talk to them, . . . [and] you see a pattern of it. It's a tone in their voice and it's every time, and I just see it escalating and I don't see it going back." Or patients exhibit extreme emotions at odd times, like "when I'm just sitting talking about general fertility things and they start breaking down a lot" (Dr. Don West).

Such extreme emotional displays are so worrisome to providers because of the many unknowns within patients' health histories. It's difficult to ascertain a patient's mental health: "I've had patients that I've told them that they just gotta do a time out . . . or they've gotta go see somebody for counseling, and we're only seeing people when they have their best face on, as a rule. So we don't really know what's going on" (Dr. Sachie Keefe). Since many patients alter their behavior before providers, it's understandable that they might be unwilling to acknowledge and discuss stigmatizing mental health needs: "it's hard enough to make the acceptance that they need help getting pregnant, but then taking another step and saying, 'I need emotional help' is very hard" (Dr. Don West). Thus, a patient's psychiatric diagnosis can go undiscovered unless she discloses it, displays obvious symptomatology, or it is diagnosed through treatment. In rare cases, it isn't clear how much stress a patient can stand and what she'll do when pushed too far.

Professionals' concern intensifies when patients display symptoms of a more serious mental health condition. "People who have borderline personality disorders can be a real difficult challenge for anybody to deal with because they're very unpredictable; . . . they have no problems lashing out at people," Dr. Roselle Suarez said. Other troubling signs include "an increase in depressive symptoms, they maybe are beginning to miss work, they're having a lot more arguments with their husband, of course if they were reporting any sort of suicidal ideation [as well as] . . . even things like increased social withdrawal, increased panic attacks" (Psychologist Rory Frei). Infertility stresses and medications aggravate preexisting issues.

Mental illness can trigger provider concerns or judgments; providers might question whether certain patients can care for the children they could conceive. Psychologist Marcel Park recalled one patient with a "longstanding psychiatric history, [who] . . . didn't have the wherewithal to be able to care for a child, yet she got to the point of almost starting a cycle. . . . It was almost psychopathic behavior, lying about what they were doing."

Fortunately, most patients don't need to see a mental health professional to proceed with treatment: "Are there some who could probably use it? Yeah, but not the vast majority; they don't need that psychological vetting" (Dr. Connor Gibson). Thus, mental illness is rarely a treatment barrier; rather, it requires patients and REs to work new factors, like medication, into treatment plans: "Sometimes people are on psychiatric medication that are very well controlled and they've tried repeatedly to . . . get off them and they become completely dysfunctional and they'd have to be hospitalized again. [Some are on] medicine . . . known to be teratogenic [that can interfere with fetal growth and cause birth defects]. So we've occasionally refused treatment [or] we work with the person's psychiatrist for [a] very prolonged period to get them change to something new [and safe for pregnancy] and get them re-stabilized" (Psychologist Colin Bulle). Such delays mirror those for other health conditions, ensuring patients' fertility medications don't conflict with other prescriptions: "we're not going ahead until the psychiatrist writes a note that says you're okay. . . . The same way that if [a patient's] . . . kidneys aren't working, I'll say the kidney doctor needs to write a note that says you can get pregnant" (Dr. Heike Steinmann).

Because they have broad discretion in making mental health referrals, providers are understandably comfortable handling most issues themselves, at least temporarily: "I'm occasionally willing to start low-dose antidepressants that are safe. But I really recommend that they actually establish care with someone" (Dr. Jie Hu). When REs do make referrals, it's usually to build patients' support structures, not obtain clinical diagnoses: "it's years that they're trying to conceive and it doesn't happen, and they just need to speak with somebody. . . . they could probably use somebody to talk to other than their partner or their family" (Nurse Iola Lowry).

But REs don't hesitate to make referrals when patients might have a more serious condition: "We try to identify ahead of time and have them see a health psychologist, and get an opinion as to whether or not they're stable enough to go through infertility treatments, . . . [which] usually refers to, "Do they have an active psychiatric diagnosis; severe depression, or fear that they're going to harm themselves or something?" (Dr. Stefanie Burgstaller). For instance, one clinic wouldn't treat a woman who "tried to kill herself with cuticle scissors when she was on hormones last time she was trying to get pregnant" for six or seven months (Nurse Nylah Chen). Here, postponing a referral could have deadly consequences.

Mental health professionals routinely involved in fertility care try to work closely with physicians to ensure patients are stable enough to proceed: "even people with mental health problems have the right to become parents, even if I don't think they're going to be good ones. If I feel that their mental health is such that they're incapable of giving an informed consent, then I'll state that very explicitly" (Psychologist Haylee Randell). Such policies ensure that patients with other health conditions enjoy more equitable access to fertility treatment.

Domestic Conflicts Between Patients and Partners

Trust must exist not only between providers and patients, but between patients and their partners. Professionals closely observe how couples behave toward each other; as Dr. Sebastian Alfaro explained, "There's a very good reason why the place where you're sitting doesn't have a desk in front of me. . . . I need to see the whole human interaction among the two of them. . . . The interaction between both of them tells me a lot. . . . Who is asking the questions, the tone of voice, the speed of the voice, the posture, the movements, the connection in the eyes with me, especially when [asking] questions." Worrisome couple behaviors could include a "subtle, argumentative nature, distance, disagreements on what they want to do with therapy, and what they're willing to do" (Dr. Jie Hu).

Professionals are concerned if a patient's romantic relationship appears unusually strained or contentious. Dr. Connor Gibson stressed that neither patients nor partners should blame each other, or strip the other to their base reproductive selves: "I'd really like to have [a patient] for whom her relationship with her partner is equally as important, if not more so, important than kids. . . . The relationship shouldn't be for the purpose of having kids but because they want to be with [each other]. . . . A female shouldn't be looked upon as fruit-bearer, and the male partner shouldn't be looked upon as the stud or sperm [provider]."

To avoid the blame game, Dr. Don West said, "I prefer working with couples where I have a little female factor and I have a little male factor." Naked hostility is also disquieting. "Sometimes you're talking with a patient and they're arguing back and forth; the husband's like, 'No, I don't want to do that,' and the wife's all, 'No, I want to do that,'" said Nurse Nylah Chen. "You just sit and go, 'Do you or do you not want to have a baby together?'" Clinical Coordinator Mira Durham grew wary when patients grew very aggressive toward [each other]: "if I think there could be some verbal abuse going on, I just really have a hard time stomaching trying to bring a baby into the world when it isn't the ideal." Such interactions "might suggest worse things that might be happening at home" (Dr. Denzel Burke). Here, as with patients' preexisting health conditions, providers often have to determine whether their caution stems from personal biases or medical concern.

Providers are troubled when one partner dominates the other, like "when the couple comes in together and one does all the speaking" (Nurse Arya Muller), or when "I ask questions about her menstrual cycle and he knows all the information about when she ovulates and she doesn't" (Dr. Connor Gibson). Conversely, Dr. Alexandra Sanford grew cautious "if the woman doesn't pay attention to or discounts the contributions of her partner." Here, doctors' subjective assessments of what's "normal" in relationships govern. "I have a same-sex couple where the one that supposedly wants to get pregnant never talks, and . . . I've sent her through psych[ological] screening and . . . apparently every-thing's OK, but . . . I'm always going to be on heightened alert for it, just because it's not a normal interaction," said Dr. Don West. It's often unclear whether domination or submissiveness indicate relational dysfunction: "you wonder how much are individual or even cultural issues versus actually being pathologic . . . it's hard to ferret out" (Dr. Denzel Burke).

On the other end of the spectrum are disengaged partners who appar-ently want to be anywhere *but* the fertility clinic. "Infertility in itself takes two people, takes two gametes," Second Year RE Fellow Dr. Peter Gore observed. "But the patient who comes in by themselves and in the initial workup talks about problems with the other partner understand-ing the issue, or there's some disconnect between the two about the goals going forward, . . . that's always a concern." "Sometimes, I've had patient's husbands on cell phones while we're trying to talk. . . . I've taught a class where the husband is constantly talking, or there's a cou-ple that's constantly talking and not paying attention," Nurse Nylah Chen remarked. It's worrisome when patients' busy schedules can't accommodate treatment cycles, and "there are constantly roadblocks for why things can't happen" (Dr. Connor Gibson). Dr. Gibson recalled, "I had one couple where . . . she was on [a] regular predictive 28-day [menstrual] cycle, and on the weekend when she should be [trying to conceive], he was always going off fishing with his buddies and she was going to [the city] shopping with her girlfriends. So that made her rethink whether that was really what they wanted."

Perhaps one partner is ready to undertake certain procedures or treatment decisions for which the other is still unprepared. These situa-tions, though rare, arise often more when couples are using donor eggs, sperm, or embryos. "We might be right at the point of doing embryo transfer, and you've got a patient that's saying that they're not comfort-able," said Senior Embryologist Lizbeth Norton. "[I] immediately left the room [where I was] consulting the patients, and [went] to the physi-cian to make them aware of the comment that was made." As with aggressive or difficult behaviors, REs are buffers for domestic disputes.

Partners might even feel they can't communicate certain information or feelings to their mates, and so they become dishonest or inconsistent. "I got another infertility patient who has AIDS, and she knew she had AIDS, but she never had her husband tested, and as far as we know, he doesn't know that she's got AIDS," asserted Dr. Errol Walter. "I just refused to do anything until she brought him in and we had a discussion. She never brought him in." Partners may not even be honest with each other about not wanting children. Recalled Lab Technologist Samuel Hurst:

> Only once I had a patient that made me uncomfortable. He came into the lab and shut the door and he said, "I just want you to know that I don't want to have any kids. If my count is low, that's what God wants for me, and [my wife] just wants a baby because her sister wants a baby." Now these are issues that I as the embryologist can't really deal with. . . . The day we did the retrieval, he went out to the car and sat in the car. And they did have twins. And I just hoped that when she got pregnant and when he saw the heartbeats [and knew] that he'd become a dad, that that would change him.

One partner might even go so far as to sabotage a cycle. Instead of providing a sperm sample in a specimen cup, one man was ejaculating on the floor, ostensibly because "his wife was driving the show" (Lab Director Keane Schultze). Thus, when they accept new patients, providers often land right in the middle of patients' complicated relationships with their partners. Hopefully for better (but maybe for worse), providers become part of that relationship before moving forward into treatment, which will trigger additional changes.

Sociocultural Factors

Personal characteristics like race, ethnicity, class, and spirituality or religion can also influence how trust develops in nascent treatment relationships, since IVF, like other life experiences, is embedded within sociocultural and medical contexts. Potentially problematic issues grow more worrisome if they widen power differentials or cultural divides between patient and provider. Social and economic inequalities place reproductive medicine beyond the reach of many. Those who can access IVF might find that they come from different backgrounds than their treatment team members. As Dr. Bret Sternberg observed, "that can be through language or socioeconomics; the greater that spread, probably the less satisfactory the relationship is going to be for both parties."

Socioeconomic differences can be uncomfortable even when patients and providers are of the same race and speak the same language. Providers might react differently to patients who can't easily afford fertility treatments, since wealth overlaps with both parenting circumstances and parental education levels: "Someone [can] come in [and] financially have no money, and they can barely afford the HCG [trigger shot] that's $100. Us nurses will kind of just vent to each other, going, 'If they can't afford a $100 shot, how are they going to afford diapers?' . . . I'm not saying that people can't have kids if they can't afford it. I'm just saying it just seems that [these patients] aren't as highly educated, and there maybe is a reason you aren't getting pregnant right now" (Clinical Coordinator Mira Durham). Once again, to minimize these differences, providers must police the line between personal biases and treatment-related concerns.

Tensions can also arise if patients' spirituality or religious beliefs prompt interpretations of cycle outcomes that contradict providers' scientific or medical explanations. Is an unsuccessful cycle God's will, or the result of a bad protocol, or both? Should patients consult a minister, a medium, an acupuncturist, a holistic medicine expert, an RE, or some combination? Conflicts exist between spiritual, secular, and scientific understandings of fertility outcomes, between lay and professional systems of knowledge and proof; and between homeopathic or "alternative" fertility treatments and reproductive medicine:

> [Some regard] an infertile marriage . . . as one that was cursed by God, or not acceptable in God's eyes. . . . That's a difficult situation because . . . we don't have a shared language, experience, or culture to feel that we're on the same page. And the same thing happens when I talk to practitioners of nontraditional medicine—the acupuncturists, the herbalists. . . . There's no medical word for Chi, and I can tell they're earnest and they believe in what they're doing, but [I have] no way to evaluate it or have any conversation with them about it, so they might as well be from another planet. (Dr. Bret Sternberg)

These effects are even more pronounced when patients and providers hail from different countries or ethnic backgrounds. Dr. Bret Sternberg explained, "The more culturally separated you are from patients, particularly with a language barrier, I find that difficult. I have some Middle Eastern patients now, devout Muslims . . . they won't let me do ultrasound; you can't touch them." Given privacy issues, some patients who hail from other countries don't want to use interpreters, making it difficult to assess comprehension: "I don't think sometimes they fully understand what we're saying" (Nurse Jaylen Abbott). Here, treatment relationships themselves can be lost in translation. This heightens providers' responsibilities. "I always want to make sure that language barriers are being addressed, learning issues, education issues," Third Party RN Prasad Singh urged. "I'm making sure if somebody's from another country or culture, that we're paying special attention to their needs."

Meeting these patient needs might require creativity, flexibility, and modifying clinic practices. Couples from some cultures might request preimplantation genetic diagnosis (PGD) to select embryos of a specific sex: "it's a cultural thing where they want strictly a boy, [so they request] gender selection, and we can't do that" (Insurance Specialist/Surgery Coordinator Emelia Zimmerman). Some providers understand other cultures as having different, gendered norms of social interaction: "we have a lot of Indian patients, and the male speaks for them; the women don't speak to us. I mean, they listen, but it's the men that you talk to on the phone" (Nurse Iola Lowry). As Dr. Bret Sternberg put it, "that's not a difficult patient; that's a difficult situation." Relationships are easier to build as providers learn to anticipate and manage certain patient behaviors, but the risk of stereotyping is always present. "Sometimes you have cultures that are a little bit more difficult because they don't want to fork out the money [for IVF]," one clinic staff member noted. "I think more of the Indian population has probably [tried to negotiate pricing]. We call it the 'Indian shake-down.'" Here, providers must be especially vigilant to keep personal biases in check when walking the thin line between anticipating certain patient behaviors and prejudging patients themselves.

Finally, patients might try to use reproductive technology to attain cultural goals, like a male child. Using donor gametes introduces several issues in the most pedestrian circumstances, and these issues are compounded when a multiracial couple seeks a donor who closely resembles them. A bad match can have drastic consequences. One patient feared that her unborn child's physical appearance would expose her use of ART and donor gametes, and she almost took drastic steps:

> A woman . . . was pregnant, and she had used a donor. She was Asian, her husband Caucasian. . . . and they chose a donor who was half Asian and half Caucasian, because for them, logically, that was what they'd be creating. But then after she's pregnant, then she decides, "Well, this child's going to look far too Caucasian, and my family doesn't know, and . . . how will I explain this to them." . . . And she was seriously considering aborting. And for me, though I can't tell someone what to do or what not to do, I thought that was unconscionable. To have finally been able to create a life, and be able to just say, "Well, sorry, this is going to be too Caucasian, can't do this?" (Fertility Counselor Alivia Warwick)

This anecdote reinforces the critical importance of informed consent and skilled counseling about genetics and third-party reproduction in these situations.

Again, patients and providers should address these issues with flexibility and cooperation. Medical professionals try to avoid judging patients, or inadvertently erecting barriers that prevent certain types of patients from accessing treatment: "We aren't social engineers. . . . so who are we to judge . . . with the exception of not treating drug abusers?" (Lab Director Farran Ibbot). Working through these issues in clinical situations means that providers must skillfully use the very tools and resources that are hardest to use when patients and providers are so vastly different: trust and informed consent.

Professionals attempt to strengthen trust by trying harder to meet patients where they are: "we just go above and beyond for those patients, because there's a reason for them being in that stage" (Nurse Iola Lowry). Regardless of why patients are difficult, accommodating them often requires changes to professional routines and increased resources. "We just try to do our best to calm them and make this experience as easy for them as possible," said Nurse Iola Lowry. Professionals build extra time into their schedule for patients who might require extra time and information: "I do spend a lot of time with them on the phone or . . . I'll sit down and meet with them for however long it takes" (Nurse Jaylen Abbott).

A little understanding often goes a long way. "I just try . . . to always come back to the common goal of why they're here. And I just try different things," Dr. Shel Kruger said. Sometimes the best strategy is empathy: "by just acknowledging that they're angry and that they're going through a really difficult decision-making process . . . giving them a chance to vent about it and talking about [it], we can just look forward and see how we can address this problem" (Dr. Corwin Summers). Nonetheless, some patients remain unresponsive to these overtures: "You try to do everything that they ask, but then . . . you just get to a point where you don't like dealing with them at all, because their demands are so great, and [because of] the amount of time you have to spend" (Lab Director Keane Schultze). It's at this point that providers can lose patience, and treatment relationships can quickly degenerate. But when these tactics are unsuccessful, there might be only one solution: discharging, or firing, a particular patient.

LOSING PATIENTS: DISCONTINUING TREATMENT RELATIONSHIPS

The relationship between fertility professionals and patients is unique. While it is more enduring than many other treatment relationships, it isn't intended to be permanent, at least not for patients seeking pregnancy (versus chronic conditions like endometriosis). Pregnancy marks a natural exit point from fertility care; these lucky patients are referred to obstetricians, who provide prenatal and postpartum care. Entering these fertility treatment relationships, then, most parties hope they'll be brief. But in reproductive medicine, these hopes are often dashed, and these associations last longer than expected, making trust particularly important.

But just as patients switch doctors for any number of reasons, doctors may end their relationships with patients before they've conceived. Slightly more than half of REs have terminated patient relationships; they consider this option to be very unusual, a last resort, particularly over serious issues like inappropriate or disruptive behavior (32%), substance abuse (8%), divorce or relationship issues (12%), and patients who don't—or can't—listen (12%). "I can't say that over 18 years that I haven't fired one or two patients, but it would be very rare," observed Dr. Gerard Gabler. Similarly, Dr. Heike Steinmann estimated she's dismissed "maybe one or two in the last 15 years. . . . it's usually people who are just absolutely obnoxious or who ask you to do things that are illegal or immoral or whatever." Dr. Jie Hu has wanted to dismiss patients who "find a way to my private email and daily emails, and things that get way over the top in what they request."

Sometimes patient and doctor just don't click. Dr. Teagan Shepherd told one patient, "There are other people you can see. . . . I just don't think that we were a good fit to work together." Doctors might also dismiss patients who persistently make medically risky decisions, like not terminating a potentially fatal ectopic pregnancy: "it was medically dangerous; she could've died, and she wouldn't come in and do the things that I asked her to do. I mean, we could talk about options or different ways to deal with it, but she just wouldn't do it. And then once I got her through it, once she survived it, I wrote a letter and said, 'I don't think we can do this anymore.'" Similarly, Physician's Assistant Nora Stanton refused to treat a patient with "completely uncontrolled diabetes" to the point "they had a malformation in [a prior] baby that was the result . . . so the baby passed away." She resumed care once the diabetes was well managed.

Other grounds for discharge include patients who insist upon problematic treatment arrangements, or persist despite unstable relationships. Dr. Abbie Walther described an ethically dicey donor sperm scenario: "I had a single woman who wanted to get pregnant, which is fine, but she wanted to use a friend's sperm, and he was married, and she didn't want to tell his wife. And I was like, 'No, you have to have counseling, and that's the rule.'" Or marriages could be problematic: "the wife tells you in the intake room . . . 'If I don't get pregnant he's gonna divorce me.' You have to act on those things" (IVF Coordinator Meredith Haynes).

Excessive dishonesty also warrants dismissal. One woman repeatedly visited a fertility clinic with "conflicting information" about her mysterious partner: "the partner that she came in with isn't the same one [as] . . . the husband, and was different from the one listed on insurance, . . . and the story kept growing and growing; at some point it was clear that we'd never be told the truth" (Dr. Cary Priestley). Others might try to manipulate providers into performing certain procedures: "a patient . . . was convinced that she needed a surgical procedure. . . . I did the testing to see if she needed it and she didn't. . . . She ended up going to lots of other people and asking for the same procedure and telling them I said she needed it" (Dr. Sachie Keefe).

But the most frequently fired patients disrupt clinics, harass other patients, or even threaten treatment providers themselves: "[a patient was] disrupting my entire front office in the waiting room for patients. . . . I can withstand almost anything until they start interfering with other patients too much" (Dr. Errol Walter). Those rare patients who are excessively angry, hostile, or high-strung can lower staff morale and interrupt clinic functioning, posing both personal and financial problems. Irate patients can even make clinic staff feel unsafe. Nurse Tricia Peters admitted there were times when she wondered, "is that person going to bring a shotgun in here and kill us," and that "I've gone to . . . our office manager [and said], 'That person scares me and they're yelling at me . . . and they're calling me names and I'm physically afraid.'" Pushed too far, medical professionals must switch tactics from being patient and empathetic to self-protective. Dr. Jaxon Arnaudo described one such incident:

> I had a patient who came in to see me, and she thought one of our front desk staff who's never rude was being rude to her, and she started yelling at my staff member in front of me. And I said, "Don't talk to my staff member that way." . . . And that pretty much ended our relationship. . . . There just can come a point where I have to defend our staff members. And we tend to bend over backwards and say the customer is always right. . . . But sometimes it gets to a point where you can only take so much. You have to make a difficult choice for the sake of the well-functioning of the clinic.

If a provider does dismiss a patient, it could be only temporary; providers may condition future treatment on patients' behavioral changes or other terms. Lab Director Farran Ibbott had a problematic patient escorted off clinic premises: "We had one patient who was extremely aggressive with a technician. . . . It was on a weekend, and our techs are alone on the weekend. She felt threatened, and so the patient was told, 'We'll only provide you service on a weekday, and you'll have additional staff accompanying you, and this behavior won't be tolerated.'" Dr. Terrence Trumbauer said. "We've had a couple whose husband threatened one of our lab workers, and [we] said that, if they were going to come back, he'd have to go through counseling and have to be chaperoned throughout his entire visits here. They never came back." To make these conditions as explicit as possible, Third Year RE Fellow Dr. Peter Gore proposed creating a patient-provider "contract": "I just . . . tell them this is what my contract is. These are the terms of our relationship. If you break any one of these rules, this contract is terminated, and I'll no longer take care of you." Thus, firing a patient, while rare, gives providers a trap door by which to escape from a problematic treatment relationship to protect their own integrity and maintain a calm clinic environment and healthy staff morale.

CONCLUSION: BANKING ON TRUST

Trust and the provider-patient relationship are influenced by and in tension with substantive aspects of medical practice, patients' health needs and relationships, and other factors. Patients' and providers' remarks demonstrate that reproductive medicine is situated within two contexts that can impair trust: within a competitive medical market, subject to market forces, and within a legal bureaucracy, subject to both judicial case law and legislative regulation. Certain elements within each context create new incentives for developing trust, improving bedside manner, and deepening provider-patient relationships; yet, other aspects undermine these same goals.

Though patients often choose to focus on reproductive medicine's interpersonal dynamics rather than its commercial aspects, they are very aware of providers' profit motives. Cost-conscious patients might be especially wary of market incentives, lest providers take advantage of their open wallets. Watchful patients might misinterpret provider kindness as predatory intent or profit motive, or mistake a provider's emphasis on consent documents for professional anxiety over malpractice. For instance, Dr. Bret Sternberg followed a certain routine to set patients at ease: "when they first come in they're never smiling and [they have] a little bit of a wary look on their face. . . . The first ten seconds where you shake their hand warmly, you look them in the eye, [you have] a friendly, open look on your face is the most important ten seconds in the whole interview. . . . These are considered tricks, but I don't consider them tricks, I consider them part of starting the doctor/patient interaction." Even empathic behavior, then, is caught within tensions between the treatment relationship's commercial and interpersonal dimensions, forcing providers to explain that these gestures aren't "business-boosting" tricks.

For their part, professionals realize a "good" bedside manner and satisfactory treatment experiences have commercial value as well as medical benefits and use these assets to distinguish themselves from competitors. For instance, Dr. Sebastian Alfaro described the patient experience his clinic attempts to cultivate, in part to attain a market edge:

> There's three main competitors here . . . and I'll be lying if I tell [patients] that we have a better pregnancy rate . . . it's the same. Cost, it's the same. There's something that's called customer experience. Right there, I can tell you, nobody can beat us. We've focused [on ensuring] that the environment is friendly [to] the eyes, the colors. There's a consistency with this office [and] the office that you visit before, the same painting is there, the same colors, the same staff; everybody's in a good mood. There's absolutely no negative vibes because we believe that that'll create an emotional environment where everybody can trust each other.

When a reputation for sensitive patient care enhances a clinic's competency and facilitates trust, it also attracts more patients, and more dollars. Trust is a commercial asset *because* it is so desirable, the hard-won product of authentic interpersonal relations motivated primarily by patient care, not profit-seeking. Yet, these commercial and caring motives are inextricably intertwined. This might seem intuitively wrong, even disturbing, until we realize that market forces are not always problematic. So long as these commercial and caring motives remain in balance, just because a clinic provides excellent patient care, facilitates trust, and is therefore commercially "in demand" doesn't mean patients are worse off, taken advantage of, or subject to greedy providers. Providers enjoy working at outstanding clinics for other reasons than profit motives. As Dr. Denzel Burke remarked, "I think making sure you take a job and feel proud of where you work and trust the people around you in the institution [is important, as is] just walking in the door of an institution that has a good reputation for evidence-based medicine." But even as trust is worth more because it's authentic, it's cheapened by this high valuation, which seemingly strengthens commercial temptations. If priorities change and commercialism outweighs care, then providers lose perspective, and patients and interpersonal relationships suffer, sacrificed for ever-greater profits.

Thus, although they're intertwined, patient care and profit-seeking as values always seem at odds and are in precarious balance; trust's authenticity enhances its commercial value, which in turn undermines its authenticity. Patients know it's in providers' financial interests to continue treatment relationships, and professionals know skeptical or unhappy patients will likely begin treatment elsewhere. This motivates providers like Dr. Rory Fontaine to work hard to sustain patient trust from cycle to cycle, investing in continued relationships to help their patients, not line their pockets:

> I have very few patients—I can probably count on one hand—that haven't gotten pregnant that have stuck with treatment. I really attribute that to our relationship. That they trust. . . . And so what I think is rewarding is when somebody has a failed cycle and we can change it and they stick with it and you're able to affect positive change. . . . I find it very discouraging when patients give up. They fail one cycle; they give up; they lose trust and they don't go forward with treatment. I really feel like treatment is built on learning what went wrong in the previously cycle and tailoring it accordingly.

Thus, patients must not only maintain trust that physicians are acting in their best interests, but sustain faith that these efforts might succeed. But patients who too readily endow physicians with trust and faith may be vulnerable to manipulative and profit-motivated professionals. Ironically, a provider's market success can be as persuasive an indication that patients' trust is well-placed as bedside manner.

These tensions between trust, treatment quality, and commercial success mirror other patterns at work in reproductive medicine and other medical fields. Throughout the health care industry, patient satisfaction now has monetary value. Market forces motivate health care institutions to quantitatively assess the quality of patient care; these incentives join new requirements set by health insurance companies, practice administrators, and others, as well as legal and regulatory schemes like the Affordable Care Act. Patients can "grade" physician performance on clinic or health system evaluations and independent online websites, spurring providers to comply with patient requests, lest refusing treatment generate a negative review. Dr. Alexandra Sanford ruefully said, "[I]t's really bizarre, and it took me quite a few years to understand that, again, at our institution, good medicine's what the patient thinks is good medicine, not what you as the physician think is good medicine." These developments reinforce the market's impact on bedside manner and trust, potentially cheapening it in the process. "At our institution, we get graded . . . and part of our ratings at the end of the year go into a little performance bonus; so we have to many times pretend that we like or care about or [are] interested in patients' completely irrelevant perspectives or reactions," Dr. Sanford emphasized. "So I just put on my best Eagle Scout smile and . . . do a lot of validation of feelings."

At the same time, reproductive medicine is situated within a legalistic bureaucracy that establishes requirements for providers, like obtaining a license to practice and following informed-consent-as-ritual. This bureaucracy also has teeth; it provides enforcement mechanisms and punishes noncompliance. Reinforced by professional ethics training and perhaps the looming threat of a malpractice suit, these requirements encourage safeguards like lengthy consent forms and signing appointments. Consent documents, in turn, educate patients not only about treatment details and protocols, but also what will happen should something go wrong and grievances arise, perhaps inadvertently planting ideas of legal redress while proscribing remedies. But these documents are inserted into the treatment relationship at a point when this bond is likely still nascent and fragile. Though consent forms are intended to be educational tools, patients often regard them as talismans of distrust. Ironically, then, trust might be undermined by the very legal practice designed to encourage it.

Trusting patients might be less likely to read consent forms. "With the consents, I think that patients trust that we'll kind of explain everything to them," Nurse Nowell Waterman said. "They know that they don't necessarily have to read all of the consents word for word, because they put trust in us and they know we'd never do anything to harm them." Yet, trust legitimizes forms' authority and enforceability in the first place. Patients must trust their providers and the medical institution writ large to accept these documents as credible. And consent conversations will likely fail without trust. What, then, is the relationship between trust, commercial interests, bedside manner, and informed consent? How do patients and professionals experience the informed consent process, and how do consent forms and conversations in turn strengthen or weaken their treatment relationship? And how do commercial and legal interests impact these processes?

PART THREE

Documenting the Informed Consent Experience

CHAPTER 7

Is Informed Consent in Reproductive Medicine in Critical Condition?

Every human being of adult years and sound mind has a right to determine what shall be done with his own body; and a surgeon who performs an operation without his patient's consent commits an assault.

—Judge Benjamin Cardozo[1]

Entities may do things only *with* consent, which must be solicited through another grueling barrages of disclosures. . . . Consider HIPAA's incessant disclosure requirements. My hospital distributes seven pages of disclosures in print so small I can't read them with my glasses on. One analysis placed these forms at a college reading level. . . . But what does the language matter, since no one reads the forms? One "covered entity" told me that in three years I was the second patient to ask for a copy of his HIPAA disclosure form.

—Carl Schneider[2]

These days, it's easy to overlook the human elements within the informed consent project, to forget it's a product of relationships and not just a litigious culture, and a process of communication and not merely bureaucracy. As Judge Cardozo's idealistic portrait of informed consent suggests, its importance hinges on many factors that promote patients' and providers' well-being and protect their relationship—including safeguarding autonomy, dignity, and decision making. Yet, these lofty goals can be undermined by informed consent's "dark side," to which Schneider alludes, the idea that consent is little more than a bureaucratic ritual designed to protect doctors and medical facilities at patients' expense. Informed-consent-as-relationship can disappear in the no-man's-land between the right to choose medical treatment and how that choice is carried out. Consent in IVF takes place against conventional expectations that posit that consent forms are incomprehensible and protect doctors at patients' expense, and that patients don't read or care about them. Are these expectations accurate for patients undergoing IVF? And, regardless, how do they affect patients' and providers' informed consent experiences?

Answering this question requires interrogating how patients and providers (including physicians, nurses, and mental health professionals) define and experience both informed-consent-as-ritual and informed-consent-as-relationship, dissecting it into its constituent parts of documents (rituals) and conversations (relationships). Informed-consent-as-ritual is conventionally thought to be problematic. The consent project in reproductive medicine brings unique challenges; forms are longer, and choices present different ethical and moral questions. Moreover, most patients don't experience informed consent as conventional assumptions suggest, but believe that it begins before forms are signed and is influenced by treatment relationships, and many consider themselves well-informed beforehand. Having mapped the larger relationships in which informed consent takes place, it's now possible to turn to the informed consent project itself.

This informed consent project can be understood as both a bureaucratic practice (discussed in this chapter) and as an experience (discussed in chapter 8). Both perspectives are critical. On the one hand, bureaucratic institutions like law and medicine determine what informed-consent-as-ritual must achieve and how, creating particular consent practices to meet these goals. On the other hand, experience clarifies how formal bureaucracy and informal relationships influence one another. Understanding how informed-consent-as-relationship and informed-consent-as-ritual work together helps us to identify more realistic consent goals, assess why current consent practices hamper these objectives, and design practices that are more responsive.

IS INFORMED CONSENT INFORMED?

Informed consent to medical treatment (as ritual) is a legal and ethical imperative, connected to the four moral principles of medical ethics: autonomy (respect for persons), beneficence (do good), nonmaleficence ("first, do not harm"), and justice (be fair).[3] These same principles also apply to healthy interpersonal relationships, where participants respect and look out for one another. But somehow, they've become lost in translation from theory into practice. While legal and medical experts have emphasized "informed-consent-as-disclosure"[4] of material information, this focus overlooks the patients' understanding and autonomous choice. An inclusive definition of informed-consent-as-ritual, in contrast, includes several other dimensions: *threshold* elements (patients' ability to understand, competency to decide, and ability to make a voluntary decision); *information* elements (disclosing material information, recommending a plan, and patient understanding); and *consent* elements (outlining a treatment plan and giving authorization).[5] This definition accommodates the complementary roles of patient and physician, as well as the many behaviors, technologies, and stages the informed consent project involves.

The all-weather, tried-and-true definition of informed consent (here, informed-consent-as-ritual) requires providers to disclose information material to treatment decision making, like risks, benefits, side effects, and alternatives,[6] as well as providers' treatment recommendations and consent's nature and limits.[7] Within this definition, legal standards differ; for example, physicians might have to disclose what the *reasonable physician* would disclose, or what the *reasonable patient* would want to know. If patients' health circumstances allow, these disclosures typically occur in consent forms and conversations, where patients can ask questions before signing. But patients can have trouble understanding medical documents and consent forms, including technical or legal jargon.[8] The average consent form is 12 pages long,[9] tempting patients to skim through rather than read carefully. Moreover, more information isn't always better;[10] patients might give consent documents short shrift if they think that forms legally protect providers, and they might be in the habit of signing forms in doctors' offices quickly, without reviewing them. Thus, there is great tension between the sad reality of what informed-consent-as-ritual often is (or is conventionally expected to be) and the idealistic conception of what it could and should become. These tensions are palpable even within something as basic as professionals' definitions of informed consent (as ritual).

REFORMING INFORMED CONSENT

Many professionals practice reproductive medicine because they enjoy helping patients to build longed-for families. But the same potentials that make this field attractive to professionals also expose it to criticisms that practitioners are playing God and taking advantage of desperate patients: "It's just the stigma about childbirth. . . . It's a billion-dollar-a-year industry. [The assumption is that] people are out there to rip you off. You've got a vulnerable population, so [critics assume that we're thinking that] the way to resolve that's just to give them so much information that they don't even know what to do with it. I think that's behind a lot of it. It just gets a lot of scrutiny" (Lab Director Keane Schultze).

In patients' and professionals' comments, their opinions and preferences about informed-consent-as-ritual align; both strongly prefer effective interpersonal partnerships and honest and transparent communication. Both also tend to view signing consent forms as a bureaucratic ritual. For most, an ideal consent interaction unfolds like Natalia Payne's visit: "with [the] first doctor that we love, when we went in for our consultation on IVF, it was in a conference room. When they talked about things, they had slides and brochures to go with every single page so we understood, they actually discussed with us and let us ask questions and read the whole document before we signed, and we actually did that with about seven different consents."

In IVF, informed-consent-as-ritual mixes formal and informal elements, relying extensively on lengthy (and bureaucratic) documents and interpersonal provider conversations. Patients and professionals know that these conversations are integral to the informed consent project, that they function differently than documents, and often prefer conversations to forms outright. But conversations have a critical legal shortcoming: unless they're recorded, they're undocumentable and provide poor evidence of what occurs. This creates an impasse. Patients recognize they're emotionally, physically, and financially vulnerable, but most believe the best protection lies in healthy relationships with trusted physicians, not in consent forms. But while these treatment relationships are enormously effective in *preventing* adverse outcomes, they carry little credibility within law and medical administration, the rule-based institutions that create, mandate, and monitor consent practices. And outside of these institutions, consent forms have little weight *because* they are seen as bureaucratic and even inspire cynicism. This, then, is the question: how do patients and professionals negotiate and experience informed-consent-as-ritual using both interpersonal communication and bureaucratic documents, given each tool's advantages and disadvantages?

Answering this query requires assessing how bureaucracy shapes the informed consent project. The term "bureaucracy" connotes a formal system that prioritizes rules and rationality, with time-consuming and document-intensive routines and policies. Bureaucracies rely on formalism, or excessive adherence to prescribed principles. Extremely bureaucratic organizations are impersonal, unemotional, detached, and rigid, mechanistically based on fixed, absolutist roles, routines, and rules. But in the "real world," formalism is in tension with its opposite, informality, which is personal, emotional, and flexible. Because relationships and interpersonal communication have informal qualities, they threaten to disrupt and undermine bureaucratic institutions.[11] In practice, most patients dislike bureaucratic medical care and view the "fertility factory" as nightmarish. Instead, they seek treatment in clinics that offer individualized, flexible care through partnerships with emotionally sensitive providers.

Informed-consent-as-ritual is conventionally seen as a formal process in which professionals ensure their patients review and sign consent forms before treatment. Medical bureaucracies tout informed-consent-as-ritual's educational benefits and legal protections at the same time as they support strong doctor-patient relationships (informed-consent-as-relationship), but realistically they treat these ends as distinct and largely unrelated. And signatures are different from authentic patient understanding; as Simone Henry noted: "I'm not convinced that that paperwork really showed that I was a well-informed patient, so to me, that's . . . where it becomes [focused on] legality."

But in practice, informed-consent-as-ritual is not entirely formal; its most important goals are at least partially informal in nature, or accomplished through partially informal ends, including educating patients, obtaining consent, coordinating clinic practices, and establishing procedures that safeguard patients from doctors and doctors from lawsuits. These tasks all require human relationships, not merely paperwork. Informed-consent-as-ritual's informal qualities are even more apparent in its more subtle accomplishments. Informed-consent-as-ritual defines and reinforces doctors' and patients' hierarchical roles in treatment relationships, confirming structures of power and authority. It informs patients that bad things sometimes happen and tells them where and how to seek redress afterward. Informality makes this news more palatable and less threatening. Simply put, informality is more comfortable. Patients want to know they're protected if something bad happens, but they don't want to be continuously reminded that formality or bad outcomes exist, and they dislike being confronted by reminders at odd times, like when they're entering an informal doctor-patient relationship.

These tensions between formality and informality explain why patients might feel that informed-consent-as-ritual does a poor job of educating them and protects doctors at patients' expense. Consent forms, after all, are like other papers that people often disregard before signing, like HIPAA forms or mortgage documents. Patients might not regard conventional consent rituals as very important: they trust their providers; think nothing bad will happen; or find consent forms too time-consuming, technical, lengthy, and overwhelming. Informed-consent-as-relationship starts to break down when informed-consent-as-ritual is the butt of patients' and providers' suspicion, skepticism, cynicism, and humor, further decreasing consent forms' authority and perceived usefulness. Bureaucrats argue that these breakdowns can destabilize the informed consent project's legal protections, exposing doctors and clinics to lawsuits. After all, bureaucratic processes only work if users believe that they can effectively advance well-being and protect patients. If bureaucratic processes can't accomplish these ends, then users will pursue their goals through informal communal relations, further undermining formality and bureaucratic organizations' authority.

Indeed, patients do try to circumvent informed-consent-as-ritual as their respect decreases (especially forms), inadvertently depriving themselves of important (albeit bureaucratic) protections that require compliance to work. If patients circumvent consent forms by not reading them, they'll likely lose malpractice claims in court because judges will presume that patients read the documents they signed and should be held to their terms. Patients don't intend this result; they think they're merely opting out of an ineffective routine, instead relying on treatment relationships and communication, and they don't think they'll ever end up in court. Meanwhile, health bureaucrats who create and administer consent aids know that patients might circumvent consent procedures and use several strategies to discourage this behavior, like shortening and simplifying forms. Conventional strategies double down on formalism, making consent forms longer and more technical, emphasizing documentation, and discouraging conversations. Only recently have they begun to adopt new techniques.

But these conventional, overly formalistic strategies don't increase compliance; they diminish it. The more forms with which patients are confronted, and the more thorough these forms become, the less likely patients are to read and engage with them. From the formal, bureaucratic perspective, *this* noncompliance seems even less reasonable, under the logic that people can't rationally ignore forms that are so lengthy, informative, and clearly important to their well-being. From patients' perspective, however, it makes perfect sense. Why would anyone waste their time on consent documents that are incomprehensible, misallocate priorities, and fail to protect patients—the most vulnerable parties, with the most to lose and the least power? Moreover, overformalism brings bureaucrats into patients' lives in ever more intrusive ways, transforming the provider-patient dyad into a reproductive rumpus. Fertility care thus comes to resemble other contentious practice areas like abortion care, where bureaucrats have already staked out a permanent presence. And without patient buy-in, informed-consent-as-ritual, and thus the informed consent project, becomes ever weaker and ineffective.

Finally, overly formalistic tactics like longer, more technical consent forms also change treatment relationships, distancing doctors from patients, reinforcing professional detachment, and strengthening traditional power structures. Certain levels of interpersonal distance are appropriate and productive in medical treatment, but distance becomes dangerous when it encourages providers to view patients as diagnoses rather than as people: the endometriosis case in Room 2, the ectopic pregnancy in Room 3. With professional detachment comes a renewed commitment to technical aspects of care, which traditionally stress pathology and physiological needs, not illness's social and personal dimensions.[12] This is the last thing patients want; such distance threatens those qualities patients prioritize most in fertility care experiences.

Thus, put simply, when patients think that consent offers weak protections and misguided priorities and try to opt out, their attempts to circumvent consent processes can trigger more formalist tactics that only reinforce patient cynicism and contravention. Ultimately, this vicious cycle erodes public trust in existing rules, processes, and institutions, weakening their legitimacy and authority.[13]

Thus, innovation, not overformalism, is the best response to patient circumvention—why not change those elements of informed-consent-as-ritual that don't seem to work, potentially by swapping documentation for new consent technologies, like multimedia or e-learning applications?[14] While overconformity's pressures can stifle creativity and innovation, they can also serve as a crucible, forging new improvements to the informed consent project.[15]

Patients' and providers' reflections on whether consent forms are important or bureaucratic and whom they protect illustrate the advantages and disadvantages of formality and informality. These comments explore the social, cultural, and institutional contexts in which informed-consent-as-ritual takes place and how these settings influence participants' experiences, for better and for worse. The formality of certain consent routines—especially signing documents that may appear voluminous, authoritative, and legalistic—inspires gravitas, while the informality of other consent practices—like consent conversations tailored to specific questions and needs—provides individualized support and information. The most promising consent improvements incorporate aspects of both.

(NON)WORKING AGREEMENTS: PATIENTS' THOUGHTS ON INFORMED CONSENT'S IMPORTANCE

Patients have nuanced opinions on whether they consider informed-consent-as-ritual to be important, on the one hand, or bureaucratic and redundant, on the other. Half deemed consent important because it educated them about IVF procedures and medications. Many felt consent fit within both categories; 38% noted that it seemed less relevant when they didn't anticipate problems in treatment cycles or relationships. Only 12% of patients judged consent processes to be entirely bureaucratic or redundant. These reflections are complemented by surveyed patients' divided opinions on whether they felt the consent ritual was something to "get out of the way" and whether they took consent forms seriously. While 95% took forms seriously, 45% said they were something to get out of the way, implying that some patients didn't spend much time with the consent process.

To many, informed-consent-as-ritual is bureaucratic because it's synonymous with paperwork. "It feels so bureaucratic, because you do it at every doctor you go to; you have your HIPAA consent," noted Marta Lyons. The trope of informed-consent-as-bureaucratic-ritual goes hand-in-hand with the idea that patients sign consent forms without reading them. After all, if "no one really reads them and no one really takes them seriously" (Anne Kelley), why should patients invest more effort than a signature? Cecelia McBride alleged that the entire informed consent project is flawed: "I think the people who actually acquire the signatures usually don't do a good job of explaining the significance of informed consent. . . . I don't think informed consent is very valid in most cases." But others, like Nicole Bell, suggested that other (informal) measures fill gaps in understanding: "[the forms are] very wordy; most people aren't sitting down reading all of them. But the nurses . . . summarized [them]." This implies that formalist consent forms by themselves are inadequate.

Most patients regard consent forms as important and useful. Cautioned Lena Coleman, "you've got to sign a contract of some sort; you've got to . . . say that you understand what's going on." Jenna Moreno found it educational: "I do think they're important, because there were a lot of questions that I hadn't considered. . . . There were things that my husband and I had to sit down and talk about because I didn't know." And forms ensure everyone's literally on the same page, moving forward with a common understanding. "I think the patient should if anything be reminded of what they're getting into, reminded of what they're responsible for, and what the doctor's responsible for, and to be aware of what the risks are," asserted Kelley Bates.

Informed-consent-as-ritual might be more important for some medical procedures than others: "[for] giving blood or getting a flu shot [informed consent] is more of a bureaucratic, redundant thing . . . versus elective surgery, where they're going to sit you down and talk you through everything" (Christopher Franklin). And informed-consent-as-ritual often seems more relevant in reproductive medicine than other medical contexts. "Outside of infertility, I would say they're redundant and bureaucratic because they're always 'You could die from this procedure' type of forms. But with IVF, I think they actually were informative," Danielle Greene clarified. "It really did say, 'OK, here's the possibilities of twins and triplets and more. And think about selective reduction. Think about what you're going to do with the embryos that you don't use.'"

Several patients describe informed-consent-as-ritual as both redundant and important. "I think the bureaucracy part is they're very wordy. But certainly it's important that everybody understands that the patient understands," observed Nicole Bell. While Ethan Reeves believed "the forms themselves are kind of redundant and bureaucratic," he felt "the discussions that they prompt are very important." Some patients noted that consent precautions were theoretically important, but personally irrelevant. They believed all would go well: "To me, they're bureaucratic because we don't need them . . . but if things took a turn and lawyers got involved or something, I'm sure things will come back up, but now, I don't see significance in the paperwork" (Rodney Hughes).

Patients often take informed-consent-as-ritual only as seriously as their providers do; professionals' approach to the consent process and how much time they invest in it matter enormously, as 29% (interview) of patients observed. Shannon Ward complained that her physician didn't emphasize consent forms enough, because there was no informal discussion of consent information: "If we had had a better relationship with our doctor, I would've been able to make a significantly more informed consent. His attitude was like, 'It's all there on that paper.' . . . I felt incredibly informed about the process in general, but not to my specific case."

Having been a patient at two different clinics, Simone Henry observed many differences in how each conducted informed-consent-as-ritual; her first clinic "had such a casual attitude: 'OK, this is just paperwork, you have to sign.'" But consent seemed much more important at Simone's second clinic, largely because of consent interactions: "they read everything to you and they go over it, but you wind up having more of a conversation, and it changes the relationship. It's not, 'Here is something that you need to sign before you can see the doctor'; it becomes almost, 'Okay, we're going to go through this together.'"

Informed-consent-as-ritual also seems more consequential when patients feel they can realistically decline treatment, or when forms require them to choose among several options. Anne Kelley felt consent forms' value could vary: "I think . . . when they actually contain decisions . . . they're very important . . . but if they're just like, 'Hey, take this drug; here's the multiple side effects and you could die,' no one really reads them and no one really takes them seriously." Then again, at this time, patients' minds may be preoccupied with IVF's benefits—conceiving—and not its risks, and certainly not its alternatives: "you're going there to get pregnant, and it's all about having a baby. . . . That's a sidestep; . . . it's like a game show; you're to the end, and you're almost about to win. The rest of it's secondary" (Luke Holloway). Related Deanna Douglas, "I think I'm just too wrapped up with my own . . . emotions to think about what paperwork I signed."

No doubt the timing of informed-consent-as-ritual—of necessity, before treatment—also matters, because patients aren't yet far enough along to know why such protections might be necessary. Cynthia Gardner recalled, "I didn't think I needed to be protected in most cases." Before treatment, forms seem to disproportionately benefit doctors. Patients' perspectives are also influenced by their good health; they are generally young and unlikely to have experienced serious health complications or medical errors. And chances are, even if a problem occurs, it won't result in liability; such medical errors rarely produce lawsuits in fertility care.

Moreover, patients' remarks suggest that formalism does lead to patient noncompliance, but not for the reasons critics suggest. Because patients resent the bureaucratic and litigious cultures that they believe necessitate informed-consent-as-ritual, they take documents less seriously and are more likely to dismiss the real risks these forms describe. Consent violations and malpractice seem a problem that *others* experience when exploited by *other* providers. Few patients think that *their* physician could perpetrate such acts. "Unfortunately, there are some not-[so]-good people in the world," Christine Zimmerman opined, "and I think that lawsuits are for people that feel like they didn't have informed consent." Some patients resent that *they* have to endure such tedious routines, but make the best of it nonetheless. "I just wish we didn't live in such a culture where the doctors are so afraid of being sued that they have to explain every slightly possible bad outcome in a consent form," related Jackie Carson. "But since we do, I think they're very important. If I were a doctor, my consent forms would have every single thing that could possibly go wrong in them." Thus, many patients regard informed-consent-as-ritual as a by-product of a culture of civil liability in which doctors are its victims, not its violators.

DOCTORED INFORMATION: PERCEPTIONS OF INFORMED CONSENT PROTECTIONS

Perhaps the more nuanced (and perhaps more cynical) question wasn't *whether* informed-consent-as-ritual was important, but *for whom*—essentially, whether patients felt protected by formalist consent processes. Patients were almost equally divided on whether consent forms protected doctors (40%) or patients (47%). The remaining 13% of patients thought informed-consent-as-ritual protected both parties.

Patients regard the signed documents as shields doctors can raise for protection against a civil suit: "they're afraid of getting sued, and so they need something to say, 'No we told him the risks, and he signed off on them.'" (Andre Baker). Brooklyn Knowles was more blunt: "it seems like a CYA [cover your ass] thing on the medical profession's part." Luis Torres believed forms protected doctors, because doctors created them and distributed them to patients: "otherwise I [as the patient] would be having them sign something if I was trying to protect myself more." But this doesn't make informed-consent-as-ritual worthless; it might have a different type of value. As Deanna Douglas asserted, "I guess it's helpful in the sense of just knowing what you're getting into. . . . It still made me feel better, I guess, that he's still legally obligated to do something for me, since I'm giving him all this money." This is a more transactional view of consent and the treatment relationship—as a contract, triggered by payment of a fee.

Those who think doctors receive the lion's share of protections from consent forms also observe that consent forms' legalistic structure and fixed provisions favor providers and clinics. The legal terms of Racquel Kennedy's consent forms struck her as inequitable: "I didn't really like the part about where you're . . . releasing [the clinic] from damages if they do something wrong. . . . If we get eight eggs and we have extra embryos and they drop them on the floor, then that's nobody's fault." One-sided terms left patients like Rodney Hughes feeling unprotected: "if something serious were to happen, [some] huge error, I don't feel that we'd . . . win."

Similarly, patients' lack of control over consent document provisions —together with formalist rigidity—also suggests that forms disproportionately protect providers: "I think it's there to protect the doctor, because it's not like you can write in your own little clause" (Rosa Grant). Christopher Franklin observed that some clinics didn't allow patients to make changes: "any time that you're not given an option to change . . . or negotiate the terms and conditions, obviously it's meant to protect the person that's handed you the paper." He noted that many patients may feel uncomfortable suggesting changes, but wished more would:

> I think a lot of people don't understand that they can negotiate terms and conditions . . . and this situation is, in most senses, a business arrangement. . . . You don't want to create waves . . . [and] they probably don't get that question [about changing the forms] a lot. . . . You absolutely, I think, are within your rights to go back to him, [saying] "There's something I'm not comfortable with, and I'd like to strike this." And then that office can always say, "Forget it, there's the door." If they're showing you the door, then that paperwork's meant to protect them.

But if patients think the only way they're permitted to engage with forms is to sign them, there is little incentive for them to take more initiative. To these ends, a few said consent processes would be more meaningful if they required patients to exercise more responsibility: "I think in most cases it ends up being more protective for the doctor, just because patients treat it so lightly" (Cecelia McBride).

A smaller group of patients felt that forms protected both doctors and patients. Sergei Bennett, an attorney, believed consent protections might have a larger impact on patients, most of whom wouldn't otherwise consider adverse outcomes: "I know most people don't think about what happens if you get divorced and have a frozen embryo somewhere, but I know the legal implications of that and how critical it is. So it's very important to have all of that decided up front." Sara Harper believed its protections were slanted in providers' favor: "I think that in some ways it's biased, because they're trying to avoid malpractice. And I think that it is also important to know what the risks are going in."

Ultimately, these reflections on informed-consent-as-ritual confirm that, when patients believe consent is largely a bureaucratic ritual that benefits providers, they don't think it's effective. Consequentially, patients pay less attention to consent procedures and seek more informed protections in treatment relationships. "It's about being sued, and so that's why, when I view it that way, I'm not paying attention as much," Marta Lyons explained. "So I didn't feel like it was as much of the medical process, which it should've been." This, then, is one of the informed consent project's greatest ironies—a procedure meant to protect patients ends up making them feel more vulnerable, either because the consent form terms seem biased toward professionals, or because no lawyers would take such a case, as Anne Kelley discovered. Since her uterus was half-size, Anne's consent forms stated that only *one* embryo could be transferred. But her provider transferred *three*, giving her triplets:

> [Informed consent] didn't do much for me. It didn't protect me. I still ended up with the triplets and absolutely no basis to have any retribution or whatever the right word is for that. . . . I definitely did consult a lawyer because I just needed to for my own psyche, because I needed to know what my options were. And they basically said, "You have none because there's no guarantee that you could carry a pregnancy to term anyway"—and that was before I did. . . . I was like, "No, there's an informed consent [form] there [that] spelled out O-N-E, one embryo should be transferred." . . . We were told, "Oh sorry, you can't pursue any justice based on informed consent." . . . Why did I sign that then?

Patients may be surprised to learn that many professionals also hold consent forms in low esteem and believe they disproportionately protect providers. If anything, professionals are *more* likely than patients to regard consent forms as legalities: "I think the documents that they sign are important from a legal point of view. Nothing you really tell them really stands up in court unless you've got written documentation" (Dr. Gerard Gabler). This diminishes consent forms' perceived importance within care relationships. Documents may even seem like "more of a formality" (First Year RE Fellow Dr. Yazmin Kuhn). Dr. Nicole Potter opined that forms are "somewhat meaningless," and Dr. Don West observed that the "written part is to cover your back, unfortunately." Some professionals even question whether consent forms effectively accomplish these legal aims: "I'm not an attorney, but from what I understand, it really doesn't matter if they sign it or not" (Dr. Don West). And several doubt whether consent forms can simultaneously deter malpractice *and* educate patients. These contrasting purposes—education and protection—capture two clashing images of the provider-patient relationship—an interactive, trusting treatment relationship versus one that is suspicious, adversarial, and legal. The question is, which one is the most authentic?

CONCLUSION: THE FORMALISM IN THE FINE PRINT

For these reasons, informed-consent-as-ritual is at something of an impasse. As patients react to overly formalistic consent reforms like longer and more thorough documents with avoidance and cynicism, the continual tug-of-war between formality and informality threatens the entire project. We may laugh at informed consent bureaucratic banalities, but this laughter is a symptom of despair, a warning sign that we regard these problems as intractable within medical practice.

But both formal and informal processes are necessary for the informed consent project to work. Formalism is the reason we have consent procedures and routines in the first place; informality explains why consent can be an especially effective patient protection. Bureaucratic, formalistic elements may often inspire cynicism and a lackadaisical attitude, but they ensure that such consent procedures are followed, and the consistency of consent routines might prompt patients to fully engage in the consent process and have confidence in its protections. Meanwhile, in other contexts, informality might make providers seem unprofessional and undercut their authority; but here, informal, interpersonal dimensions can encourage trust between patient and provider and encourage providers to tailor generic consent forms to patients' individual needs.

The adoption of patient-centered care—in effect, a sustained focus on informed-consent-as-relationship—stands to become a new, larger battleground in the war between formality and informality. In the past two decades, medical standards have grown to encompass a patient-centered philosophy, the conscious adoption of the patient's perspective.[16] Patient-centered care respects patients' values, preferences, and expressed needs; attempts to coordinate and integrate different types of medical care; provides information, communication and education; prioritizes patients' physical comfort; provides emotional support and alleviates fear and anxiety; involves family and friends in care processes, and ensures continuity of care when patients leave clinical care settings.[17] Focused on compassion and empathy, patient-centered care keeps bedside manner, communication, and doctor-patient relationships at the heart of the care experience. It represents a formalization of the informality that patients seek, in a sense using informality to preserve and secure formalist systems, while providing the compassion that enhances credibility. Such bureaucracies can seem empathic rather than cold and recognize how treatment relationships are as critical to informed consent as its rituals.

But many patient-centered care principles are at odds with older formalist conventions; for instance, long, technical, consent forms brimming with jargon are the opposite of shorter, easier to read aids. But because patient-centered care is a comprehensive *model* of patient care, not merely a reform affecting one aspect like informed-consent-as-ritual, it might be strong enough to compel a new formality, one very different from older, repudiated care models like paternalism. A new patient-centered formalism could effectively wage a slash-and-burn campaign against cumbersome arrangements of authority and bureaucratic busyness; this new formality could prioritize patient education and understanding while continuing to build in effective provider protections.

For now, however, having a basic understanding of formality, informality, and the tensions between them makes it possible to assess how they interact in practice, and in particular with different types of consent forms: those describing IVF protocols and those recording patients' embryo disposition decisions.

CHAPTER 8

Filling in the Blanks

How Patients and Providers Experience
Informed Consent

With an understanding of how patients wrangle with informed-consent-as-ritual's bureaucratic dimensions, and of how a successful informed consent project requires both the informal relationship dynamics of informed-consent-as-relationship and the formal routines of informed-consent-as-ritual, we can turn to how providers and patients experience the informed consent project. Consent experiences are where informed-consent-as-relationship and informality have their greatest impact—including enabling current consent practices to work despite themselves.

The status of informed-consent-as-relationship depends on what happens in informed-consent-as-ritual. And conventional assumptions about what happens in informed-consent-as-ritual leave little room for hope. Medical professionals, policymakers, and others frequently deem the informed consent ritual ineffective and the informed consent project unrealistic on the grounds that patients don't read or comprehend consent information. Consent forms themselves are stereotyped as sign-don't-read documents, alongside others like HIPAA privacy forms, mortgages, and end-user license agreements.

But documents, like tools, each fulfill distinct purposes, and users can use the same types of forms in different ways to achieve diverse ends. Even the different consent forms signed before IVF are means to different ends; patients view some as more relevant than others. A victim of identity theft likely pays more attention to her HIPAA form, and a patient nearing the end of ovarian stimulation probably studies her IVF procedural consent form longer than a general consent covering egg retrieval surgery. Consent documents don't just inform patients about material information; they can be anything from confirmations that fertility Expeditions are underway, to reminders of a litigious culture. Consent interactions can educate and clarify, but they also strengthen or weaken treatment relationships.

In practice, then, neither informed-consent-as-ritual nor consent forms are as narrow as stereotypes suggest. Informed consent can't be reduced to recall and comprehension: it is situated within human relationships, so why and when and how it fails is complicated. Patients might not trust their doctors, or don't trust forms that appear to protect doctors over patients. Or consent tools might fail, such as when patients prefer conversations to generic forms that seem long, legalistic, and technical.

Examining how patients and providers experience informed-consent-as-ritual and informed-consent-as-relationship through forms and conversations yields new insights and unsettles conventional assumptions. Providers define informed consent in surprising ways and place varying emphases on different elements of consent like information delivery, understanding, and interaction. Moreover, they believe their patients are generally well-informed, even if this education occurs primarily through research and conversations. For their part, patients explain that, while they read and understand consent documents, they already know much of the information therein and, like providers, dislike forms' legalistic qualities and find conversations more meaningful.

"DOCTOR, DOCTOR, GIVE ME THE NEWS": HOW PROVIDERS DEFINE INFORMED CONSENT

Informed-consent-as-ritual has a standard definition that all medical professionals should know by heart. But many professionals' definitions of "informed consent" are much broader. Ideally, informed-consent-as-ritual educates patients, but many providers focus instead on its practical role in managing legal liability, ceding talk of patient education to informed-consent-as-relationship. Dr. Alexandra Sanford insisted that consent's legal dimensions have swallowed all other considerations: "whatever the lawyers say. That's it." Psychologist Janine Dedrick distinguished informed consent as a legal practice from the interpersonal consent practices she followed with her patients: "it's a legal term. . . . I

have to do the best job that I can to explain what it is that they're consenting [to], and that's not the legal side." Dr. Oliver Evans asserted that
this medical need for consent existed independently of any legal mandates and persisted long beyond the consent ritual:

> It's the process of actually explaining and the patient understanding the risks
> and benefits and alternatives to treatment. So, it's not necessarily the signed
> piece of paper. . . . [Informed consent involves] that continuing process of
> the patient being aware of what's happening, and then the more formal por-
> tion of that is bringing it down to the risks and the actual consent form sign-
> ing. And that's more of the medical, legal part of it, but aside from that, if we
> knew a patient absolutely would not and could not sue . . ., we would still
> do that part of explaining the whole process.

Nonetheless, Dr. Evans admitted, consent's legal aspects are tremen-
dously consequential: "here, an attorney can sue you for anything, and
they don't even have to be right, and it can cost you."

Informed-consent-as-ritual's legal dimensions would appear to make
forms more important, not less. But Physician's Assistant Nora Stanton
frankly admitted that, in practice, medical professionals emphasize
quality treatment relationships and interactions (and thus informed-
consent-as-relationship) over consent forms: "I know there are forms to
sign, but we generally call them CYA forms, you know, 'cover your ass.'
I don't think they really hold up; I mean we're trying to document that
the patient is understand[ing], so they're signing, thinking 'Oh, I should
be paying attention here.' Hopefully, when I've done my job well, I
don't need any form." Therefore, professionals don't assume a patient's
signature successfully demonstrates patient understanding. Instead,
most see it as confirmation that informed-consent-as-ritual has occurred,
that "they've had a chance to ask questions and that in the end . . . they
really feel like you've explained everything to them, and that they're
okay, and they aren't afraid of something" (Lab Technologist Samuel
Hurst).

To some, informed-consent-as-ritual is a rights-based process, where
patients are entitled to material information; others see it as a status
at the end of an educational process, where patients have been "con-
sented" or made aware of material information. If patients and physicians are "actors" in the informed consent encounter, these remarks
cast them in certain roles: information deliverer, information receiver,
or conversational participants. Some accounts are one-sided, emphasizing the professional's or the patient's role in packaging, delivering, or
receiving consent information. For example, Dr. Elihu Brant remarked,

"[i]nformed consent means that *you've conveyed to the patient* the nature of the procedure, the potential complications of the procedure, the alternatives to the procedure, who will be doing the procedure." And for IVF Nurse Coordinator Meredith Haynes, it's all about the patients: "informed consent means that the *patient is aware* of what they're undertaking. . . . And that *they have a chance to ask questions* about this at any point in time or stop their treatment if they want to." In these statements, only one participant is active—the provider giving the information, or the patient receiving or comprehending it. Significantly, a participant (usually a patient) can be described as passive in a consent interaction, even if he is its focus; for instance, Insurance Specialist/Surgery Coordinator Emelia Zimmerman remarked, "[T]he procedures *have been explained* to [patients] in depth, that they haven't only *been talked to* by the physician, but that now they're *being talked to* about the procedures by the coordinator. And that's when we sit down with the patient and *have them sign* whatever paperwork needs to be signed."

In contrast, other accounts emphasize mutual actions like conversing, exchanging information, and asking and answering questions. Nurse Tamara Isaacson's definition stated, "It means that *you've educated* the patient [on] what procedure they're going to be having and *allowed them to ask any questions* they might have." Here, information delivery substitutes for the consent process, although it's distinct from patient understanding and agreement.

Other professionals' definitions mention other resources besides information that are important to informed-consent-as-ritual: "I think that it means that the patient is provided with *adequate time* and information to reach the decisions" (Nurse Melanie Simons). Clarity, too, is a precious (but perhaps scarce) resource: "it needs to be transparent, and you need people to understand that there aren't any guarantees. . . . I think what happens is that we put so much into informed consent that people get lost in the detail and so they don't really understand what you're asking them, but it sounds good and it sounds very professional and so they say, 'Yes'" (Dr. Abbie Walther).

But what exactly patients are supposed to understand through the consent process also varies across professionals' replies. Most focus on whether patients understand the medical and legal terms to which they are agreeing, as did First Year RE Fellow Dr. Yazmin Kuhn: "informed consent means to me that, whether you're doing a surgical procedure or treating a patient medically, *they understand* what you're doing; *they understand* the reason you're doing that. *They understand* their alternatives to the treatment or surgery or whatever you're doing for them. And *they understand* the risk involved." Nurse Tricia Peters prioritized deep understanding of specific terms: "we use so many legal and medical terms in those consent forms that I think it would be very confusing to patients. . . . I just want to make sure that they understand exactly what I mean by ICSI . . . what do I mean by 'You're the responsible person for a child created by a donor sperm,' do you understand exactly what it is you're signing?"

But another medical professional described understanding as a different type of objective: not information comprehension, but patients' receipt of all the information that physicians have on a topic: "Everything that we know of and that we can think of, we've informed you of that. We haven't only stated it, but we've given it to you in writing. . . . And you have opportunities to ask and get questions answered. . . . Once you sign on that, that's saying . . . 'Yes, I've been given all this information. And yes, I want to move forward with this. *And I understand that you've given me everything that you know: pros and cons'*" (Donor Coordinator Assistant Louise Whitaker).

The informed consent project also requires medical professionals to assess patient comprehension. Patient explanations of treatment information might reveal whether they comprehend what will happen: "I like [my patients] to tell what [the procedure, process, and risks] are and articulate them and that they have a pretty realistic view of all of that, and I think if they can do that, that's informed consent" (Psychologist Robbie Leavitt).

A final component to the informed consent project—patient competency—is usually presumed. But mental health professionals assess competence more carefully than other experts, likely because they are often asked to "weigh in" on problematic situations. For Psychologist Geoffrey Bourke, informed-consent-as-ritual entails "evaluating . . . can they actually make a decision. Because if they're not in a pretty good place, I'd say, 'Let's delay it until they're in a spot where you get a chance to think about it.'" Patient competency itself can be difficult to define; Psychologist Colin Bulle describes it as "the capacity to process information and weigh it and make decisions. It [also] means that they're free from coercion." In reproductive medicine, competency goes a bit farther: "As a baseline, informed consent means having the cognitive competence to understand the options that are presented and weigh their relative merits. . . . Informed consent in infertility practice, I think, has a second layer, for me, about whether you had an opportunity to think through the sort of social and emotional aspects of a choice. I think the medical aspects are sort of the front line, and then beyond that having a chance to sort of chew on the complexity that exists beyond these choices" (Psychologist Rory Frei).

Providers who emphasize information delivery or reception likely consider informed consent bureaucratic, based on informed-consent-as-ritual; those that focus on patient understanding and dialogue envision it as a relationship, like informed-consent-as-relationship. These two outlooks create very different consent interactions, representing the difference between giving patients forms to review and sign and prioritizing mutual conversation.

MATTERS OF FACT: IS INFORMED CONSENT DIFFERENT IN FERTILITY TREATMENT THAN IN OTHER MEDICAL FIELDS?

Informed consent to IVF covers issues far beyond procedural details, reaching into financial well-being, family building, emotional stability, and nearly every other aspect of a patient's life. About one-third of professionals didn't believe informed-consent-as-ritual in reproductive medicine differed significantly from that in other medical fields. "Obviously the content is going to be different, but the concept is the same," opined Nurse Melanie Simons. Some regarded informed-consent-as-ritual as a universally important process, where "people need to know what they're doing and what they're getting involved in," regardless of what treatment they're considering (Nurse Wright Yu). And, they noted, fertility patients should have the same informational concerns as patients undergoing other, nonfertility procedures: "why would you sign a consent in surgery if you didn't understand what could happen? . . . I wouldn't want a procedure and sign a consent form if I didn't know what the heck was gonna happen to me" (Nurse Nylah Chen).

But most medical professionals—nearly two-thirds—describe informed-consent-as-ritual within reproductive medicine as different—and more ethically significant—than in other fields, making it more difficult to achieve. Fertility care entails unique ethical issues. "What we're doing with ART is totally unnatural, and that includes both the stimulation and what happens in the laboratory with the embryos, so I think . . . that that's a little different and that deserves attention and respect," said Dr. Bret Sternberg. Patients aren't merely making decisions about their own health, but also about the health of their potential offspring; as Dr. Sebastian Alfaro related, "the principles are the same, but I think the execution and the nuances are different because . . . there's different sets of values—is there a life there, is there not a life."

These complexities are compounded by the extensive discretion that fertility professionals enjoy in how they present and describe consent information to patients. What's ethically troubling to one provider may be acceptable to another. It's unclear sometimes what should be up to providers, and where patients should have a say. Another distinctive aspect of reproductive medicine is that its procedures have uncertain outcomes: it's unknown what effect a medication will have upon a patient's ovaries, or how many embryos will fertilize, or how many fertilized embryos will implant. Consent forms can't spell out these unknown implications when they describe treatment scenarios; they can only inform patients that these risks are indeterminate before they consent. Thereafter, patients essentially proceed on the basis of educated guesses. Professionals readily acknowledge that "we have to pay a lot more attention to alternatives. . . . When you come in with a broken leg, your orthopedist is normally not going to discuss the option of not doing anything. But with fertility issues we deal with probabilities" (Dr. Gerard Gabler).

Not only are these probabilities more variable, but they can affect future generations, not just patients themselves: "there's another human being that's brought into this planet; . . . it's not just about themselves. We're requesting them to think about another person" (Psychologist Valerie Ness). And when patients lack complete information, the consequences can be tragic:

> If a surgeon is going to remove a gall bladder, the complications are knowable, generally, but a complication of having a gamete [egg or sperm] donor isn't as knowable. The patient relies on the person screening the gamete donor, and they kind of presume this pristine egg or this pristine sperm. And in my child practice right now, I have two brothers . . . both from the same [sperm bank] donor. . . . And both boys have really, really severe genetically inherited problems. I read the documents from the sperm bank on the donor, and there isn't anything . . . that would indicate that these problems existed. The interview from the sperm donor w[as] really cosmetic and superficial. . . . And so the parents are now obtaining . . . services for these two dimpled adorable little boys. . . . Fortunately [they] are in a financial position to obtain the services that'll help these little boys, but if they'd been aware that this person had carried these risks for really severe learning disabilities, I'm sure they'd have chosen a very different donor. (Psychologist Haylee Randell)

To complicate matters, patients' perspectives toward their potential offspring change over time: "the disposition of embryos, that's very unique to what we do. And I think it's hard to know what you'd want to do. . . . I'd gone through IVF, [and] I think what I would've done with those embryos is very different now that I have children as opposed to before I had children" (Dr. Corwin Summers). For instance, after patients have children, they often value embryos differently, as potential lives, not merely reproductive resources, and might be reluctant to destroy them. Patient wealth also affects values and the decision-making process. "I had a couple the other day that said, 'We can afford multiple cycles, and we're only implanting one embryo because we don't want those risks,'" explained Psychologist Robbie Leavitt.

And these uncertainties are compounded by new technology, options, and problems. In contrast to other medical fields where innovation rates are slower and there are lags in scientific progress, reproductive medicine attracts substantial research, leading to rapid scientific advances and innovation. "The technology changes so quickly that there may be things that we're not even prepared to deal with that'll be there in ten years," observed Third Year RE Fellow Dr. Wilma Sumner. Similarly, Psychologist Robbie Leavitt opined, "[T]here are so many studies out there, there's studies coming in week after week after week, that the thing that would make it different would be the speed of the science and the difficulty of keeping up with it."

Even without rapid scientific innovation, IVF's technicality might be hard for patients to understand: "A lot of things aren't nearly as complicated; . . . when you're talk[ing] about surgery, it's a lot easier for someone [to understand], 'Oh you're gonna cut me open, take out the bad part and put me back together'" (Dr. Bryant Rowe). IVF is unique because the subject of the consent process—a child—is "not tangible right now; that's hard for a lot of people to wrap their arms around because they can't see it. They can't touch it. They have stuff in a freezer" (Second Year RE Fellow Dr. Peter Gore). Therefore, patients undergoing IVF may need a different type of informed consent process to effectively evaluate risks and benefits.

But not everyone characterizes informed-consent-as-ritual in reproductive medicine as more difficult. Some professionals find it easier, because patients are generally more informed and have the luxury of time to spend reading consent materials. "Our patients are better informed than their fertile counterparts," remarked Dr. Jaxon Arnaudo. And, because fertility treatment is elective, "patients have adequate time to consider and ask the questions they have" (Head Nurse Melina Draper). Moreover, most reproductive medicine treatments last not hours or days but weeks, in contrast to other procedures, where "they have you sign [the consent forms] in the hospital, the day of your surgery" (Nurse Jaylen Abbott). And IVF consent forms are more thorough than others: "the standard surgical consent form is so general as to be nearly meaningless, whereas the consent form for this process is very specific" (Dr. Heike Steinmann). Forms must strike a balance between being under- and over-informative. Consequently, REs may be more thorough about consenting patients than their peers in other fields: "the degree of information is much greater, the discussion is more involved, and the risks are lower" (Dr. Kerry Kushner). This creates a paradox, as Dr. Kushner noted. Patients undergoing IVF are getting *more information* about fertility treatment procedures that are carry *less risk*, while other patients are getting *less information* about other, *more risky* treatments. Instead, patients could use more information on risks like multiple births that come about because of IVF rather than risks of specific IVF techniques. And perhaps this information should be presented differently, such as through patient stories instead of generic statistics and clinical language.

BREAKING NEWS: INITIATING INFORMED CONSENT

The timing of the informed consent project—when patients believe the process begins—partially determines whether they find it meaningful, since consent's value decreases sharply if it's too early or too late. Most patients—74%—think consent begins before they sign documents. Some believe it starts with personal information-gathering through books, the Internet, and social networks. For others, it begins when they seek treatment in an RE consultation. Many connect it to acts identified with informed-consent-as-ritual, like receiving and signing documentation or paying for treatment. The multiplicity of patient answers reveals that the informed consent project is complex and nuanced, encompassing many different behaviors besides signing documents or conversing with care providers. As Ethan Reeves reflected, "[F]or me, informed consent is educating about [the IVF] process, and . . . I feel like through the beginning, . . . they talked about all the various options and things that might happen. So I feel like it was a process, not just signing off [on] the forms and reading through it."

A handful of interviewed patients (7%) trace the informed consent project's origins back to before their first fertility clinic visit. For Stella Madison, it began when she traveled to her first appointment: "flying into another state [to visit a clinic] . . . was when it began." Monique Strickland, on the other hand, associated it with early information gathering: "I did a lot of research ahead of time. I spoke to a lot of people ahead of time. So [I] kind of knew everything to [an] extent when I walked in."

Most interviewed patients (65%) reported that the informed consent project began a little later, during their first consultation; Brittany Watson placed it "right away during the first consult, making sure just that we understood even just what we were getting into," and Stella Madison noted, "I think it's really real with the doctor." This makes sense since, as Patrick Shields explained, "the first appointment was really about getting information, asking some questions, trying to get an understanding of things"—all activities directly relevant to consent. Initial appointments are also often when patients receive informational packets: "we went into a conference [room] with the IVF nurse coordinator, and she presented us with a big binder of information and all of the consent forms" (Gillian Matthews).

Of course, the informed consent project can also begin with signing documents, the act with which it's conventionally identified. "That's when they actually went through them in detail and what everything meant," noted Danielle Greene. Patients can complete this paperwork any time from months to days before treatment; Adam Woods completed his consent process "two months, two and a half months prior, I think, to the actual retrieval." Others—particularly returning patients—sign forms much closer to a cycle's beginning. "They had me sign it on the first day of my cycle when my new cycle began. When I'd come in for the first time for blood work, that's when they'd ask for the consent form," explained Megan Cooper. Or consent may start with actual patient education; Ashley Carpenter's clinic initiated informed-consent-as-ritual when they presented her with documents during her injection lesson: "we didn't really feel like we were really in it until we were in that injection lesson, and it was like, 'Okay, you're going to start these shots in a week,' and that's when we signed everything."

While the informed consent project usually begins at some point when patients receive information—personal research, patient education, or receipt of consent forms—it's also linked to other activities. Sheri Lopez linked the informed consent project's beginning to an event usually tied to informed-consent-as-relationship, allowing her provider to examine her: "I don't know the law school definition of informed consent per se, but . . . once they're touching my body, I'm giving them consent." It might take place when patients schedule or pay for IVF: "We were committed to the process and we'd made the decision . . . almost to the point when we took the loan out," April Baldwin related, "at that point, [we said] 'All right, we're in, let's do it. Let's see what happens.'" And the later that patients sign consent forms, the more likely they are to believe the informed consent project begins at an earlier stage. This seems logical and confirms that patients feel educated before they commit to paying thousands of dollars for an IVF cycle.

Providers' consent duties persist long after consent forms are signed. When they don't fulfill these responsibilities, informed-consent-as-ritual can fail, with consequences for informed-consent-as-relationship, like distrust in providers:

> I didn't feel out of control within decisions I was making or what I was doing, but I felt very out of control in that I wasn't consistently made aware of what decisions were being made, why I was having certain procedures. . . . No one was explaining things to me; I was just told to do and expected to do whatever they said. And when I would ask there was . . . a significant pushback. . . . I was willing to surrender to the process in order to have a child, but there were limits to what I was going to do. (Shannon Ward)

The earlier the informed consent project beings, the longer providers have to uphold their consent obligations, and the more expansive they become.

A MEETING OF THE MINDS: DO TREATMENT RELATIONSHIPS INFLUENCE INFORMED CONSENT?

It's no coincidence that most patients (51%, interview) link informed-consent-as-ritual's beginning to initiating treatment relationships with providers (informed-consent-as-relationship); these two processes are intertwined within the consent project and strongly reinforce each other. When the informed consent project works well for both parties, patients confirm that the treatment relationship, not providers' liability, is at the center of consent interactions. Respecting one's RE often makes the consent process easier. "I think I was more willing and less burdened by them [the forms] because I liked the doctor personally," explained Zoe

Pearson. "I think I would've been more annoyed if I didn't like him." Or a physician's reputation and consent documents' standardization can reassure patients: "I read them. . . . I was like, 'Okay, fine. If this is a standard informed consent, this is fine.' . . . [H]er reputation was good" (Victoria Santos). Conversely, negative emotions can make informed-consent-as-ritual more difficult. Ethan Reeves scrutinized his consent documents more closely because he was "angry": "We were already kind of angry, and not at anyone in particular, but angry, and [that] made us feel like we probably needed to read the informed consent closer."

The role of trust in informed-consent-as-ritual builds upon what we already know about trust's critical importance and treatment roles. Patients' trust in providers profoundly influences both parties' experiences of informed-consent-as-ritual, making it smoother and more effective. Lindsey Burton recalled, "I felt so at ease with him that it wasn't hard for me to sign the documents. Obviously, I read what I signed, but the fact that I trusted my doctor—that made it easy to sign the papers." Providers' manner during consent interactions can further enhance (or undermine) trust: "the nurse that did [the informed consent] was very motherly, and whenever she calls me, she calls me 'Sweet Pea' and she's really loving and supportive and nice and holds your hand and everything. So during the informed consent process, she tried to make it as serious as she could and explain everything. . . . [M]y kind of trust with her is that she wouldn't lead me astray" (Ashley Carpenter).

Ironically, this trust that patients crave and doctors cultivate may undermine patients' regard for consent forms or even the entire informed consent project, depending how complacent trusting patients become. In awarding their trust, patients essentially grant their providers a certificate of worthiness that diminishes their own perceived needs for informed consent protections, like information disclosure: "I trusted him, I trusted his staff. And so the way I thought was just, 'OK, let's just sign these.' I just didn't really see the need to really double check, to really read through them that well" (Kendra Figueroa). Brittany Watson felt trust made her more compliant: "the more trust I gave to the doctor, the more willing I was to be agreeable and understand anything, whether it was a particular test or a particular process." Or this compliance can grow into extreme deference: "I think when you have trust in the doctor, [it becomes] 'Yeah, yeah, yeah, yeah, yeah'; you just sign whatever he tells you to sign, because you trust this doctor and you like the doctor" (Monique Strickland). To well-informed patients who thoroughly discuss consent information with providers, consent documents might seem redundant: "the document signing wasn't really a major thing in our eyes. I think it was just a formalization of what we'd already been told" (David Reid). And little about consent forms disturbs this trust. Tyrone Crider thought his consent documents seemed straightforward, not the type of legal form meriting suspicion and close scrutiny: "I didn't really look at [informed consent] as being something [where] they were trying to pull a fast one on me. There are legal documents that I kind of suspect I need to look [through] for a loophole . . . but this just didn't really seem [to be] . . . a confrontational kind of document [or] . . . all that contractual." Trust, then, can suppress patients' self-protective instincts, as can consent form characteristics, like format.

There's a delicate balance between excessive caution and excessive compliance; while too much trust can diminish the informed consent project's significance for patients, too little can endanger care relationships before they reach that stage. The patient-provider relationship must be a mutual connection, where trust is a two-way street and both parties are engaged participants. This is where informed-consent-as-relationship matters. If respect, liking, or a detailed, dialogic consent process can improve traffic flow in the treatment relationship, negative feelings or a detached, rushed, or mechanical consent presentation can block traffic in one direction. An overly clinical consent presentation actually decreased Christine Zimmerman's liking for her doctor. "I think it put a negative spin on our relationship. That was the first doctor I saw, and it was very rote: 'This is the risk chances, this is the worst-case scenario, you could go to the hospital and die.' It was just matter-of-fact. There was no emotion behind it." Similarly, Andre Baker's disconnection from his provider made informed consent seem more bureaucratic: "[b]ecause of the lack of personal connection we had with the doctor, . . . I don't remember her ever sitting down and having a conversation with us about that. So it felt . . . like some red tape that they had to go through."

Others also frankly acknowledge that diminished trust in providers would change their perceptions of informed-consent-as-ritual. Several would ask more questions: "I might have more questions . . . if you don't trust someone and they're trying to give you information and you're going to consent to letting them do something, I would probably be more hesitant" (Darla Clarke).

Similarly, a lack of trust would prompt many to review the consent documentation more thoroughly. Distrust makes forms seem more significant: "if I didn't trust my doctor, I'd feel like the informed consent process was more important, like I'd need to see it in writing rather than just hearing it from him" (Keira Wilkinson). Or consent forms would deserve more attention or time: "I skimmed over some parts, but I would've been just a lot more careful what I read" (Amber Butler). This could make decision making more difficult: "I think then you would be second guessing every decision he made. I think it would be more emotionally stressful." In particular, consent would be longer, more tedious, and more adversarial: "without that kind of trust, it would be a much more negative experience. And probably drawn out longer . . . the sort of thing where [we] have a lot more questions, not really sure if we're actually getting either accurate answers or maybe even just hearing answers that we might . . . be less apt to listen to" (Patrick Shields). Perhaps the entire encounter would change: "I think it would've been a little more strained, going into it. The documents wouldn't have been any different, but if I didn't trust them, I don't know if I would've gone in to sign them that day," Natalia Payne noted. "I probably would've asked for them beforehand, to go home and really look and think and digest, and then brought them back to sign."

But a lack of trust wouldn't necessarily derail informed-consent-as-ritual, even if it damaged the informed consent project. As Nick Hall was quick to note, it's impossible to obtain treatment without signing the forms, regardless of how patients feel about the process: "we signed them because that was the only way to get it done." This intimates that patients might feel they have little choice whether to undergo IVF if they want to conceive a child, just when choice matters most. These feelings could also be interpreted as desperation, with all the baggage that term brings.

The informed consent ritual is inevitable, and patients can negotiate it with either equanimity or discomfiture and unease (or choose not to sign). This led Christine Zimmerman to note that even trust wouldn't distract her from her patient responsibilities: "I trusted him. But I still read it. I know when some people trust their doctor, they won't read it, but I wanted to read everything because I wanted to know what's going on." And other interpersonal dynamics besides trust, like time and politeness, influence how consent interactions unfold: "The person is telling you what the form is about, and I start to read through it, and she's explaining at the same time, but then you feel like you don't want them to wait while you read the entire form, so you just sign it."

And because they believe the informed consent project predates the treatment relationship, many patients (47% interview) don't believe their treatment relationships necessarily influence informed-consent-as-ritual. Stella Madison saw no connection between the two because she didn't condition her consent on interaction, and felt "the minute I walked into your office to talk to you, I'm giving you my consent, unless I change my mind; I have that privilege as a patient, but . . . in my mind it's assumed. I'm ready."

If an informed consent ritual appears highly standardized and can just as easily be carried out with a computer, patients' feelings about their providers may seem irrelevant, since this type of consent experience is not interactive or individualized. For Luke Holloway, other, more weighty concerns, like worries about unsuccessful cycles, dwarfed the rather humdrum, uneventful consent interaction: "I remember . . . the one where they're talking about whether we're going to freeze eggs, and looking at pricing for it. Other than that, I just don't remember that much about it. So to me, it just wasn't that big an issue. There was just so much else going on that felt like it was more important."

Thus, most patients link informed-consent-as-ritual with initiating and developing treatment relationships and trust, not just signing documents. This relationship in turn influences informed-consent-as-relationship, motivating patients to dig deep and thoroughly consider particular information and choices about *how* they want to undergo IVF—even when they have already decided to undergo the procedure, largely because it's their best—or only—option for conceiving a child.

OVERINFORMED CONSENT: ARE PATIENTS WELL-INFORMED ABOUT FERTILITY TREATMENT?

Given conventional doubts over whether patients read and understand consent forms, it's surprising that the vast majority of reproductive medicine physicians, nurses, and clinic staff (61%) perceive that patients were generally well-informed by the time they complete informed-consent-as-ritual. This makes sense, however, if patients get their information from sources other than consent forms, as 21% of providers report. As Psychologist Rory Frei observed, patients seeking fertility treatment are uniquely incentivized to become educated about infertility: "they're a very collaborative, highly educated, goal-directed clientele, and so they often have done a lot of thinking and looking and reading in advance." And patients likely receive forms comparatively late in the educational process so that information is no longer new. "We do so much education before they get to that point where they're signing, that I think they're pretty well-informed," Nurse Tamela Isaac-son opined. "I would say probably most of our patients have done some homework even before we've seen them here for their first visit."

Because so many educational opportunities are built into clinics' treatment protocols, patients are frequently exposed to information about risks, benefits, side effects and alternatives. Dr. Don West said, "We talk to them a lot. . . . My IVF presentation is 30 minutes long, and then they have an IVF teaching class, and then we see them every single monitoring session. So even as they're going through, they're getting more and more informed throughout the process." Third Party Concep-tion RN Prasad Singh estimated patients at her clinic get "three hours, four hours of education between" two classes on IVF processes. There's good reason for building so many informational opportunities into the treatment process. "I think in a medical facility . . . we can't assume that someone's gone over this with them. It is each person's responsibility to go over that information," emphasized Senior Embryologist Lizbeth Norton. "Unfortunately for the patient, it becomes redundant. But I hope that they have an understanding of our side of the sheet of paper, so to speak."

The question of whether patients are well-informed prompts the issue of what exactly this phrase means. How much information must patients know before they meet this standard? And, for that matter, how well must they understand it? It would be ridiculous to suggest patients must become experts on IVF, mastering everything down to the least detail, and equally absurd to contend they need to know nothing. "I don't think you have to understand all the nitty-gritty of everything to provide informed consent," explained Dr. Don West; "you're supposed to get the basic knowledge of risks and benefits that the average person is going to understand and expect to know, and I think you get that here." But Dr. Teagan Shepherd argued that patients might not be well-informed about some of these basic risks: "Some of our patients have done a lot of research, but by and large, no. Even if they come in informed about the IVF process, they aren't necessarily aware of the potential birth defect risk, the potential malignancy risk."

Patients also consider themselves well-informed, many times well before informed-consent-as-ritual took place. Several—84% (interview)—asserted they were already familiar with most, if not all, of the infor-mation, making informed-consent-as-ritual more of a review or even a "formality" (Phoebe Paul). Prior knowledge prompted Shelley Lawrence to all but disregard her consent documents: "there was nothing they were going to tell me that I didn't already know. . . . I don't even think I looked at them that carefully, because it wasn't new to me." This suggests that patients regard informed consent more as a project than as a single event or ritual; in other words, informed consent is bigger than informed-consent-as-ritual. To these ends, Maria Craig reflected, "I think you get more of the information throughout the whole thing, rather than just at what they call the informed consent time," and Ethan Reeves related, "I feel like it was a process, not just signing of the forms and like reading through it . . . [it] started kind of from the beginning."

Irrespective of providers' duties, some patients feel that it's their responsibility to become well-informed before the consent appointment. Tracey West thought it would be worrisome if patients weren't already familiar with these details: "If you didn't know anything about the procedure, you might think it was kind of overwhelming. But at that point, if you're going through the procedure and you don't know enough about it anyways, I think you got a bigger problem there." But thereafter, patients can't be well-informed if providers don't fulfill consent responsibilities, as Simone Henry felt when she didn't receive needed information after an unsuccessful cycle and had to quickly decide whether to start a new one:

> After my first IVF, I had started spotting before my pregnancy test, so I was pretty sure that that wasn't going to work out. . . . They called with the results of my pregnancy test, and she said, "Well, I'm sorry to tell you it's negative. . . . So, [your doctor] would like to know if you would like [to] go again." Then I said, "Okay," then she said, "Okay . . . today is cycle day one, can you call me Tuesday and pick up your new calendar." And that was essentially the entire conversation about what's gone wrong . . . on the first cycle. No one said, "Let's discuss the changes to the cycle." . . . That's not how you make a decision about an IVF; you don't make a decision in a 30-second phone call. . . . And so, there was no consent, there was no conversation.

Education thus is both a professional duty and a patient responsibility.

But perhaps the only way to become truly well-informed was to experience IVF firsthand. Dr. Jaxon Arnaudo explained, "If they're first-time IVF patients, [they're] probably not [well-informed]. And it sometimes depends on how much time they've spent as an infertility patient before they've read that consent form." "You can read as much as you want, but until you start going through it, [you won't] get it," May Weiss explained. This is especially true for issues many patients will encounter but don't foresee. Anne Kelley recalled that, during her informed consent appointment, she and her husband were "thinking about the embryos . . . about what to do in different scenarios that we probably hadn't really thought through until we got those forms." And Dana Gibbs recalled "new information in regards to the selective reduction; that wasn't something that I discussed with the doctor beforehand."

A few professionals, however, felt some patients aren't well-informed. Patients' diagnoses might play a role, particularly if patients learn right after beginning treatment that IVF is their only option. But getting them up to speed doesn't take long. According to Dr. Jaxon Arnaudo, "[male factor patients going straight to IVF] are kind of the most naïve going into it . . . so they probably spend more time reading the informed consent documents than our other patients." Compared to other reproductive medicine professionals, mental health experts are less likely to believe patients are well-informed, either as to IVF in general or about specific issues. Psychologist Delphine Darby blamed "misinformation" on emotions and distress:

> you've got somebody who's essentially in a crisis state, if they're really distraught having to sign a piece of paper. . . . I realize that happens in other situations as well, whether it's cancer or what-not, but . . . I would say that it's not ideal. . . . And [fertility care is] not a situation where somebody's necessarily going to take a family member in to be able to sit through and listen to all of it to get the accurate detail[s]. It's usually the husband and the wife, or the wife and her partner, they're both stressed out, and therefore they're getting information and they're not necessarily processing it correctly due to their level of anxiety.

Information gaps, too, may play a role; most patients may lack the specialized knowledge to negotiate trouble spots: "In general, I think that people don't understand statistics, and they don't understand the terminology," Psychologist Haylee Randell observed. "I would say that they're generally informed, and if everything goes okay, they have sufficient information, but I would say that a great many people aren't adequately informed if something would go wrong." How information is explained affects how patients understand it; even a statement like "You have a 50% chance of getting pregnant" can be misinterpreted. "I would say [instead] that they have a 50% chance that you won't get pregnant. But the doctors won't say that," Randell explained. Psychologist Marcel Park believed repeat exposure to the same information often surmounted this consent issue: "I do think that there's a lot of things in place to get people to listen. To get to hear it, it's done several times. . . . If they don't know it, in all probability, it's because of the emotional aspect of it." Thus, being "well-informed" might come down to what patients are ready—and able—to hear.

PATHWAYS TO KNOWLEDGE: ARE CONVERSATIONS OR DOCUMENTS MORE EFFECTIVE?

Different tools affect consent experiences; consent conversations are altogether different from reading and signing consent forms. Though informed-consent-as-ritual can't be segmented into neat packages like "conversation" versus "document," or "spoken" versus "written," it is possible to break it down to better understand patients' and professionals' reactions to diverse consent tools and their characteristics, consequences, advantages, and disadvantages. Proceeding into the informed consent experience itself, do parties find consent documents or conversations more effective, and why?

While 84% of patients found consent documents helpful, most (55% survey, 53% interview) found conversations more useful, and many (22% interview, 40% survey) rated them equally helpful. Patients prefer conversations to documents because they can ask questions; conversations better match learning styles, clarify information, or are more comprehensive; and human interaction is more enjoyable. Conversation can make the consent act more real, immediate, and necessary. Moreover, patients frequently discussed consent information with providers (87% interview, 83% survey).

Conversations can make consent more memorable. They're easier for auditory learners, like Luis Torres: "I can learn things ten times faster in a ten-minute conversation than I can by reading pamphlets and books and whatever." Providers can simplify consent forms, explaining relevant information in more comprehensible terms. "Sometimes when I read things I need to hear things again in a different way," Joanne Johnson explained. "[T]o hear something from someone two times would've been [more] helpful than just reading something that says the same thing." These additional explanations are especially helpful for scientific or technical information. "I think it was more helpful for one sheet in particular, the one where they were talking about rescue, ICSI, assisted hatching, and a couple of other things," recounted Ida Olson. "We didn't understand why it would fit into our cycle, and so when the doctor went through it, it just totally made sense." Then, too, conversations are often less intimidating than a veritable avalanche of documents: "[documents were] probably more overwhelming than helpful. I think it would've helped to have . . . a caring person sit down and go through them with you, [rather] than, 'Here, sign these papers'" (Maggie Copeland).

Along with tailoring *consent* for particular patients, conversations let providers tailor *treatment recommendations*—in Rochelle Rowe's case, guidance on how many embryos to transfer: "he looked at what past results we've had with IVF . . . and made informed decisions on how many embryos to transfer, and he'd be like, 'You should transfer four.' And in my wildest dreams, I would've never done that, but for the complete faith that he had looked at my records." Similarly, Jackie Carson's physician altered the course of her entire IVF cycle by persuading her to freeze embryos, which insurance didn't cover:

> We went into that thinking "We're not going to do cryopreservation," and then when we started discussing it more, [the doctor] said, "I just want to make it *clear* to you, that if you don't do the cryopreservation, he isn't going to fertilize all of your eggs. He's going to throw the ones that don't look as good away. And he's going to fertilize two because that's how many you want. And then they'll divide as they're going to divide, and we'll transfer what we have to transfer." . . . I remember very clearly saying, "How often does it happen that you don't do cryopreservation, you only fertilize two, and you don't have anything to transfer?" And she just looked at me and said, "Almost all of our patients do cryopreservation." And so at that point I was just like, "God, I feel like we don't have [a choice] . . . we have to do the cryopreservation in order to have the best chances of a successful cycle."

Jackie obviously felt pressured by circumstances, including finances, but she also hadn't known how important cryopreservation was within IVF, and she viewed it as a choice. Jackie's provider was able to learn about and discuss this misconception; Jackie's forms probably didn't cover that information.

Thus, conversations also provide moments for interaction—after all, "you just can't interact with a piece of paper" (Natalia Payne). "I don't think that you read a form the same way that you have a conversation, so you're able to ask questions in a conversation," Maggie Copeland emphasized. "If you don't understand something that you're reading . . . that's the end." And conversations allow providers to tailor consent to patients' unique needs and concerns. "It was more personalized . . . more individualized," noted Monique Strickland. Marie Byrd, who was Catholic, very much appreciated how her physician was able to address her religious concerns in consent conversations: "he could [speak to] us as Catholics. . . . And he could give us a lot more information based on our beliefs and our particular situation. . . . When I said to him not wanting to freeze necessarily, he said, 'You're not going to get 30 eggs.' . . . Because it was based on me and my medical background and my husband's medical background and religious preferences, we digested [it] a lot better because it meant something to us."

Thus, conversation's biggest strength is its humanity: "just the human . . . touch, the human tone. Almost like, 'You can do this. It'll be all right'" (Nicole Bell). These interpersonal dimensions deepened emotional dynamics within the patient-provider relationship. "They can calm you down if you needed to be calmed down," asserted Patricia Beck. Human interaction makes informed-consent-as-ritual something other than a provider's duty, grudgingly carried out. Remarked Ashley Carpenter of her provider, "She's been there a long time, so I just felt like she was telling me . . . these things from experience rather than, 'This is just something we have to tell you.'" A provider's physical presence underscores the importance of the consent process: "when a doctor's sitting there . . . when he's saying it, he's experienced it, he sees it, he does it. . . . It's more real when it comes from the doctor that's going to be doing everything. And you're listening to him. You're sitting in his office at his chair, and he's at his desk, and you're listening to him. It's not one of those things where you're on page ten and just trying to get through it" (Luke Holloway).

Because conversation requires a tangible investment of human time and energy, conversations add gravitas to the consent procedure. "Sometimes when you're reading something, you just gloss over it," related Antonia Hughes. And conversation can also redirect patients' attention back to proper decision making roles, the consequences their choices might have, and the need to have additional—and very different—discussions. Stella Madison recalled a clinic visit when she and her husband were choosing embryo dispositions, and she asked for a clinic staff member's opinion on what to do. "[The staff member] was like, 'I can't really tell you; it's going to be up to you and your husband. . . . But understand what you decide today, should anything go south, [will be] a legal binding document now,'" Stella explained. "In hindsight, they . . . were absolutely right to present it as 'This isn't something we can decide for you.' . . . It protects them, and it probably gets the conversation going between spouses."

Because they are interactive, thorough consent conversations can remind patients to take the informed consent project more seriously. Though Simone Henry admitted she had not read her IVF consent forms, which her provider had not discussed, she reacted differently to the interactive consent process for her fertility-related laparoscopic surgery:

> [W]hen I had my laparoscopy, it was really probably like an hour that we went through it. . . . I had a printed copy in front of me, she had the computer, and we went through every single thing. . . . They had a question that said, 'Do you understand that there are other options besides this surgery; would you like to discuss them now prior to signing?' And I hadn't, I thought it was an interesting way of putting it. . . . That was very different than at my clinic . . . where it was just sort of like, "These are your consents," and *no one went through them*. I was glad that I went through it. I've had the dye test twice, I had two IVFs, and signed whatever they put in front of me, and never looked at what I was actually having done. So, unfortunately I think I've treated it as medical redundancy, *but having been through it more carefully now to have an operation, I would hope to take it more seriously in the future.*

Despite the many advantages of conversation and consent interactions, a much smaller group of patients prefers documents, often because of their backgrounds and learning preferences. Visual and textual learners appreciate seeing information rather than hearing it: "What I teach is English, so I'm a big reader, and I read really fast and digest a lot of information. . . . I think the conversation probably wasn't as important to me as what I read, because I digest information really well" (Rosa Grant). Others said their provider's conversation was much less detailed than the forms: "the document contained more information that I could read later when I wasn't so caught up in it" (Tia Bishop). This is particularly true when consent conversations are largely one-sided. Christine Zimmerman's physician gave only "a quick synopsis" of what IVF entailed, pausing only to obtain their embryo disposition choices.

Patients also find documents to be useful resources over time, especially before they have a formal consent conversation, or when providers are unavailable. Angela Cox noted, "I can read it more than once; I can digest it," and David Reid recalled, "I think that the information in the document was more helpful just because I took the time to read it at home and sort of understood what they were saying." Documents are also more tangible than conversations, a difference Doreen Fernandez found critical in both symbolic and practical senses: "I like information so much, so it helped me to have something in my hands that was like tangible, 'Okay, this is real, this is starting.' It gave me more to look up online, and Google all the terminology and things like that. I was glad to finally get my hands on something tangible."

Approximately one-third of patients feel that both documents and conversations are equally important, often because they reinforce one another, going "hand in hand" (Jessica Frazier). "We really used the conversations to fill in the gaps of the documents," said Cecelia McBride. Clay Padilla believed the conversation "maybe cleared up the big picture," while the documents "let us understand the details better." The different mediums accomplish distinct tasks and have unique advantages. "[They] kind of went together. Because had I not had the consent documents, the conversation would've been very lax, and this is what these people do day in and day out," May Weiss observed. "It was nice to kind of have the written [information] and then hear the perspective of the doctor as well."

Conversely, if conversations and documents contain the same information, there is sometimes no real difference between the two: "I don't think [conversation] really added to anything that was in the documents. . . . It's like when you're in a meeting and someone's reading a PowerPoint, and you're reading the PowerPoint; . . . they're not really adding anything to it" (Bridget James). And neither format is particularly helpful if patients are already familiar with that information: "by that time, we'd already read them, so it was kind of a moot point" (Kyle Vargas).

Like patients, most reproductive medicine professionals have strong opinions as to the respective efficacy of consent conversations and documents. Approximately two-thirds feel that both documents and conversations are equally important, though often in different ways. The remaining providers prefer conversations by a vast majority; only three prioritize documents.

Most professionals consider both conversations and consent forms to be useful: each conveys information in unique ways, for different purposes, or for different learning styles, like visual or auditory learners. "I don't think that you're truly getting informed consent without accommodating both written and verbal exchange," asserted Lab Director Farran Ibbott. "You can't ask questions when you're reading the document alone, so the verbal exchange provides explanation . . . and [the] responsibility to respond to patients' questions as you review the consent." Dr. Jaxon Arnaudo observed that forms provide crucial general information, while conversations address individual needs: "I think that the informed consent documents we use are very much population-based, and they speak a lot about relative risk and even absolute risk. . . . [Conversations] allow us to . . . develop a plan for achieving the goal of a healthy pregnancy." Or forms satisfy legal requirements, while "the conversation is important in gauging how the patient understands" (Third Year RE Fellow Dr. Wilma Sumner). Thus, using both documents and forms allows professionals to "verbalize and discuss with them and [have] the documentation to back up that the patient has no questions and understands everything completely" (Nurse Sharalyn O'Keefe).

As different but potentially redundant mediums, documents and conversations often reinforce one another, saving time and using it effectively, and ensuring important information doesn't slip through the cracks. "It's very detailed; . . . there's no way I can do that level of disclosure face-to-face. It would be a half-a-day seminar," Dr. Roselle Suarez explained. "I think they need to be invited to read up on this process, but then I think you need to also meet back with them and say, 'Now that you've read it, what questions do you have?'" Consent forms can act as a checklist, ensuring that a verbal consent presentation is thorough. "The documentation helps with the consistency of it, . . . so that every person is always seeing the same thing, whereas if you relied only on conversation or your presentation of it, it could sometimes not get across," related Dr. Shel Kruger.

Consistency in consent processes serves two purposes. Like patients, providers want to ensure consent tools convey all important information. But professionals use documents as reminders in a different sense, to confirm that conversation and consent have occurred, in order to avoid legal liability: "At least with a hard copy of a document, if they question anything, obviously, you can go back and say, 'It's written here. You signed here'" (Insurance Specialist/Surgery Coordinator Emelia Zimmerman). Unsurprisingly, then, reducing the informed consent project to reviewing and signing a written document profoundly misrepresents it—potentially to patients' detriment:

> [T]he patients are consenting every moment that they're here. . . . And so their understanding is constant. . . . There's been a few times where they've got all the way to me, which means that they're going to have an embryo transfer within a day or two, or that day. And they'll make a comment like, "I don't know how my wife is going to deal with it. That's not her egg, and I'm really worried about it. . . . She doesn't think she can bond." And . . . regardless of if they've signed a consent, right there is a flag that the signature means nothing, that maybe she's not emotionally consenting to what she's about to do. And both of those instances, I've gone to the doctor . . . [and] the doctor has sat them back down and rehashed it all. (Embryologist Chalise Jones)

In fact, conversations are so important that some professionals prefer them hands-down to documents. Conversations might allow them to counteract the possibility that patients don't read or understand forms, and they can customize explanations to improve understanding. There's even the sense that "real" consent takes place in conversation, and documents are more of a formality or confirmation—that "the oral informed consent is really what gives it . . . a more personal relationship" (Dr. Gerard Gabler). Providers feel that conversation heightens consent forms' efficacy: "they don't even read them if we don't go through [them]. They just sign it because they have to, to have treatment. . . . nurses have to go through it with them one-by-one, so that they're legit" (Clinical Coordinator Mira Durham). Providers realize that consent documents' formalism may be a drawback after thinking of how they react when confronted by documents. "I sign stuff all the time, like your [cell] phone agreement, and do I sit down and read every piece of it? And I would probably say no," confessed Dr. Wes Hoffman. Thus, they expect little more from patients. Dr. Ronnie Avery related, "[I]t's very, very uncommon for patients to come in and say, 'I see on page 12 you have this written. What does that mean?'" Conversation's informality may therefore be its strongest asset.

But documents are far from useless; providers count on them to be helpful reminders for patients who can't realistically remember every fact about IVF and treatment protocols. "There's typically far too much information for them to retain. So having a resource that they can go back and look at or even refer to in the future [is useful]," explained Dr. Oliver Evans, "I think at some point they pull those documents out and they go back through." Moreover, consent forms may have a contractual effect, making patients take consent procedures more seriously: "I think they view them more as a commitment when they're reading it," Dr. Evans observed.

But documents aren't much help if they're too long or obtuse for patients to understand. "The documents are in Chinese. . . . it's like reading your mortgage, right?" Dr. Heike Steinmann quipped. "We've rewritten a lot of these things. . . . But they're very long and very detailed, and I'm sure people get lost in them." Understanding takes time and attention from all participants. Dr. Wes Hoffman observed, "I spend a lot of time talking to patients about treatments, and specifically in IVF talking about the whole process, and trying to bring it down to terms that anyone would hopefully understand." Lab Technologist Samuel Hurst emphasized: "I think you can't digest [it] until it's read out loud, because, especially when the cancer patients are coming to me, they're not really paying attention. They really couldn't care less; they have so many more serious things on their mind. But this is to me a very serious thing, and I would feel terrible if they left and I felt that they didn't have . . . that time from me that they deserved to have to really understand the consents."

While patients' understanding is a goal belonging to the informed consent project, it's confirmed by patients' signatures, through informed-consent-as-ritual. Signatures "show that that verbal part was done" (Donor Program Coordinator Ranjit Gadhavi). Thus, it's all too easy for both patients and providers to confuse the two. This is especially true when providers and patients sink too deeply into their stereotypical consent roles of delivering or receiving information. This reduces informed-consent-as-ritual to a transaction instead of an interaction and encourages providers to pursue (and patients to provide) signatures, without thinking deeply about the communicative interaction that truly advances patients' understanding, which should occur before anyone reaches the dotted finish line of the signature page.

CONCLUSION: BEYOND THE DOTTED LINE

Patients and professionals' perceptions of the informed consent project, and in particular informed-consent-as-ritual, are suffused with tensions— between medical and legal safeguards, trusting and adversarial relations, informality and formality, comprehensibility and thoroughness, comprehension and time constraints, and current optimism and potentially troubled futures. Ideally, informed consent is a long-term project, not an event, that patients perceive begins long before they sign documents. Hopefully, providers come across as empathic and patient decision-making partners, with different motives than self-protection. And when patients trust their providers, they're likely to already be well-informed.

Even as they complicate the stereotypes of emotional patient and profit-hungry provider, patients' and providers' reflections also belie stereotypes of informed-consent-as-ritual, where an underinformed patient rapidly signs a generic document replete with legal and medical jargon. If different documents fulfill different purposes, providers and patients have shown that consent forms can be used for many different purposes than conventionally assumed. Consent forms shouldn't be brief flirtations, but objects with which patients ideally have long-term relationships. Patient-provider conversations are most often what makes consent documents more attractive to patients, who then develop more respect for these forms, and for the consent process as a whole.

Informed consent interactions are most effective when providers prioritize patient understanding over signed documentation and patients' questions complement provider explanations. At best, informed-consent-as-ritual is a multimedium interaction, a blend of formality and informality in which both parties use communication to achieve specific goals. Patients may be more inclined to take the consent process seriously when it cultivates mutual respect and trust. This type of consent process actively seeks to dispel suspicion and distrust and defuse confrontation and adversarial relations. Adversarial elements reinforce the assumption that consent processes and aids are only products of a litigious culture, of little value in protecting patient autonomy and advocacy. Such antagonistic themes are incompatible with goals like patient understanding and consent. These adversarial properties can easily throttle trust and collaboration, overshadowing and potentially nullifying consent's educational dimensions.

Little research has focused on how patients experience informed-consent-as-ritual; but the one prior study that exists, published in 1980, suggests that these trends are not new. Researchers found that patients looked to providers for information first and often felt that legalistic consent forms weren't personally relevant. As the authors concluded, "Patients spontaneously expressed the feeling that official documents seemed out of place and counterproductive in the clinical setting. . . . 80 percent of the patients studied viewed consent forms as a protection for the physician. The consent form's legalistic, perhaps even adversarial, overtones may appear inconsistent to the patient who has a fundamental orientation to and preference for a doctor-patient relation based on 'trust.'"[1]

Some professionals and patients are no doubt still uncomfortable with a more informal and interactive consent process. These individuals may argue that trust is dangerous when it prompts patients to relax their vigilance, necessitating more stringent, formal protections. But formalist solutions to this problem, like longer and more technical documents, encourage patient circumvention and noncompliance, strip the interpersonal grease that eases friction within treatment relationships, diminish trust, and therefore threaten treatment outcomes. Protecting patients while promoting trust are two goals in delicate balance. Longer documents stuffed with more technical information upset this equilibrium, eroding patients' trust, imperiling understanding, and provoking ignorance and ridicule, undermining the consent process altogether.

Thus, instead of highlighting informed consent's failures yet again, patients' and professionals' remarks celebrate its surprising successes within a culture of formality and skepticism and hint at ways to harness informality to make it even more effective. Trust may partially explain why consent forms fail, but it also is why the project as a whole succeeds. If patients don't trust their care providers, why would they believe that these professionals will give them accurate information in the first place? Moreover, without trust, how would physicians accept patients' assurances that they understand consent information? Without trust, what value does a patient's signature hold?

Solving the problems of informed consent necessitates digging deeper than the document. We tend to forget that consent forms as tools don't spring fully formed from pen or printer, but are created and revised by professionals according to institutional guidelines and precedents, and modified as necessary through patient use. Formal bureaucratic principles establish the need for informed-consent-as-ritual and perhaps set procedural guidelines, but creating, revising and using consent documents take place in more informal spheres. But with this crucial understanding, how do patients use the various consent forms they must sign? Do forms describing the IVF process merit the same attention as those requiring patients to choose what happens to their embryos if they die or divorce? And how do patients' feelings about these diverse forms influence their consent experiences?

CHAPTER 9

For Forms' Sake

Comparing IVF and Embryo
Disposition Forms

For most of us, the term "informed consent" conjures up informed-consent-as-ritual, done badly: documents brimming with dry, clinical discussions of risks, benefits, side effects, and alternatives, language that can mute the importance of potentially life-or-death decisions. In other treatment situations, patients' poor health leaves them little freedom to refuse treatment. Thus, patients undergoing elective treatment like IVF have more time to read consent documents and consider next steps.

But within the pantheon of IVF consent forms—including consents to the IVF and embryo transfer procedures, embryo cryopreservation, assisted embryo hatching, PGD, ICSI, and other forms for donor gametes —one particular consent form can bedevil even the most careful and well-informed patients: the embryo disposition form that requires them to choose the fate of their frozen embryos. Embryo disposition decisions are highly specialized consent forms, triggered only by a precise, and perhaps unusual, sequence of events—*if* IVF produces embryos, *if* these embryos are high-quality and can be frozen, and *if* these embryos aren't ever used, or *if* patients die or divorce. These choices can seem surreal to patients, who may not even believe they'll ever have such reproductive resources: "it was odd to be actually writing down what you're going to do, for something you actually didn't have" (Patricia Burns). Comparing IVF and embryo disposition consent forms illustrates that different forms can inspire diverse patient reactions and prompt disparate amounts of patient attention, trust, and consideration.

IVF consent forms are mostly informational; they provide important definitions, explain key concepts, outline how an IVF cycle unfolds, and detail possible outcomes. If IVF consent forms can sometimes spark emotional reactions from patients anxious to build families, embryo disposition forms strike at the very heart of their most ardent desires. It's hard enough for a patient to decide the fate of nonexistent embryos, let alone contemplate her own death or divorce, when she questions whether her eggs are even viable. Embryo disposition forms also educate patients, but go further, requiring them to plan for the future in unique ways resembling end-of-life care. Asking patients to confront these choices early in treatment broadens the informed consent project in novel ways, increasing their awareness of values and relationships that affect treatment decision making, and alerting them to the unpleasant realities of potential medical and legal pitfalls.

Patients understandably use and react to IVF consent forms differently than embryo disposition documents. Forms describing IVF protocols receive more attention than general surgical consents or forms detailing embryo cryopreservation, either because patients treat these decisions as a given or because most have no moral, ethical, or religious opposition to freezing embryos. For instance, Rodney Hughes contrasted the embryo disposition decision with the choice to freeze embryos: "For the cryo[preservation] stuff, I remember I didn't feel odd about it, [since it's] a realistic option. But for the frozen embryos, we haven't been there yet, so we haven't emotionally crossed that bridge." Embryo disposition forms receive the lion's share of patients' attention because they capture situations where the future bares its fangs most threateningly, and deal with events over which patients feel they have the most control—and the most at stake. Their decisions will determine what happens in the event of unthinkable possibilities. Thus, the embryo disposition form and its serious real-world implications are very different from stereotypical consent documents.

Given these high stakes, it's especially ironic that it's here, in the depths of the informed consent project, that we meet the cousin of the desperate, ideal, and difficult patient stereotypes: the dull and unengaged patient, who doesn't read or understand consent forms. Though this stereotype usually represents patients less wealthy and well educated than the average IVF patient, it doesn't discriminate, and embraces patients undergoing fertility treatment along with everyone else. Placed alongside one another, the stereotypes of desperate, difficult, and uninformed patients illustrate the evolution of a particular type of patient over a stereotypical IVF Expedition. Presumably, desperate patients are so distraught and single-minded that they'll become difficult once they enter treatment, and in their haste to conceive they will want to skip or rush through necessary steps like informed-consent-as-ritual without "rational" consideration of risks, benefits, and alternatives.

Across numerous medical contexts, patients have many logical reasons for not reading, understanding, or engaging with informed-consent-as-ritual. No doubt some patients, schooled by prior consent experiences, give the process short shrift because they're eager to begin treatment or believe the process unhelpful. Demographics and education also matter. Patients might lack the literacy or vocabulary to read or comprehend consent information. Other patients might feel too anxious, fearful, angry, or sad to care about what a medical procedure involves. These psychological and emotional reasons for noncompliance receive little attention from experts, who primarily focus on reading and comprehension. Yet, it's vital that these issues receive more attention, since they exert such strong effects, but can likely be easily remedied.

Comparing providers' and patients' perspectives on IVF and embryo disposition consent forms suggests answers to two questions. First, do individuals undergoing IVF engage with and satisfactorily complete informed-consent-as-ritual? If consent fails for this generally privileged patient group, we can expect it will also fail for other, less advantaged patients in other medical fields. Second, *why* and *when* does informed-consent-as-ritual for IVF succeed or fail?

One note of caution is in order. This research relies on patients' self-reports of how they reacted to and used IVF and embryo disposition consent forms. While reliance on self-report measures can unlock otherwise inaccessible treasure troves of data, it can also be problematic: patients are subject to biases and may overreport the extent to which they read, understand, or engage with consent forms. To attempt to minimize bias's presence and power, responses were obtained from two different patient populations through surveys and interviews. Yet, in many instances, both groups gave nearly identical answers to the same questions. This suggests that any biases were at work to the same extent in both populations. But more importantly, shockingly high percentages of patients in both groups reported reading and understanding their consent forms, intimating that most patients likely fulfill informed-consent-as-ritual quite thoroughly; such behaviors are often associated with high socioeconomic and educational backgrounds. Moreover, several patients describe authentic, active engagement with informed-consent-as-ritual, usually because of informed-consent-as-relationship and provider partnerships. It is useful, therefore, to first investigate how consent documents are created and how physicians use their own consent forms. Do *they* read these documents? Who decides what to include in them and when and how they are completed?

TAMING PAPER TIGERS: PHYSICIANS' PERSPECTIVES ON FORMS AND FORM REVISIONS

Well-run informed-consent-as-ritual is like a symphony performance, at the center of which stands a conductor (the provider) who directs how and when participants play their instruments (consent aids). Before and after (consent) performances, reproductive medicine professionals orchestrate forms' structure and content, creating and revising them. Thus, it matters enormously to informed-consent-as-ritual where these forms come from, what providers think of them, whether doctors are aware of what's in them, whether patients can change them, and how providers present these forms to patients.

Until recently, providers obtained forms from other medical professionals: "I think I brought a lot of my initial forms from where I was before. . . . And then they've just sort of evolved over the years to what we use now. . . . It may have been like picking and choosing from a lot [of others], going to other places in the early years [and asking] 'What are you guys using? Can I look at your consents?' And you'd exchange material." Now, however, the most obvious place for physicians to obtain forms is the Society of Assisted Reproductive Technology (SART), which has recently promulgated model forms for several reproductive medical procedures, including IVF. Several physicians work in practices that have either adopted the SART model forms wholesale or used them as a template. "There's sort of a base form that was made available to all [SART] members, and on the other hand there's state laws," explained Dr. Roselle Suarez. "Sometimes you have to go back in and tweak it a little bit to bring it into conformity with what your particular state says." Dr. Oliver Evans adapted useful portions of the model forms into his clinic's existing ones and revised them when necessary: "as the model forms were coming out, I incorporated changes and also if there are any times that I come across a consent, if we got records in from someone else, you look through it and, 'Oh that looks good, let's put that in.' And then, as questions come up from patients, there's things I could bring up later, we go back and model the forms. They're always evolving."

Other practitioners, however, haven't adopted these model forms. "I actually downloaded it and distributed it to everybody and said, 'Are you interested in going to this?' and [got nowhere]," Lab Director Keane Schultze related. "If the docs don't even read it, how do you expect patients to read it? . . . It's too long, too much information." Yet, Dr. Teagan Shepherd preferred his forms to the SART model forms because "our forms are actually more thorough."

Many providers regard certain consent form characteristics, particularly their length and level of detail, as necessary evils. "I wish that it could be a little simpler for patients. But yet, on the other hand, I do understand [why they aren't simpler because of] all the legalities and the potential ethical things that may come up in the future," emphasized Nurse Meredith Haynes. "You have to provide for the possibility that there could be a divorce or a death later on, and those things do have to be covered up front, unfortunately." Some feel their hands are tied. "I think they're too damn long, and that there's way too much stuff there, [but] they don't have any other ideas on what to do with them," explained Dr. Bryant Rowe. And even though they're far from perfect, current forms are an improvement over past generations of documents: "I think over time we've gotten even better at making better forms that really try to give better explanations, that are more thorough and more detailed . . . in language that I think patients understand better than consents we used 10 years ago" (Head Nurse Melina Draper).

A few providers admit they aren't familiar with what is in their consent forms, especially if they have practiced at the same clinic for several years. "I haven't gone through and read every word of the consent form," acknowledged Dr. Shel Kruger. "I know at my previous practice we went through and redid all the consents, so I read every word, but after joining this practice I haven't read every word of the consent. I probably should." Dr. Don West had also never read the consent forms at his current practice, but demurred on the grounds that he had given detailed consent presentations to many patients over the years: "I can sit there and give you an IVF presentation, and within probably a 5% margin, you're going to hear the exact same thing that I told the last 150 people. . . . Consistency in how you counsel your patients is almost as valuable, if not more valuable, than anything else you put on paper."

Whatever their forms' source, providers frequently review form content. "They've been updated as things come and go," added Nurse Emilee Powell; "we'll hear about it in our weekly meetings, you know, 'I've had this situation arise. I think we should change the form.'" Dr. Bryant Rowe described the process of revising his forms—originally from a colleague's fellowship program—to incorporate information about PGD: "We took our consent forms and, when we wanted to do PGD, we took it [to] our ethics committee, and they had a big meeting and we discussed it there [and incorporated changes and] added it to our consent forms. Then we took it to our legal team and they went through it all. So we try to cover it all, but, oh lord, it's hard."

When providers aren't satisfied with forms, they revise them. Fed up with his consents, Dr. Ronnie Avery made them simpler. "There's a consent form for each kind of procedure, and it's very repetitive with all the legalese in it, and so . . . you have to dig into all the jargon words to find what the specific procedure is about," he recounted. "So I met with our hospital lawyer to revamp to use the SART consent or SART educational bulletin, and then just a one-page consent that says 'I've learned about ART from this educational bulletin.'" Other revision opportunities arise if patients ask for clarification or changes when they don't understand or disagree with form provisions. Ultimately, however, providers know a perfect consent process is elusive: "I don't know if there's ever going to be a perfect form" (Dr. Wes Hoffman).

Patients do in fact ask providers to change certain consent form provisions they find problematic; approximately half of providers have fielded such requests. "Patients do things like line things out and stuff like that. Not very often," related Dr. Sachie Keefe. "Our [embryo] discard policy . . . that's the one thing that's most likely. They'll write in the margin '[donate to] research' or something like that." Senior Embryologist Lizbeth Norman also felt such challenges were rare: "occasionally you'll have the patient who feels that they have to dissect it, even making comments and addendums. . . . But those patients are few and far between." Patients' responses support these intuitions; only a minority of interviewed patients wanted to change the forms (28%, vs. 9% survey), but the vast majority felt that they couldn't make changes (68% survey), while 71% of patients didn't want to make changes; perhaps more would want to if they believed it were possible. Ultimately, only 7% of interviewed patients were allowed to change their forms.

Most patients try to change forms because they dislike certain provisions, not because of emotion. Thus, it makes sense that many challenges usually come from patients who are attorneys. "We don't get a lot of disgruntlement," noted Dr. Jaxon Arnaudo, "maybe from some attorneys every once in a while." Attorneys like Christopher Franklin read certain provisions more closely, specifically looking for problematic provisions:

> [The sections on] IVF, what that was, medication, that would've been what I would've just skimmed right through. . . . What I read very carefully were the terms and conditions that applied to our business relationship, the financial conditions and what applied there. Because that was something that I could change, and that was something that I needed to understand. I wasn't going to not sign the form because they didn't clearly articulate everything about IVF. We knew what we were getting into, and we trusted— again, trust was important there—we trusted that they knew what they were doing.

Sometimes these changes seem bizarre; as Dr. Corwin Summers noted, "half of [the modifications] weren't even really pertinent to the cycle at hand. I think they just wanted to feel like they had control over something. Because God knows, when we go to the doctor, we're horrible patients." Usually patient dissatisfaction only extends to a few provisions. For instance, a handful of patients may dislike an arbitration provision requiring parties to submit disputes to a neutral individual instead of a judge and to accept that person's decision. "[I tell them] there's somewhere on there where you can put on there, 'I'm not in agreement, but I'm signing this saying I'm not in agreement,'" Donor Coordination Assistant Louise Whitaker explained. "[They're] acknowledging that they've been presented with this information."

Some providers do, however, allow patients to make sensible, benign changes. Dr. Jaxon Arnaudo related, "[I]f the change were to be something that would go against medical prudence, then we'd need to have that discussion with them. If, on the other hand, it's something relatively minor, then most of the time we allow them to make the change." Patients' requested changes might actually improve consent forms: "We did just have . . . a patient who . . . had one dose of the donor sperm left, [and] they had a child from that same donor. [They] wanted to thaw it to use sperm from that last sample for ICSI, but knew there'd be some left over. . . . So they wanted to refreeze the portion of the sample that didn't need to be used. . . . I found that out on a Wednesday midmorning and by 6:30 p.m. we'd [created] . . . a consent for refreezing."

Most providers discourage modifications. Dr. Don West recalled one couple: "[S]he wanted the embryos if he died, but they had to be disposed of if she died. And that's not an option on our consent form. . . . For the most part we've really discouraged them from changing." And some women with frozen eggs have wanted them destroyed immediately if a physician couldn't retrieve their partners' sperm through testicular biopsy. "I've had to talk them into just leaving them in storage a little bit longer so they have time to really come to terms with the decision before we discard them," Dr. Corwin Summers recalled. Professionals are unlikely to approve most modifications:

> I had one patient a few years ago. The husband was an attorney; he went through and marked the whole thing entirely up and sent it back to us. . . . I just sent that right back over to [our office manager] and said, "What do you think?" . . . Of course she took it to [our attorney] and he said, "No, he can't change that." . . . Pretty much they had to go with our form if they're going to go through our thing. It depends on what they're really asking for. If they rewrite the whole entire thing, then it isn't gonna work.

And some providers veto *any* changes. "Occasionally they do [want to make changes]," Dr. Kerry Kushner remarked, "and we won't." One clinic actually had a strict "no changes allowed" policy: "I was in a different practice before and that was a big thing. They couldn't make changes to the consent. . . . We had questions like 'Where would you want the disposition of the embryos,' and people would try to write in 'my mom' or something. And it's like, 'That's not a choice. It's either you, or your partner'" (Erika May). Nurse Nylah Chen observed that patients' requested changes were often impossible because of cycle protocol, not legal ramifications: "everything else was pretty straightforward about what happens in the IVF cycle and what you do for a retrieval and transfers; it's not a lot of wiggle room to change anything in those." Thus, whether patients might attempt to change forms for ethical reasons, self-protection, or simply exercising some control over the process, they likely will encounter stiff resistance from providers.

IN FINE FORM?: NEGOTIATING IVF CONSENT DOCUMENTS

Patients usually review and sign consent forms describing IVF procedures before they choose surplus frozen embryos' fates. As Figure 7 illustrates, the vast majority of patients in both survey and interview populations—87% and 82%, respectively—reported reading their entire IVF consent forms. "Yes, I read everything cover to cover. Everything they gave us," Sarah Harper asserted. In fact, many read the form repeatedly, most often because it described cycle protocols. "I probably read that form, who knows? Fifty times," quipped Nicole Bell.

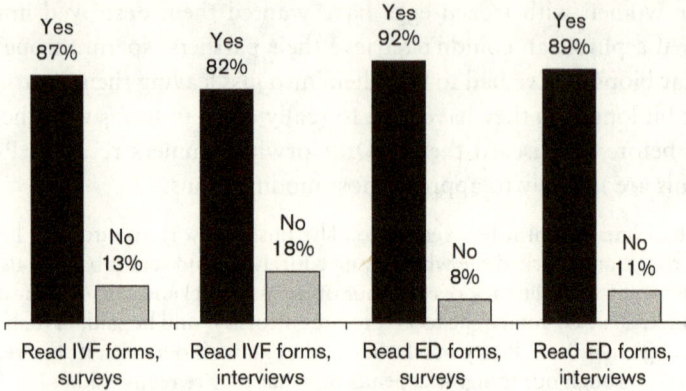

FIGURE 7. Patients' Reports about Reading the Entire IVF and Embryo Disposition (ED) Forms. Source: Jody Lyneé Madeira

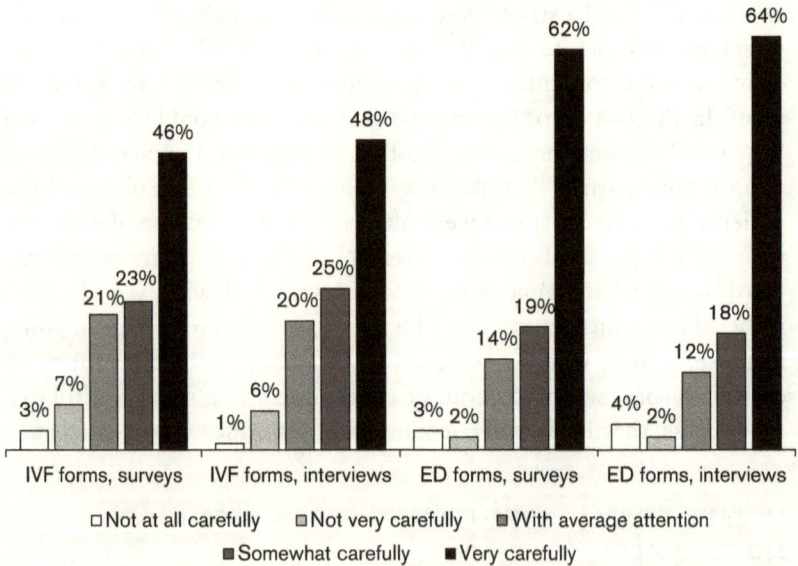

FIGURE 8. Patients' Reports on How Carefully They Read the IVF and Embryo Disposition (ED) Forms. Source: Jody Lyneé Madeira

Patients' willingness to read forms depends on *why* they're asked to do so; many, like Antonia Hughes, read it because it's useful: "Because it wasn't all legalese stuff. It was, 'This is what's going to happen. This is what to expect.'" Patients often think their IVF consent forms are more informative than other medical consent forms: "in general, at the

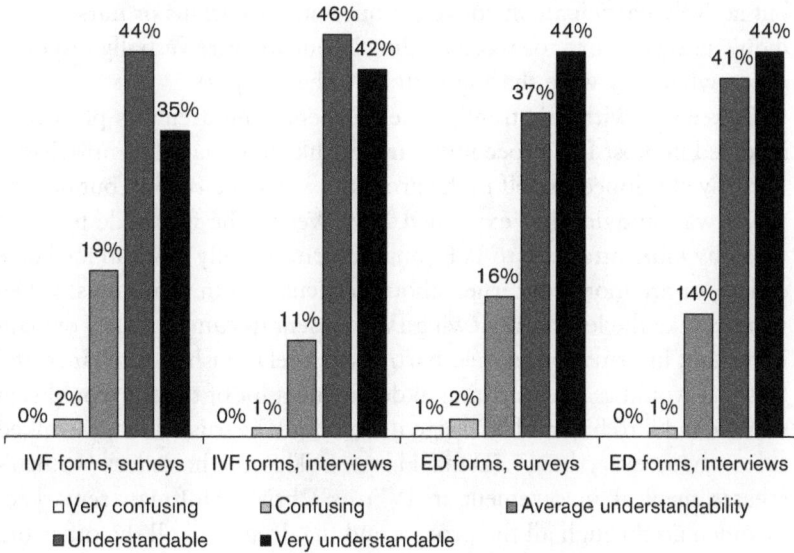

FIGURE 9. Patients' Reports on How Understandable They Found the IVF and Embryo Disposition (ED) Forms. Source: Jody Lyneé Madeira

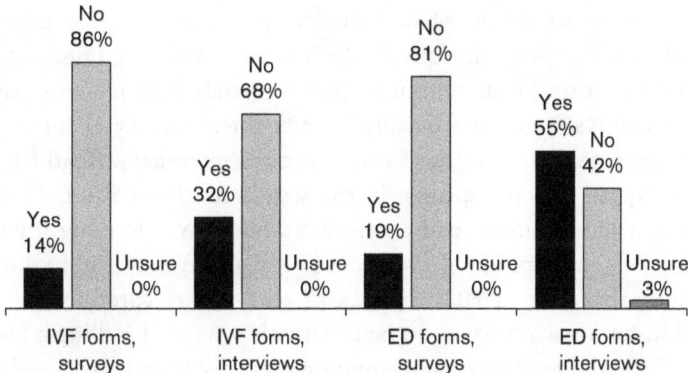

FIGURE 10. Patients' Reports of Whether They Were Surprised by the Information in the IVF and Embryo Disposition (ED) Forms. Source: Jody Lyneé Madeira

doctor I just sign whatever they hand me, but in this case I read it pretty thoroughly" (Tia Bishop). Predictably, then, they are less likely to read the entire form if they've already undergone IVF: "the second time, because I think I'm a know-it-all and I'd already done it once, I proba-bly skimmed it" (Stella Madison). And still others glance over the forms, but actively participate in conversations with physicians or nurses: "we didn't sit there word for word reading it, but we were verbally responding to what they were sharing with us" (Sheri Lopez).

In keeping with this trend, male partners, who aren't as physically involved in most IVF procedures, are less likely to read the entire form. "I really enveloped myself in the process. . . . He did read it, but not the way I was studying it," explained May Weiss. The few male partners who pay *more* attention to IVF consent forms usually work in medicine or law, or are more concerned about particular form provisions. When women take the lead in reviewing IVF consent documents, they explain important information to their partners in a relationship of reliance and trust: "I would read everything in detail and a lot of times I would sign it and hand it to him and he'd sign it. So I think he trusted me; we talked a lot about everything" (Dana Harper). This might reflect women's greater medical involvement in IVF; as Christy Hoffman remarked, "women go through all the process and the drugs and all the other fun stuff, and [men] just kind of go in for one day and drop off a donation."

Patients not only read their IVF consent forms, they read them quite thoroughly, as shown in Figure 8. Very high percentages of patients—90% (survey) and 93% (interview)—reported reading forms with at least average attention. Most patients (46% survey, 48% interview) read the forms "very carefully," which might involve highlighting them and taking notes in the margins. Approximately half as many patients read forms "somewhat carefully" (23% interview, 25% survey) and "with average attention" (25% survey, 23% interview). Reading documents "quite closely" means, in the words of David Reid, "I wasn't reading it like I would read a contract where I was looking for something to trip me up, like if I was reading a [mortgage], I'm looking for anything that's not what I want. . . . I read it very carefully to understand it, but I wasn't trying to make sure they weren't pulling a fast one on us." Reading with average attention meant that patients "read it like a newspaper article" (Ashley Carpenter), often discussing forms with a care provider and reading through it again afterward.

Perhaps because of this "close read," virtually *all* patients—98% (survey)/99% (interview)—found their IVF forms to be, at minimum, of average comprehensibility; as Figure 9 explains, many (42% interview, 35% survey) described them as "very understandable," while most patients (46% interview, 44% survey) estimated they were "fairly understandable," and fewer (11% interview, 19% survey) rated them of average comprehensibility. Patients whose forms are of average complexity are still comfortable reading them; for Miranda Valdez, they were "understandable enough. It was in medicalized language, but it was clear enough to understand." Darla Clarke described her form as "fairly" instead of "very" comprehensible "because of the terminology like "ICSI that we weren't familiar with," and Rochelle Rowe chose that same category because "it's just a laundry list of things that could go wrong, rather than things that are likely to go wrong versus the things that [are] remotely likely to happen."

Patients who find their forms "very comprehensible" feel they are "well-written; they didn't use a whole lot of medical jargon that most people wouldn't understand" (Tracey West). Patients appreciate forms that aren't "too technical" (Elizabeth Alvarado), so "human beings could actually read it and understand everything" (Madeline Lowe). Predictably, most patients—86% survey, 68% interview—weren't surprised by information in these documents (as evidenced in Figure 10), often because they already knew those details. Juanita Poole asserted, "I think I'd done so much research at that point, nothing was new or different."

Thus, information that seems new to patients is usually difficult to uncover through research; it might be technical, like details of assisted hatching or selective reduction, or unique to particular providers, like postprocedure activity restrictions. Patients who find other information surprising often haven't done much independent research, like Samantha Romero, who didn't research IVF since "I really didn't think I would ever do it. . . . It was the first time in my whole career of trying to get pregnant that I didn't know what I was walking into until I was given the form and the meeting to explain everything." Patients were also surprised when they actually learned how procedures would be performed. For instance, Aaron Schneider was astonished to learn how eggs were surgically retrieved:

> I'd assumed that they were going to have her on the operating table, completely cut open, and retrieving them that way, I wasn't expecting just okay, have her out in what they called like a twilight type of [anesthesia], and like inject this, pull this out in a syringe type of thing. So that was a shock, but for the most part, most of it was self-explanatory. . . . You're sitting here like, "Well, wait a minute, you're going to pull an egg out of something like that?" And in my mind, I'm thinking eggs that you cook for breakfast.

Sometimes, patients have trouble understanding information because of consent rituals, not forms. Consent isn't necessarily that informed if it occurs at inopportune times or in unhelpful ways. "My consent for transfer was done in the transfer room, and I couldn't sign it—my husband had to sign it—because they had me take Valium before I came," described Simone Henry. And Antonia Hughes made a mistake while injecting her fertility medication: "There was no pen available to actually take notes or anything. I'm a very note-oriented-type person. And, if I didn't have it written down, I don't remember. And we actually used the wrong needle at one point, and I went back [to the clinic] the next day and was like, 'I can't take that needle again.' And they were like, 'Oh my God, you took the wrong one.' . . . At that point, I was ready to give up. . . . We'd actually done it wrong, but it wasn't clearly labeled."

Fortunately, most interviewed patients—72%—felt that their IVF consent forms covered the most important details. "When you look at it as . . . a document that needs to pertain to a lot of cases or all cases, I think it was fine," noted Sheri Lopez. Forms could even be *too* detailed for comfort: "it was a little more detailed on the egg retrieval than I was expecting, because I remember getting a little nauseous when I read it. Like about the needle probe and all that" (Cecelia McBride). But patients did observe that consent forms focused almost exclusively on IVF's physiological effects, overlooking its *emotional* impact. Claudia Parsons wanted more information on "how emotional it's going to be. It says something like, 'This may be an emotional time for you and your partner,' but going into it, you have no idea how up-and-down it's going to be. I mean, that was a shock."

Consent forms' thoroughness makes some patients suspicious that providers have other, more pecuniary motives than increasing patient understanding. Or patients suspect that providers use these forms to reduce their workload: "I think they want you to use that binder and look at it so you don't call them a lot" (April Gonzalez). Others speculate that consent "laundry lists" relieve providers' fears of malpractice suits: "I really think that these are hurdles that the doctors have had to put up to protect themselves, because of the society that we live in. Did it touch on some stuff? Yeah. Did it really help explain things? No."

The few patients who feel forms aren't sufficiently thorough usually have experienced something unexpected during treatment. Dana Harper's IVF cycle was riddled with unknowns: "[the form] definitely never went through diminished ovarian reserve, stopping the cycle options, it never addressed any of the things we ended up going through."

Coming full circle, although informed-consent-as-ritual typically occurs early in the IVF process, some patients wish their forms provided more information about its end. For instance, Anne Kelley "wanted them to emphasize a little bit more that you could end up with nothing [to transfer]. . . . Everyone assumes you will, but lots of people don't." Thus, while patients are generally satisfied with their IVF consent forms and knowledgeable about the procedure, they are able to identify several areas of improvement. These changes would make consent documents even more useful, perhaps more fully engaging patients who are ready to actively participate in consent interactions.

Although the vast majority of patients report both reading and understanding consent forms, most providers are skeptical that they actually do either. "I honestly think people . . . view it as an obstacle to get through," Dr. Abbie Walther explained. "Done, sign it, done. That's what people do." Dr. Sadie Blackman agreed: "I don't think that everybody read them. That's probably 1, 3, 5% that reads them." Dr. Corwin Summers believed patients just wanted to get underway: "I do sometimes worry that patients aren't really reading any consent forms or really listening to what you're saying because they really want to get into that cycle next week." But Nurse Devan Neville thought patients were more circumspect: "most of the time when . . . we're going through IVF, they usually won't sign anything that they don't understand."

Medical professionals distinguish reading consent forms from understanding them. Reading these documents may be sufficient for, but not necessary to, patient understanding, and patients can get information from other sources: "I don't get questions about the forms, but I do get questions about the process, and so I think they're informed because they're thinking about it, but not because they've read the legalese of the consent form" (Dr. Ronnie Avery). It is difficult for providers to determine exactly how much attention patients have paid to consent tools. Trust is at least in part what carries patients through informed-consent-as-ritual: "I think it's akin to [signing a mortgage] when [you have] a lot of trust in your loan officer, that you just hope they aren't having you initial things that are problematic" (Physician's Assistant Nora Stanton).

THE HARD COPY: COMPLETING EMBRYO DISPOSITION DOCUMENTS

Most patients arrive at informed-consent-as-ritual already knowledgeable and confident about their decision to pursue IVF. But they often aren't expecting that IVF entails other thorny choices like determining embryos' ethical status, or what should happen to frozen embryos if they die or get divorced. Such decisions reach far beyond conventional informed-consent-as-ritual. Nicole Bell thoughtfully distinguished IVF and embryo consent issues: "I guess I'm thinking of two different things. One is the way [the doctor's] treating me. You know, the way he's doing procedures on my body. That's one thing. And the other part of the informed consent was having to do with the embryos. So for me, the embryos was more my own ethical struggle."

Embryo disposition is a high-stakes decision: if patients die or get divorced and have unused frozen embryos, will these remaining embryos be donated to research, donated to another couple, given to the other partner, thawed and discarded, or some other disposition? Once chosen, these dispositions can't be changed, at least without completing a new form; once carried out, they can't be undone. Patricia Burns recognized this finality: "after we signed them [our embryos] over for research within the clinic, [it] gave me a little bit of apprehension. But I felt better that they were staying there, and I could still help infertile people. . . . But what if I'm wrong, and life begins at conception, and I do have 45 babies in heaven?" Patients believe the embryo disposition form is more intimately connected to their interests because of the personal stakes involved in choosing their embryos' fate. Kendra Figueroa tearfully described deciding to donate a donor egg embryo back to her clinic for another patient to use, and then changing her mind:

> It's [my husband's] genetics [in the embryo]; it's actually not mine, but I feel more attached to the embryo than he does. . . . I guess another thing that maybe swayed us [toward donation], which is a silly thing that maybe shouldn't have, is whenever we were deciding whether or not to donate, we'd gotten the bill for the cryopreservation, which was $400 a year. . . . So we were like, "Well, do we [donate]? . . . Are we gonna use it? If we're not gonna use it, we might as well just go ahead and donate it." . . . We just talked about it extensively, and my husband . . . didn't have the emotional attachment that I still have, obviously. And then . . . we signed the consent form . . . and had it notarized to donate, knowing that we won't know the outcome. . . . I changed my mind after the consent form was signed. . . . The next Friday is when I went in to say, "I want to tear up the consent form, I want to keep our embryo; here's the money." She said, "It's already been transferred." . . . My heart shattered into a million pieces.

Kendra's experience illustrates what might be at stake in the embryo disposition decision and how unique and emotional these choices can be.

As with IVF consent forms, the vast majority of patients—92% (survey) and 89% (interview)—read the entire embryo disposition form, as Figure 7 illustrates. Completing this document often requires more time and attention than the other consent forms: "I read it . . . several times, and I think my husband and I kept going back to it. I think we signed the other parts of the forms first and [went] back to it" (Megan Cooper).

Likewise, very high percentages of patients (95% (survey) and 94% (interview)) read the embryo disposition form with at least average attention (see Figure 8). More patients (62% survey, 64% interview) read these forms "very carefully," as compared to IVF consent forms. Patients read embryo disposition forms more closely because these documents seemed so novel. Rochelle Rowe, who read her form "fairly closely," said, "[T]hat's the most useful form; you make sure you agree on that stuff." Patients are also more likely to read embryo disposition forms more closely if they and their partners disagree on what should happen.

Patients ask questions about embryo disposition forms less often than with IVF consent forms, likely because this decision rests primarily on their own values: "it was more talking about it ourselves than us asking questions of the doctor's staff" (Penny Hill). When patients do ask doctors about something, they are attempting to understand particular disposition options. Or patients might ask whether they can add a particular possibility: "the next one about the embryos didn't have the donation [option] on there, and so I asked if I could write that in there, and they said yes" (Patricia Beck).

But providers can also be unfamiliar with such details and might have the wrong answers to patients' questions. In one case, a provider told a patient—incorrectly—that her embryo disposition form wasn't "legally binding" in the event of death or divorce: "When we got to the actual section on what would happen if we got a divorce, there was a separate thing for each type of scenario, and she was like . . . 'If you changed your mind it wasn't gonna matter. You can fight it out if you were to divorce'" (Inez Griffith). But that's the very purpose of embryo disposition forms—to choose embryos' fates if such circumstances arise. And courts enforce these forms, even against one party's objection. In the New York case of *Kass v. Kass*, a wife sued her husband for possession of frozen embryos created before the couple's divorce. The court upheld the preconception agreement and said that such documents were enforceable: "Agreements between progenitors, or gamete donors, regarding disposition of their pre-zygotes should generally be presumed valid and binding, and enforced in any dispute between them. . . . Indeed, parties should be encouraged in advance, before embarking on IVF and cryopreservation, to think through possible contingencies and carefully specify their wishes in writing."[1]

Unlike the IVF consent form, which patients generally find easy to complete because they've already decided to proceed, the embryo disposition form is more difficult because it requires them to make complicated and potentially emotional decisions. Intensely focused on their upcoming IVF cycles, patients may not have thought through what to do with surplus frozen embryos in the event of death or divorce, and this choice often catches them unawares, even if they're fairly well-informed about the IVF procedure. Yet, despite their research, many patients still aren't aware they'll have to make such choices. As Figure 10 explains, more patients (55% interview) were surprised by information on the embryo disposition forms than on the IVF consent documents (32%); these patients learned new information from this document. Deanna Douglas recalled, "[T]he rest of it, like the whole IVF process, I'd already Googled so extensively, and watched TV, and [did] all the research I possibly could." Others, like April Gonzalez, felt too buoyant to consider options carefully: "I felt sort of excited . . . we were on our way to going through the procedure. So I didn't really think a lot about what it meant to have extra embryos or kind of the ethical issues."

Many individuals find it surreal to choose the fates of nonexistent embryos—especially if they've never been pregnant and perhaps doubt they ever will. "I know we were capable . . . but some of it just seemed so out of the realm of reality. . . . The whole embryo thing itself is kind of sci-fi," said Nicole Bell. These feelings can make this decision seem less immediate and important.

Patients are initially mystified about why they have to contemplate worst-case scenarios. If IVF consent forms introduce the notion of distrust into proceedings, embryo disposition forms can inject an air of tragedy: "it felt really overwhelming to make that decision on the same day that you were just trying to start a process" (Sheri Lopez). The embryo disposition choice seems to negate patients' heartfelt reasons for undergoing IVF:

> I think the most surprising thing was the fact that they were asking that right off of the bat. When you go into it, it's like . . . "We're going to have a person physically make a baby for us." . . . You don't go in there thinking to yourself, "Well, is it going to work, is it not going to work . . . " you're like, "Well, wait a minute here; isn't it just automatic that we're going to have a kid because you're doing this, so why do we need to sign this page?"

Keira Wilkinson superstitiously felt signing such forms would be tantamount to inviting failure: "I wasn't excited about that [form] because I felt like I wanted that first round to work, so I . . . felt like if I signed that, then I was okay with it not working." For pessimistic patients, it's hard to contemplate one might ever have viable embryos at all: "You didn't have the possibility of human life before the IVF cycle; you just don't think about it. So now you have to think about this and make a good decision" (Heather Stewart).

Patients negotiate this weirdness in several ways. Some take a somber approach: "The most difficult document for us to sign w[as] what to do with the embryos should something happen. . . . It's just tough and then you kind of have to rationalize it in your head and talk it out" (Penny Hill). Others use humor: "My husband and I were joking about all that stuff. And he was saying that if I died he'd take the embryos, and I'm like, 'What, you're going to get married again and have my embryos put in some other woman?' I'm like, 'That's just crazy!'" (Racquel Kennedy). And some just dodge the bullet; Monica Hansen simply couldn't think that far ahead:

> I remember discussing it with my partner for about 15 seconds; we signed it and moved on. . . . We don't feel like, going into a cycle, that . . . it's going to result in divorce or something. Something could happen to one of us, but we're not thinking that far right now. We're thinking about whether or not we can even make an embryo. It's a very stressful thing, so to be thinking about what to do with the embryos afterwards. . . . It seems too far out and it just seems like . . . a distraction right now.

Even though completing these forms is a weird experience, patients appreciate the need for embryo disposition forms and realize they're important for different reasons than IVF consents: "I know it's necessary because they have to know what to do with it [the embryos]. I've seen TV and stuff where it's a huge fight . . . and I'm like, 'Oh, that's nasty—you need those forms'" (May Weiss). Patients understand these kinds of choices protect both themselves and their clinics: "It's logical for the clinic to have to know ahead of time what's to be expected with the embryos because they have to . . . act in such a way that protects them from being sued and also protects us from them doing something we didn't want them to do. . . . They're dealing with a very delicate, emotional [topic]. . . . It's different than going to get your appendix removed" (Luis Torres).

Moreover, completing the embryo disposition forms can provoke useful discussions between partners, and most patients readily accept this responsibility: "[we] chose to create these embryos, and we need to be responsible and mature enough to make decisions regarding their future" (Nicole Bell). These unfortunate events do happen, however hard it is to imagine on the cusp of an IVF cycle: "my biggest thing is the whole divorce thing, that they need to add these embryos to the divorce decree because this is their property. . . . And a lot of patients are like, 'Oh no, that's not going to happen.' And then sure enough, here comes the wife, three years later, trying to transfer those embryos, and [her] husband calls [and says], 'Don't transfer those embryos.' Every once in a while, we'll get a patient that does that" (New Patient Coordinator Aston Reinhold).

Couples usually work through these decisions together; 93% of surveyed patients discussed the embryo disposition form with their partners. "That was one of the things that we had a big long talk about," Elizabeth Alvarado recalled. Though most partners agree on a disposition (90% survey), these tandem efforts are especially important when they don't: "that one was . . . very helpful because I realized . . . that we . . . had different views about what we wanted to do with them. So it made us at least think about it and come to an agreement" (Christy Hoffman). Patients may even strategize about how to persuade their partners to choose a particular disposition. "I didn't want to dispose of them because of my age should something happen, so I let him open the conversation, and he was very supportive. I'd read through everything very carefully in case I had to give some kind of convincing argument" (Christy Hoffman).

Many factors play a role in choosing an embryo disposition; surveyed patients cited emotions (45%), partner's wishes (35%), morals (32%), religion (14%), a desire to help others (20%), and finances (3%). These concerns motivated patients to choose the option that most closely matched their values and needs. Most surveyed patients would give their embryos to their partners in the event of their death (43%) or, surprisingly, divorce (19%); the second most popular option was donation to research (14% death, 18% divorce), followed by destruction (8% death, 14% divorce), and donation to another patient (8% death, 7% divorce). Only a handful of patients would keep them frozen (3% death/divorce), or simply thaw them (2% death, 4% divorce),

Sometimes, patients have particular religious, moral, or ethical concerns about specific disposition options. "We had to look at our church's website and stuff to see what their stance was on it" (Madeline Lowe). Similarly, Jackie Carson's husband was wary about a few aspects of IVF: "my husband wasn't super comfortable with cryopreservation in general. And even still now, we have one embryo frozen. I think he just feels a little icky about it, and using it, and it being there in general. But he just kind of came to terms with the fact that that's how this IVF process works, and there are lots of babies born from frozen embryos and they're healthy and everything. He had more reservations up front than I did." In general, men are more reluctant to allow others to adopt their surplus embryos than women: "I wasn't opposed to donating embryos to another couple; he wasn't okay with that" (Jessica Frazier).

Deciding what to do with potential embryos prompts many individuals to humanize them in ways they might not have before and even make choices about them "like they were children" (Keira Wilkinson). Madeline Lowe remarked, "[I]t made you really think of these a[s] real human beings, and what would happen if we had leftovers." But other patients feel that their embryos are treated as so much old furniture. "It was kind of weird that your future children were property already," said Elizabeth Alvarado. Several feel these choices are unsavory, however necessary: "it's like doing a will; I mean, it's something that you don't really want to think about" (Sean Gray). Their emotional reactions to this decision often take patients unaware: "The one about what to do with the embryos, that stayed with me for a while. . . . [Choosing] 'Yes, I'm giving you permission to destroy the embryos' feels weird, because you're fighting so hard to get them. . . . Is this now like organ donation? Do I have to let other people know? 'By the way, call the fertility clinic and tell them to destroy our embryos?' Are they going to get a death notice? How does all of that work now?" (Simone Henry).

Humanizing embryos is especially common after patients have children. "Before I had a son, I would've been totally comfortable with [donation to research]. Now that would be a tougher question," acknowledged Luis Torres. Ashley Carpenter came to feel after her first's child's birth that her embryos were potential lives deserving a chance: "I think once you had a baby through IVF, and you realize that, if you have one child and three frozen embryos, I have three other humans, how much love you have for that child that was once just an embryo. I think that's really difficult to say, 'We're not going to give those a chance,' and my thought process is we're going to transfer every embryo we're going to get. . . . Statistically they're not all going to work, but we feel we need to give them all a shot." These changed feelings might translate into altered disposition preferences, as Phoebe Paul found: "now that I've had children, I know for a fact that the decision that I made on that form is one

I wouldn't make now that I actually have embryos. So, I guess I felt like I wasn't really equipped to make that decision."

And for couples who use donor gametes, the stakes are different if one partner is related to the embryos, and one is not. Tensions can arise if each partner asserts rights to choose dispositions based on genetic relationships versus intent to parent: "I'm pro-choice, so I pretty much feel [it's] my body, my choice [about what happens to the embryos]. . . . He kind of threw the monkey wrench into that belief when he was like, 'Yeah it's my sperm.' . . . I don't want to say that I backed down but I could . . . put myself in his shoes . . . and that's why I agreed, 'OK, we'll destroy it should we get divorced'" (Stella Madison).

Few dispositions evoke stronger feelings than embryo destruction. Patients are concerned about what this involves and about its ethical ramifications: "I know it's semantics, but the word 'destroy' is just really upsetting in that situation" (Simone Henry). Given these concerns, Rodney Hughes was uncomfortable with his embryo disposition form's unfeeling language: "I think I remember . . . the form being very cold in terms of having to execute these options. . . . [I]t was a very business[-like] deal." Joanne Johnson explained her unease: "If it fertilized but didn't look right to them, it'd be discarded, and I was horrified by that. I kind of felt like they were saying if it looked like it was developing into a disabled fetus, then they'd discard it. That was the only thing I was uptight about that, I didn't want to sign. . . . But when I worded it like that to them, they made me feel like that's not what it meant at all. I just wanted to make sure they weren't going to take a living embryo and destroy it."

Reproductive medical professionals also notice patients' ambivalence about choosing embryo destruction. According to Clinical Coordinator Mira Durham, "[t]hat would be [the] biggest thing that they ever have an issue with signing—destroying of the embryo." Moreover, donating embryos to research might be scary for those who want to know what is involved. Donation to research, for example, doesn't reveal anything about what the research is for, or what might happen to the embryo. "There wasn't a lot of information about [donating to research]. . . . And probably [because of] the fact that they didn't give a lot of information on that, [that choice] was never even an option" (Claudia Parsons). She imagined the worst possible outcomes: "You start thinking, 'Well, I don't want them to grow my embryo into a person, a baby, and harvest organs.'"

In fact, making this decision before embryos exist might make the process easier, however strange it feels: "I think [I made] as educated [a decision] as you could because there wasn't an emotional attachment to anything yet" (Jenna Moreno). Similarly, Ian Johnston reflected, "I don't think we were very emotional about that, because again, these were kind of made-up things that we could just handle on a completely objective basis. . . . It didn't have a face on it. It wasn't like we were giving up a child or something." Couples may, however, reconsider their choices after embryos do exist, if their previous choices haven't been carried out, so long as they complete a new embryo disposition form.

Though several patients find these disposition forms intriguing, novel, and unsettling, most don't find them difficult to understand, as shown in Figure 9. "I think it was black or white, you make one of the following choices. It was more just the idea of what we'd do in those situations that made it difficult to fill out," Brittany Watson reflected. Legalistic provisions can make disposition forms more obtuse: "It kind of felt like a lot of legal stuff, like, 'If you abandon the embryos, then this will happen.' So it wasn't quite as straightforward" (Racquel Kennedy). But patients' discomfort doesn't mean that they can't make this decision effectively, or that they choose badly. "I knew pretty much what I would do with them at that point; I don't think I was conflicted," remarked Krista Carrillo. In fact, most patients find this choice easy (55% survey, 58% interview). Moreover, most report having a good idea of what choice they wanted to make (87% survey)—and they make the right decision the first time. Looking back on their decision, the overwhelming majority would make the same decision again (95% survey).

But approximately one-third of patients felt they couldn't make an informed disposition decision. To some, deciding embryonic fates is a tragic choice with no good outcomes: "I don't think we'd have felt comfortable with any decision we made . . . just because there's . . . no good decision" (Andre Baker). Others feel they can't choose: "We sort of just had to wing it because we were there and we had to pick something" (Rachael Wilkerson). Many, like Angela Cox, feel unprepared: "I was concerned about signing it because I don't know what's going to happen. . . . I mean, is this written in stone? . . . I still signed it. I don't even understand why they have you sign that form at that time. I feel like that's . . . a decision that you have to make down the line. But how can you ask someone to destroy embryos when they don't even have any embryos and they don't even know if they're going to have a successful pregnancy?"

And Simone Henry felt her clinic chose a poor time—right before retrieval—to complete the embryo disposition form:

> We didn't know that we were going to be signing the paperwork. They said you were coming to see what the room looks like and to find out what the retrieval process is going to be like, and . . . we weren't anticipating taking in so much information. . . . She put that paperwork [in front of us] . . . [and] when the second piece of paper came in [she] said . . . "What do you want to happen to the other embryos later?" I hadn't even thought of that and . . . there are like these little boxes to check and I looked at it real quick. I said to my husband, "What do you want to do with them? . . . Do you want to destroy them if we die?" And he said, "Yeah, that sounds good," and that was about the extent of the conversation. . . . And I remember at that point realizing that I was definitely over my head. . . . I wished I was more prepared for that meeting, and I think, from that point of the meeting on, I really felt overwhelmed.

Placed in such a situation, some patients feel there's little they can do but consider disposition options fungible and select a "placeholder" disposition option they can later change:

> [W[hen they say, "We're going to do this IVF procedure," . . . then I'll listen to that and say, "Yes I consent to that," because that's definitely going to happen. But with the embryos, I mean, who knows if you get [embryos]. That's at the very last stage, and that's if you've had one or two or three kids and then you still have embryos left over, and I thought, "That's so far away and that might not ever happen, why do I need to make a decision about it?" . . . We didn't know what to answer; he was thinking one way, I was thinking another way. So I just said, "Let's put something down and they can't hold us to it." If we change our mind, I'm pretty sure when we get to it we can say we changed our mind, we want to do this instead. . . . We kind of closed our eyes and picked that box, to be honest. . . . We didn't really take it seriously. (Rachael Wilkerson)

But sometimes changed circumstances can also prompt patients to revisit their earlier disposition choices: "We made the decision that we'd donate them for research purposes to our physician's office. . . . Now I think my husband somewhat feels like that's kind of killing them. . . . We have a family member who's having . . . crisis-mode infertility because they've done multiple in vitro cycles without success. And so the notion has been brought up of donating embryos" (Silvia Spencer). But patients can only complete new embryo disposition forms and select new dispositions if they know of this option. Surprisingly, only 53% of surveyed patients knew that they could change their mind about their decision in the future, making this issue ripe for patient education.

CONCLUSION: WHEN FORMS FOLLOW FUNCTION

Consent forms have dual roles: educating patients and legally protecting clinics. These goals can reinforce each other when providers carefully prepare patients for informed-consent-as-ritual (through the relationships that comprise informed-consent-as-relationship), regard consent as a process and project, thoughtfully design consent points throughout cycles, use tools from multiple mediums, and answer patient questions. These goals clash, however, when providers see the informed consent project as a one-time, race-to-the-signature-line event. Then, patients might not have the benefit of a consent conversation and might be restricted to a single medium—written consent forms—that could be incomprehensible. Law, medical administration, and other bureaucracies emphasize consent forms, reinforcing this one-shot model. Patients and physicians are aware of the tensions between protection and education, bur resolve them in different ways; some see one purpose as dispositive, while others recognize consent is a delicate balancing of the two.

These tensions are woven throughout patients' and professionals' reflections on IVF consent and embryo disposition forms. IVF consent forms fulfill both legal, bureaucratic interests and medical necessity, and they resemble other commonly ridiculed forms, like HIPAA paperwork and mortgage packets. But embryo disposition forms are altogether different; here, patients are making decisions about something that's inert like property, but might feel more like their child. Embryos often seem precious because they're created through patients' intent if not their genetic materials, and patients feel obliged to make responsible decisions that might resemble nascent parental choices.

Whether or not patients sign them at the same time, IVF and embryo disposition forms are wedded together in the same consent process. They represent a marriage of the professional and personal, logistical and loving, bureaucratic and democratic, self-care and other-regard. While the IVF form maps the route to conception a patient must travel, choosing an embryo disposition is the closest she'll come to a baby before embryo transfer. Patients sign IVF consent forms because they've already decided to undergo IVF, not just because they've read and understand the documentation or participated in a consent conversation. For most, their signatures are pro forma confirmations of a choice made long ago. Patients' high motivation finds an outlet in completing their IVF consent forms as expeditiously as possible. But this doesn't mean they aren't informed, don't comprehend material information, or their choice is flawed and unreasoned. Instead, their experiences augur for a redefinition of "understanding," one predicated upon interaction and dialogue. Consent is often achieved verbally long before it is reduced to paper. It's striking, then, how things usually go so right within a system that sets them up to go so wrong.

In contrast, in choosing embryo dispositions, fertility patients must contemplate both the end of life and the end of love, just when they want to think about the beginnings of new life and new family structures. This form compels them to make a radical shift in thought, encouraging them to (re)consider opinions, values, and priorities, to contemplate beginnings, endings, and beginnings-in-endings. Patients must make real choices without overarching commitments, decisions more complex than proceeding with IVF or ceasing treatment. Nor are patients as likely to have researched or discussed embryo disposition options as they are to have investigated IVF consent details.

Thus, in transitioning from IVF consents to embryo disposition forms, informed-consent-as-ritual moves from what is foreign, sterile, formulaic, and distanced to what is personal and mysterious, refocusing from learning onto potential love. That is why patients agree that embryo disposition forms are different and feel more surreal. It isn't so much that embryo disposition forms matter *more* than IVF consents; rather, they matter in a *profoundly different way*—particularly for patients who have never undergone IVF or had viable eggs and embryos.

Of course, each form positions and engages its users in certain ways. Both are usually seen as "mundane documents" that "engender routine responses";[2] thus, "they and their consequences remain, in large part because of their very ordinariness, analytically invisible."[3] But at the same time as they educate patients and protect providers, consent documents are useful emotion management tools, particularly because they appear dry and devoid of emotion.

Law and medicine, as "rational" (and likely emotionally repressed) spaces, place a heavy burden on the shoulders of the informed consent project. Communicating information on risks and side effects means conveying descriptions of bodily invasion and violence, however therapeutic or necessary, potentially upsetting patients or inducing emotional reactions. Consent documents grapple with this task by sanitizing or de-emotionalizing potentially distressing information. Patients are asked to confront and work through this otherwise emotional subject matter by reading materials that place this violence at a safe distance through generalized statistics and a format that is impersonal, standardized, and authoritative—and therefore (ideally) reassuring. Nonetheless, consent forms are most effective when they engage patients on a more emotive level, simply because it's hard for patients to empathically extend themselves into a cold, clinical consent document. Bodies of text are very different from bodies of flesh, and scientific, statistical language literally drains the affect right out of most consent documents.

At some level, the informed consent project *is* a process involving blood, sweat, and tears. No consent tools should make patients fearful, which would be counterproductive to the informed consent project. Patients should be encouraged to engage more emotionally with treatment benefits, risks, and side effects to understand them. Informed-consent-as-ritual *should* make these risks more real, because some of the options patients consider can be horrible and scary. ART carries serious side effects, even if many are comparatively rare. Patients experience ovarian hyperstimulation, suffer terrible pain, and can potentially lose ovaries. They conceive multiples, lose their pregnancies, or give birth prematurely, with devastating results. Can current consent forms accurately convey these possibilities to that patient undergoing IVF who ardently wants to risk adverse outcomes by conceiving twins?

This is why it's difficult for clinically written IVF consent forms to achieve their stated purpose and why, paradoxically, embryo disposition forms might be more successful. Patients find it comparatively easy to consent to IVF because they want to become pregnant and haven't been able to conceive through other means. But choosing frozen embryos' fate engages patients on a different emotive level. The more challenging and more intimate embryo disposition decision in effect transfuses blood back into the consent process. Ironically, then, the most effective consent forms might be those that ask patients to confront the most difficult decisions.

Furthermore, we finally have our answer to the question of why informed-consent-as-ritual can fail in reproductive medicine: a failure to engage patients, whether through a personally relevant treatment decision, insufficient interaction, or a troubled treatment relationship. The overwhelming majority of patients report reading and understanding their consent forms, using them exactly as intended. But many *still* regard the consent ritual as unsound in the absence of interaction or a treatment relationship, demonstrating that informed consent's flaws extend beyond recall and comprehension. Simply put, informed-consent-as-relationship must be present to kindle faith in informed-consent-as-ritual, or the entire informed consent project might collapse.

Conclusion

Thinking outside the Signature Box

The past fifty years have seen a revolution in medical care—and even more dramatic shifts in our assumptions about childlessness. No longer are physicians supposed to make treatment decisions for patients. No longer must women and men who can't conceive face a life devoid of the children they so ardently desire. Now, individuals can choose from a continuum of infertility treatment options, from pills to hormones to IUI and IVF, and the choice is theirs to make. Doctors may frame the options, but they can't take away patients' right to determine their own course of treatment. Of course, to access this right, patients must be able to access IVF in the first place—a daunting prospect for many. Nonetheless, critics have questioned patients' and providers' capacities to make such reproductive decisions, charging that those capacities are undermined by false hopes in one context and greed in the other.

What these critics fail to provide is an alternative way to think about medical decision making. Many are instinctively critical of the market; they would prefer to see state- or insurance-subsidized options, together with greater overall regulation, to limit market forces' impact on fertility options. Others question patient's emotional competence because they distrust the choices women make. Some oppose IVF altogether or would prefer to see less emphasis on the biological tie between parents and children, encouraging adoption. Some voice concerns that many patients don't read, and even fewer understand, consent forms. But very few critics address how fertility treatment can be a collaboration, a partnership between patients and providers.

This book has explained how patients and providers can create such a partnership. It began by providing a unique vantage point into infertility's lived experience, illuminating not only what emotions are associated with infertility, but how these emotions affect decision making in conjunction with the relationships, institutional practices, and cultures in which treatment decision making is embedded. Because most individuals negotiating infertility spend much time and effort dealing with strong emotions, any account that omitted these emotional realities would be fatally flawed. Here, the voices of men and women who weather and treat infertility provide glimpses into these experiences. If nothing else, these reflections demonstrate that very little about the infertility experience is universal—except perhaps the need to decide what to do about it.

Professionals' and patients' experiences, then, illustrate what kind of collaborations are possible. They teach us that any effective collaboration must rest on trust. Indeed, the moral of these accounts is that true partners *trust generously*. Patients should trust themselves and their informed decision-making skills. Doctors should trust patients and partner with them in making effective treatment decisions. Interpersonal trust is more transformative and worthwhile—and scarier—than trust in paper. For "informed consent" to be real and for doctors and patients to build effective partnerships, experts must design medical decision-making procedures to enhance, not undermine, the trust between prospective parents and medical providers. These procedures need to explain matters in ways that sustain trust through what, for many, will be setbacks, failures, or adverse outcomes, which themselves occasion new and often disturbing decisions.

We can, and must, challenge the conventional assumption that consent documents support and protect patient autonomy. Relationships and collaboration depend on trust, and that is the support on which patients depend, not consent documentation. Formal documents do play a role in creating records of what took place, and in creating occasions for conversation, but they can never be a substitute for decision making that more genuinely engages patients and establishes personal bonds between patients and providers. In capturing patients' perspectives, this book explains why consent tools fail for other reasons besides reading and comprehension and explores why the informed consent project nonetheless succeeds. These contributions are in their own quiet way sweeping and revolutionary: "telling it like it is" can be a powerful pathway to change. But change requires re-envisioning the medical decision-making process.

To escape from the vicious cycle of cynicism and complacency that currently undergirds consent forms' continued importance, we must realize that idealistic conceptions of "choice"—as elective, made from a confident position with head held high and chest thrust out—will likely never accurately describe informed consent experiences for most. Instead, we should acknowledge that "muddling through" and "getting it out of the way" is what most often constitute consent's humdrum reality. Patients can agree to treatment in all sorts of ways, including ways we conventionally think of as empowered, or necessarily informed, so long as they know the risks that their choices entail. Moreover, we must acknowledge that many choices that patients face are constrained at best or coerced at worst—not by providers, but by the very reasons they're seeking treatment, whether for infertility or another health condition.

The most terrible resolution to the current problem would be to maintain our consent expectations, effectively agreeing to lower them universally and permanently from a confident, forthright affirmation to a muddling determination to complete a bothersome, tedious consent form. Yet, this is the road we're currently traveling. If patients don't emotionally engage with consent documents, it is difficult to say that they trust or respect them, their informative potential, their protective capacities, or perhaps even their providers—a key source of rupture not only in the fabric of the informed consent project but also potentially in provider-patient relations.

If the reason we're traveling this fruitless path is that we can't identify a better one, we can find a more promising route by assessing why so many feel that the informed consent project is ineffective or deserves our cynicism. This, in turn, requires a commitment to responsive reform and a willingness to change patients' and professionals' relationships with consent documents and other aids. This book has attempted to spark these processes by exposing documents' "messy and excessive potentialities."[1] Fortunately, tools that are necessary but ineffective may be recrafted. Current consent documents are like a hammer with a tiny pinpoint of a head that hits the nail squarely two attempts in ten, on average—only a fool would continue to use this device. A revised consent tool might incorporate much of the same informational content into an entirely different medium, like a well-designed multimedia informed consent application.

Multimedia informed consent has many advantages over documents, even for recall and comprehension. Visual cues, animation, and diagrams are easily integrated into multimedia formats, weaving together a narrative of disparate topics[2] and facilitating better recall.[3] Animation conveys time and dynamic processes better than static images and is especially useful for describing abstract principles.[4] Individuals with lower literacy skills can more easily understand complex concepts through animation,[5] and audio and graphics can decrease anxiety as well.[6] Moreover, computer interventions allow for individualized experiences; a computer program may enable patients to obtain more information on topics of their choice, while requiring them to proceed along particular information routes.[7] Patients might also customize interventions to accommodate anxiety or learning disorders. Finally, multimedia applications can require patients to complete quizzes (that better support recall and provide them with instant feedback) in order to move through the program.[8] Quiz results can also help physicians identify which topics confuse patients, so that they can focus on these issues later in consent conversations.[9] Multimedia consent applications might also offer convenience: patients could complete that portion of the consent process outside the clinic and submit questions to their providers before conversations.[10]

But poorly designed multimedia applications might duplicate current consent documents' weaknesses. Applications can't take too long to complete, lest patients find them tedious;[11] they should engage patients' attention without scaring them, and they should walk the fine line between repetition and boredom.[12] Important information should be placed closer to the beginning, lest patients' attention flag.

Finally, we must also avoid models of doctor-patient relationship that place the entire decision-making burden on patients. Recent research suggests that the most effective—and most accurate—models are based upon shared decision making, that is, in which patients and physicians make decisions together.[13] Consent aids should be starting points for interpersonal patient-provider conversations, and never their substitutes.

Sadly, perhaps the biggest obstacle we must overcome in reforming the informed consent project is inertia. We often permit lay and professional cultures to perpetuate misunderstandings of how effective decisions are made, especially the idea that emotions dilute reason and hamper decision making. We also continue to embrace outmoded assumptions— like the idea that consent documents alone are helpful and enhance trust—despite patients' and professionals' experiences to the contrary. These problems aren't just localized to reproductive endocrinology, but pervade all medical fields. Across the board, our inaction is retarding progress in patient education and provider relationships, thereby undermining effective decision making. Active research partnerships between patients, providers, and other experts will promote knowledge of what competency truly involves in various contexts and for diverse individuals, pushing past stereotypes to cultivate more accurate understandings of how and when emotions harm decision making.

With these reforms will come an awareness that, in our imperfect humanity, we are all equally subject to emotions and their impact on medical decisions. Our human frailties mean that all of us will eventually have to make such choices for ourselves and our loved ones. When we do, likely under arduous and heartrending circumstances, we'll want our wishes to be carried out, and we hope that their authority will be undiminished by allegations of incapacity.

Methodology

In this research project, I relied on three primary bodies of data: an online survey generating 267 responses, 127 interviews with individuals who had undergone IVF in the last five years, and 84 interviews with reproductive medicine professionals, including REs, nurses, clinic staff, and mental health professionals. Altogether, this research project involved 478 participants. All participants quoted in this book were given aliases in order to protect their identities. I personally conducted all interviews either over the phone or in person between 2011 and 2014. Professional interviews ranged in length from less than 45 minutes to 3 hours, with an average length of 1.5 hours.

In my original research, I wanted to focus on the experiences of patients and professionals who had worked through and treated infertility, drilling deep into their descriptions and making meaningful comparisons between them. Open-ended qualitative interviews allowed me to conversationally guide participants through discussions of key experiences while allowing them complete freedom of response. I developed an online survey instrument for patients that tracked the interpersonal interview, both to obtain a larger sample for quantitative analyses and to initiate comparisons between the two populations to identify where and why meaningful distinctions might exist. Flexibility comes with a price; qualitative interviews were more costly than the surveys and required transcription and more time-consuming analysis. Through these mixed methods, I was able to obtain both informational quality and depth and high response quantity. I strove to make all interviews as conversational as possible, and I was aware that my own experiences with infertility and fertility treatment would influence this project. When participants inquired into my reasons for conducting this research, I deferred these questions to the end, when I briefly described my own experiences, always acknowledging that individuals' infertility experiences are unique yet share a number of common themes. I believe my own openness and enthusiasm for this inquiry allowed trust and confidence to develop within interview settings. All participants were asked for permission to audio record their interviews and signed appropriate consent forms. Completed interviews were transcribed and analyzed through the qualitative research software package Nvivo using grounded theory methodology, in which explanatory theories are developed through conducting research instead of testing preconceived hypotheses, allowing me to privilege participants' voices.[1]

To recruit reproductive medicine professionals, I relied on several methods, all based on self-selection. The most productive method was snowball sampling; I asked each professional I interviewed to identify others who might be interested in participating. I also obtained permission to visit clinics throughout the country, where I interviewed all willing employees over the course of one or two days. Finally, I also recruited participants through e-mail solicitations. In total, I interviewed 31 REs, two embryologists, one physician's assistant, one sonographer, 18 nurses, three lab technologists/directors, 10 clinical coordinators (for donor, IVF, nurse, new patient, and surgery coordination functions), 13 mental health professionals (all referred to as "psychologists" in the text), and five administrative staff members. No professional participants received any financial incentives to complete the interview. Interviews lasted between 20 minutes and 2 hours in length, with an average length of 35 minutes.

Only brief demographic data are presented for these individuals to preserve their anonymity. Participating REs worked in a variety of practice settings across the United States, including large, multiprovider practices, single-provider offices, and university clinics. Thirteen of the REs were women; the remaining 18 were male. All nurses and the vast majority of all other clinic personnel—in fact, all but one lab director and one donor coordinator—were female. This isn't surprising, given that the overwhelming percentages of nurses in women's health are themselves women (97.2%, according to a 2008 study[2]). The vast majority are white. Participating reproductive endocrinologists vary greatly in years since the completion of their medical degree from 6 to 53 years, with an average of 23.2 years.

Interviews for reproductive medicine professionals were divided into two sections, one that focused on treatment relationships and another centered on the informed consent process. The first half of the interview began with questions on the qualities comprising successful treatment relationships, the characteristics making patients easy or difficult to work with, and the presence of a mind-body connection in fertility care. These were followed by a few questions on how patients made treatment decisions, how providers viewed trust within the care relationship, and reactions to patient assertiveness. The second half of the interview addressing informed consent issues asked professionals to define "informed consent," to compare consent in reproductive medicine with consent in other medical contexts, to explain how they created and revised forms, to describe their consent protocols, and to discuss patient consent behaviors like asking questions or requesting changes to form provisions.

I recruited patients who agreed to complete online surveys and personal interviews by posting descriptions of the research project in various forums, including the RESOLVE infertility forum, listservs like the National Organization of Mothers of Twins, Inc. (NOMOTC), and blogs like "Stirrup Queens" (www.stirrup-queens.com). This recruitment method obviously skewed a few questions I asked about individuals' use of the Internet to research and cope with infertility. Since high percentages of patients undergoing IVF already engage in such activities,[3] however, I decided this was a reasonable price to pay for such wide exposure to potential participants, following other studies' examples.[4] All interview participants received a $25 Amazon gift certificate; survey participants were entered into a drawing to win one of several Amazon gift certificates.

Table 1 represents the breakdown of participants who completed online surveys and personal interviews, for a total of 394 patients. The table only reports the data total ("*n*") for those participants who answered a particular question, or to whom the question was applicable. Thus, the totals for each question reflect only those participants who answered that question.

The statistics for the survey and interview populations mirror each other in most respects. Both populations were overwhelmingly female (94.7% and 81.1%, respectively). Most participants in both samples were between 31 and 40 years of age (61.9% cumulatively); more interview participants were at least 41 years old (40.9% vs. 14.4%). The vast majority were also white (1.3%). Both samples featured similarly small numbers of minorities; 4.1% were Asian, 2.7% were Hispanic/Latino, 1.6% were multiracial, and 1.1% were African American. Members of both survey and interview populations were highly educated, with 89.3% having earned at least a bachelor's degree. Almost half (49.7%) had completed a graduate or professional degree. Of those sharing individual income data, most participants in both survey and interview populations (64.3% and 50%, respectively) earned more than $50,000 annually, with most falling in the $50,001 to $75,000 bracket.

Through these interviews, I intended to capture the diversity of infertility experiences, from initial emotional reactions to decision-making strategies, paying for treatment, treatment outcomes, relationships with providers, and informed consent, with emphasis on how patients perceived themselves and their roles within care relationships, the development of trust, and the influence of market forces. After an introductory battery of demographic questions, questions were directed toward infertility's personal impact (emotional consequences, feelings of control, infertility's effect on personal relationships, "patient personalities," coping behaviors, and patient research activities). The interview then shifted topics to pursuing fertility treatment and the clinical experience, including how patients chose care providers and their reactions to providers and clinic staff, how they paid for IVF, what emotions they felt throughout IVF cycles, whether they became pregnant, and the outcomes of their pregnancies (multiple birth, selective reduction, etc.). Patients were then asked how they felt about informed consent processes in general—when they began, who they protected, whether they were helpful or redundant, whether they learned new information. These were followed by a battery of related questions that ascertained patients' reactions to consent forms detailing IVF procedures versus other consent forms in which patients chose surplus frozen embryos' fates. The interview concluded with a section of questions on patients' attitudes toward their embryos, including emotional attachment, preferences about disposition, and attitudes toward donating embryos to other individuals.

TABLE I   CHARACTERISTICS OF PATIENTS SURVEYED AND INTERVIEWED

		Surveys		Interviews		Combined	
		N	%	N	%	N	%
Patient Sex							
Male		13	5%	24	19%	37	10%
Female		232	95%	103	81%	335	90%
	Total	245	100%	127	100%	372	100%
Patient Age							
22–25		7	3%	0	0%	7	2%
26–30		42	17%	3	2%	45	12%
31–35		87	36%	29	23%	116	31%
36–40		72	29%	41	32%	113	30%
41–45		33	13%	36	28%	69	19%
46–50		2	1%	16	13%	18	5%
50+		0	0%	2	2%	2	1%
Not Indicated		2	1%	0	0%	2	1%
	Total	245	100%	127	100%	372	100%
Patient Race/Ethnicity							
White		215	88%	116	91%	331	89%
African American		3	1%	1	1%	4	1%
Asian		13	5%	2	2%	15	4%
Hispanic/Latino		9	4%	1	1%	10	3%
Multiracial		0	0%	6	5%	6	2%
Other		0	0%	1	1%	1	0%
Not Indicated		5	2%	0	0%	5	1%
	Total	245	100%	127	100%	372	100%
Patient Highest Level of Education							
High School/GED		4	2%	3	2%	7	2%
Some College		14	6%	5	4%	19	5%
2 year Degree		12	5%	1	1%	13	3%
4 year Degree		97	40%	47	37%	144	39%
Master's		71	29%	51	40%	122	33%
PhD		21	9%	12	9%	33	9%
Professional		20	8%	6	5%	26	7%
Not Indicated		6	2%	2	2%	8	2%
	Total	245	100%	127	100%	372	100%
Patient Individual Income							
Less than $10K		18	7%	33	26%	51	14%
$10K–$25K		12	5%	4	3%	16	4%

$25K–$50K		54	22%	26	20%	80	22%
$50K–$75K		68	28%	32	25%	100	27%
$75K–$100K		35	14%	13	10%	48	13%
$100K–$125K		22	9%	11	9%	33	9%
More than $125K		27	11%	7	6%	34	9%
Not Indicated		9	4%	1	1%	10	3%
	Total	245	100%	127	100%	372	100%
Patient Religious							
Yes		119	49%	85	67%	204	55%
No		122	50%	42	33%	164	44%
Not Indicated		4	2%	0	0%	4	1%
	Total	245	100%	127	100%	372	100%
Patient Religious Preference							
Protestant		39	16%	56	44%	95	26%
Catholic		39	16%	21	17%	60	16%
Evangelical		12	5%	2	2%	14	4%
Jewish		10	4%	4	3%	14	4%
Muslim		1	0%	0	0%	1	0%
Mormon		3	1%	1	1%	4	1%
Buddhist		1	0%	1	1%	2	1%
Hindu		3	1%	0	0%	3	1%
Other		1	0%	7	6%	8	2%
Not Indicated		136	56%	35	28%	171	46%
	Total	245	100%	127	100%	372	100%
How Often Patient Attends Religious Services							
Less than 1x week		8	3%	3	2%	11	3%
Weekly		32	13%	28	22%	60	16%
1–2x per month		24	10%	24	19%	48	13%
Holidays		10	4%	4	3%	14	4%
Few times a year		38	16%	13	10%	51	14%
Don't attend		7	3%	54	43%	61	16%
Not Indicated		126	51%	1	1%	127	34%
	Total	245	100%	127	100%	372	100%
Patient Political Views							
Republican		45	18%	18	14%	63	17%
Democrat		66	27%	31	24%	97	26%
Independent		32	13%	16	13%	48	13%
Conservative		17	7%	14	11%	31	8%
Moderate		27	11%	9	7%	36	10%
Liberal		39	16%	34	27%	73	20%

(continued)

TABLE I *(continued)*

	Surveys		Interviews		Combined	
	N	%	N	%	N	%
Libertarian	8	3%	3	2%	11	3%
Don't care	0	0%	2	2%	2	1%
Not Indicated	11	4%	0	0%	11	3%
Total	245	100%	127	100%	372	100%
Patient Diagnosed as Infertile						
Yes	138	56%	102	80%	240	65%
No	32	13%	25	20%	57	15%
No, but partner is	40	16%	18	14%	58	16%
Yes, and partner is	31	13%	31	24%	62	17%
Patient Infertility Diagnosis						
Unexplained	34	14%	37	29%	71	19%
Female Factor	5	2%	41	32%	46	12%
Male Factor	6	2%	24	19%	30	8%
Both Factors	5	2%	31	24%	36	10%
Fallopian Tube	9	4%	7	6%	16	4%
Endometriosis	18	7%	15	12%	33	9%
Ovulation Dis.	5	2%	7	6%	12	3%
PCOS	18	7%	18	14%	36	10%
Poor Eggs	27	11%	4	3%	31	8%
Poor Sperm	17	7%	20	16%	37	10%
Sperm Delivery	10	4%	0	0%	10	3%
Cancer	5	2%	0	0%	5	1%
Dim. Ovar. Res.	12	5%	17	13%	29	8%
Other	0	0%	17	13%	17	5%
Patient Current Relationship Status						
Single/Never Married	1	0%	2	2%	3	1%
Committed Relatship	5	2%	0	0%	5	1%
Married	235	96%	125	98%	360	97%
Divorced	1	0%	0	0%	1	0%
Widowed	1	0%	0	0%	1	0%
Not Indicated	2	1%	0	0%	2	1%
Total	245	100%	127	100%	372	100%
Partner's Sex						
Male	163	67%	100	79%	263	71%
Female	8	3%	25	20%	33	9%
Not Indicated	74	30%	2	2%	76	20%
Total	245	100%	127	100%	372	100%

Partner's Age						
22–25	4	2%	1	1%	5	1%
26–30	17	7%	20	16%	37	10%
31–35	74	30%	40	31%	114	31%
36–40	67	27%	29	23%	96	26%
41–45	44	18%	18	14%	62	17%
45–50	9	4%	9	7%	18	5%
51–55	5	2%	1	1%	6	2%
56+	2	1%	2	2%	4	1%
Not Indicated	23	9%	7	6%	30	8%
Total	245	100%	127	100%	372	100%

Partner's Race / Ethnicity						
White	198	81%	111	87%	309	83%
African American	4	2%	1	1%	5	1%
Asian	7	3%	0	0%	7	2%
Hispanic/Latino	13	5%	3	2%	16	4%
Pacific Islander	5	2%	1	1%	6	2%
Am.In./Alas.Nat.	5	2%	0	0%	5	1%
Multiracial	0	0%	6	5%	6	2%
Other	0	0%	1	1%	1	0%
Not Indicated	13	5%	4	3%	17	5%
Total	245	100%	127	100%	372	100%

Partner's Highest Level of Education						
Less than High School	2	1%	0	0%	2	1%
High School / GED	12	5%	10	8%	22	6%
Some College	29	12%	3	2%	32	9%
2 yr Degree	21	9%	5	4%	26	7%
4 yr Degree	94	38%	50	39%	144	39%
Masters	54	22%	39	31%	93	25%
PhD	15	6%	7	6%	22	6%
Professional	10	4%	6	5%	16	4%
Not Indicated	8	3%	7	6%	15	4%
Total	245	100%	127	100%	372	100%

Partner's Individual Income						
Less than $10K	8	3%	11	9%	19	5%
$10K – $25K	6	2%	3	2%	9	2%
$25K – $50K	45	18%	31	24%	76	20%
$50K – $75K	56	23%	28	22%	84	23%
$75K – $100K	48	20%	20	16%	68	18%
$100K – $125K	32	13%	9	7%	41	11%
More than $125K	27	11%	18	14%	45	12%
Not Indicated	23	9%	7	6%	30	8%
Total	245	100%	127	100%	372	100%

(continued)

TABLE I *(continued)*

	Surveys		Interviews		Combined	
	N	%	N	%	N	%
Partner Religious						
Yes	99	40%	69	54%	168	45%
No	138	56%	55	43%	193	52%
Not Indicated	8	3%	3	2%	11	3%
Total	245	100%	127	100%	372	100%
Partner's Religious Preference						
Protestant	33	13%	47	37%	80	22%
Catholic	36	15%	22	17%	58	16%
Evangelical	12	5%	2	2%	14	4%
Jewish	12	5%	2	2%	14	4%
Muslim	1	0%	0	0%	1	0.3%
Mormon	3	1%	1	1%	4	1%
Buddhist	2	1%	0	0%	2	1%
Hindu	3	1%	0	0%	3	1%
Other/None	24	10%	5	4%	29	8%
Don't know	4	2%	0	0%	4	1%
Not Indicated	115	47%	48	38%	163	44%
Total	245	100%	127	100%	372	100%
How Often Partner Attends Religious Services						
Less than 1x week	11	4%	5	4%	16	4%
Weekly	25	10%	25	20%	50	13%
1–2x per month	16	7%	20	16%	36	10%
Holidays	15	6%	3	2%	18	5%
Few times a year	32	13%	14	11%	46	12%
Don't attend	36	15%	51	40%	87	23%
Not Indicated	110	45%	9	7%	119	32%
Total	245	100%	127	100%	372	100%
Partner's Political Views						
Republican	63	26%	19	15%	82	22%
Democrat	57	23%	26	20%	83	22%
Independent	29	12%	15	12%	44	12%
Conservative	16	7%	20	16%	36	10%
Moderate	24	10%	8	6%	32	9%
Liberal	21	9%	21	17%	42	11%
Libertarian	14	6%	1	1%	15	4%
Other	8	3%	3	2%	11	3%
Not Indicated	13	5%	14	11%	27	7%
Total	245	100%	127	100%	372	100%

Partner Diagnosed as Infertile						
Yes	57	23%	64	50%	121	33%
No	80	33%	60	47%	140	38%
Not Indicated	108	44%	3	2%	111	30%
Total	245	100%	127	100%	372	100%
Partner's Infertility Diagnosis						
Unexplained	14	6%	12	9%	26	7%
Female Factor	2	1%	0	0%	2	1%
Male Factor	31	13%	40	31%	71	19%
Both Factors	2	1%	0	0%	2	1%
Fallopian Tube	0	0%	1	1%	1	0%
Endometriosis	5	2%	5	4%	10	3%
Ovulation Dis.	0	0%	1	1%	1	0%
PCOS	3	1%	4	3%	7	2%
Poor Eggs	3	1%	1	1%	4	1%
Poor Sperm	35	14%	15	12%	50	13%
Sperm Delivery	21	9%	0	0%	21	6%
Cancer	6	2%	0	0%	6	2%
Dim. Ovar. Res.	0	0%	3	2%	3	1%
Other	4	2%	1	1%	5	1%

SOURCE: Jody Lyneé Madeira

Notes

PROLOGUE

1. American Society for Reproductive Medicine, "Oversight of Assisted Reproductive Technology," *ASRM Bull.* 12, no. 18 (2010): 4–11. See also Naomi R. Cahn, *Test Tube Families: Why the Fertility Market Needs Legal Regulation* (New York: New York University Press, 2009), 1.

2. Resolve, *The Costs of Infertility Treatment*, http://www.resolve.org/family-building-options/making-treatment-affordable/the-costs-of-infertility-treatment.html?referrer=https://www.google.com/

3. Fifteen states (Arkansas, California, Connecticut, Hawaii, Illinois, Louisiana, Maryland, Massachusetts, Montana, New Jersey, New York, Ohio, Rhode Island, Texas, and West Virginia) have legally required insurers to cover or offer coverage for infertility diagnosis and treatment. See Resolve, *Infertility Coverage in Your State,* http://www.resolve.org/family-building-options/insurance_coverage/state-coverage.html?referrer=https://www.google.com/

4. Tom L. Beauchamp and James F. Childress, *Principles of Biomedical Ethics,* 5th ed. (New York: Oxford University Press, 2001), 79, 81. See also Nancy E. Kass, et al., "An Intervention to Improve Cancer Patients' Understanding of Early-Phase Clinical Trials," *IRB Ethics & Hum. Res.* 31, no. 3 (2009): 1–10; 1.

5. Beauchamp and Childress, *Principles of Biomedical Ethics,* 79, 81.

6. Linda Tetzlaff, "Consumer Informatics in Chronic Illness," *J. Am. Med. Informatics Assoc.* 4, no. 4 (1997): 285–300; 285, 294.

7. Yael Navaro-Yashin, "Make-Believe Papers, Legal Forms and the Counterfeit: Affective Interactions Between Documents and People in Britain and Cyprus," *Anthropological Theory* 7, no. 1 (2007): 79–98; 79.

8. Annelise Riles, "Introduction: In Response," in *Documents: Artifacts of Modern Knowledge,* ed. Annelise Riles (Ann Arbor: University of Michigan Press, 2006), 3.

9. Ibid.

10. Ibid.

11. Many excellent books and articles describe reproductive markets. See, e.g., Debora Spar, *The Baby Business: How Money, Science, and Politics Drive the Commerce of Conception* (Boston: Harvard Business School Press, 2006), 33; Debra Satz, *Why Some Things Should Not Be for Sale: The Moral Limits of Markets* (New York: Oxford University Press, 2010); Michele Bratcher Goodwin, ed., *Baby Markets: Money and the New Politics of Creating Families* (New York: Cambridge University Press, 2010); Rene Almeling, *Sex Cells: The Medical Market for Eggs and Sperm* (Berkeley: University of California Press, 2011); Kara Swanson, *Banking on the Body: The Market in Blood, Milk, and Sperm in Modern America* (Cambridge, MA: Harvard University Press, 2014); Kimberly D. Kraweic, "Sunny Samaritans and Egomaniacs: Price-Fixing in the Gamete Market," *L. & Contemp. Probs.* 72 (2009): 59–90.

12. Robert Putnam, *Bowling Alone: The Collapse and Revival of American Community* (New York: Simon & Schuster, 2000), 136.

13. Ibid., 137.

CHAPTER 1

1. Alice D. Domar, Patricia C. Zuttermeister, and Richard Friedman, "The Psychological Impact of Infertility: A Comparison with Patients with Other Medical Conditions," *J. Psychosomatic Obstetrics & Gynecology* 14 (1993): 45–52.

2. Rachel Cusk, "Rachel Cusk Reviews Two Books about Assisted Reproduction," *New York Times* (Sept. 2, 2016), https://www.nytimes.com/2016/09/04/books/review/rachel-cusk-reviews-two-books-about-assisted-reproduction.html?_r=o

3. Ellen Waldman, "Disputing over Embryos: Of Contracts and Consents," *Ariz. St. L.J.* 32 (2000): 897–940, 923–24.

4. See Gay Becker, "Hope for Sale: Trade and Consumption of Techniques of Medically Assisted Reproduction in the United States," *Soc. Sci. & Health* 18, no. 4 (2000): 105–126.

5. Liza Mundy, *Everything Conceivable: How Assisted Reproduction Is Changing Men, Women, and the World* (New York: Alfred A. Knopf Press, 2007), 190, 201.

6. Ibid., 242.

7. Deborah Spar, *The Baby Business: How Money, Science, and Politics Drive the Commerce of Conception* (Boston: Harvard Business School Press, 2006), 33.

8. For instance, Dr. Michael Kamrava, who transferred 12 embryos into Nadya Suleman in 2008, later lost his medical license for "gross negligence." Alan Duke, "Nadya Suleman's Doctor Loses California Medical License," CNN (June 2, 2011), http://www.cnn.com/2011/US/06/01/california.octuplets.doctor.revoked/

9. Mundy, *Everything Conceivable*, 239.

10. See Naomi R. Cahn and Jennifer M. Collins, "Eight Is Enough," *Nw. U. L. Rev. Colloquy* 103 (2009): 501–513; Kimberly D. Kraweic, "Why We Should Ignore the 'Octomom,'" *Nw. U. L. Rev. Colloquy* 104 (2009): 120–131.

11. Jody Lyneé Madeira, "Woman Scorned?: Resurrecting Infertile Women's Decision-Making Autonomy," *Md. L. Rev.* 71 (2012): 339–410, 347.

12. Anthony Damasio, *Descartes' Error: Emotion, Reason, and the Human Brain* (New York: HarperCollins, 1994), 167–168.

13. Gay Becker, *Disrupted Lives: How People Create Meaning in a Chaotic World* (Berkeley: University of California Press, 2006), 4.

14. For an excellent discussion of narrative and infertility, see Sarah Franklin, *Embodied Progress: A Cultural Account of Assisted Conception* (New York, Routledge, 1997), 12–13.

15. Isabelle Blanchette and Anne Richards, "The Influence of Affect on Higher Level Cognition: A Review of Research on Interpretation, Judgment, Decision Making and Reasoning," *Cognition & Emotion* 24, no. 4 (2010): 561–95, 562.

16. Ibid., 587.

17. Jennifer Lerner et al., "Emotion and Decision Making," *Ann. Rev. of Psychol.* 66 (2015): 799–823, 815.

18. Ibid., 169.

19. Ibid., 166.

20. Ibid., 172.

21. Ibid., 171.

22. Ibid.

23. Damasio refers to this as the "somatic marker hypothesis." Damasio, *Descartes' Error*, 173.

24. Ibid., 174.

25. Ibid., 196, 201.

26. Blanchette and Richards, "Influence of Affect," 577.

27. Norbert Schwarz, "Emotion, Cognition and Decision Making," *Cognition & Emotion* 14, no. 4 (2000): 433–440, 436.

28. Peter H. Ditto, Nikki A. Hawkins, and David A. Pizzaro, "Imagining the End of Life: On the Psychology of Advance Medical Decision Making," *Motivation & Emotion* 29, no. 4 (2005): 475–96, 481, 491–92.

29. Schwarz, "Emotion, Cognition and Decision Making," 437.

30. Lerner, "Emotion and Decision Making," 812.

31. Ibid.

32. Tara E. Power, Leora C. Swartzman, and John W. Robinson, "Cognitive-Emotional Decision Making (CEDM): A Framework of Patient Medical Decision Making," *Patient Educ. & Counseling* 83 (2011): 163–69, 163.

33. Ibid., 164.

34. Ibid., 163, 165.

35. Amanda D. Angie, "The Influence of Discrete Emotions on Judgement and Decision Making: A Meta-analytic Review," *Cognition & Emotion* 25, no. 8 (2011): 1393–1422, 1395.

36. Lerner, "Emotion and Decision Making," 808.

37. Ibid., 805.

38. Angie, "Influence of Discrete Emotions," 1395.

39. Schwarz, "Emotion, Cognition and Decision Making," 433.

40. Lerner, "Emotion and Decision Making," 808.

41. Schwarz, "Emotion, Cognition and Decision Making," 435.

42. Angie, "Influence of Discrete Emotions," 1396.

43. Lerner, "Emotion and Decision Making," 805.

44. Ibid., 1395.

45. Ibid., 1395–96.

46. Schwarz, "Emotion, Cognition and Decision Making," 434.

47. Lerner, "Emotion and Decision Making," 808; Angie, "Influence of Discrete Emotions," 1395.

48. Lisa G. Aspinwall, "The Psychology of Future-Oriented Thinking: From Achievement to Proactive Coping, Adaptation, and Aging," *Motivation and Emotion* 29, no. 4 (Dec. 2005): 203–235, 204.

49. Lerner, "Emotion and Decision Making," 806.

50. Schwarz, "Emotion, Cognition and Decision Making," 435–36.

51. As Franklin states, infertility is "not a seamless trajectory, but a series of reframings." Franklin, Embodied Progress, 13.

CHAPTER 2

1. Sarah Franklin traces "what ubiquitously came to be known as the 'desperate' infertile couple" back into the 1980s. Sarah Franklin, *Embodied Progress: A Cultural Account of Assisted Conception* (New York: Routledge, 1997), 89–90. Naomi Pfeffer has also noted that "the modern representation of infertility" centers around desperation. Naomi Pfeffer, *The Story and the Syringe: Political History of Reproductive Medicine* (Cambridge, MA: Polity Press, 1993), 160.

2. Rachel P. Maines, *The Technology of Orgasm: "Hysteria," the Vibrator, and Women's Sexual Satisfaction* (Baltimore, MD: John Hopkins University Press, 2001); Andrew Scull, *The Disturbing History of Hysteria* (New York: Oxford University Press, 2012).

3. Chris Summers, "The Women Who Kill for Babies," BBC News (October, 27, 2007), http://news.bbc.co.uk/2/hi/americas/6990419.stm; Edecio Martinez, "Korena Roberts Pleads Guilty to Murdering Pregnant Woman, Cutting Baby from Womb," CBS News (October 7, 2010), http://www.cbsnews.com/news/korena-roberts-pleads-guilty-to-murdering-pregnant-woman-cutting-baby-from-womb/.

4. See Brief for Amici Curiae Women Who Have Had Abortions and Friends of Amici Curiae in Support of Appellees, *Webster v. Reprod. Health Servs.*, 492 U.S. 490 (1989) (No. 88–605) (including descriptions of women's experiences with illegal abortions, in which they characterize themselves as desperate and vulnerable); Richard Delgado and Judith Droz Keyes, "Parental Preferences and Selective Abortion: A Commentary on *Roe v. Wade, Doe v. Bolton*, and the Shape of Things to Come," *Wash. U. L.Q.* 2 (1974): 203–226; 224 n.115. Images of desperate women seeking abortions still populate areas of abortion scholarship where greater abortion access is sought for certain groups, such as minors. See, e.g., Brian Z. Tamanaha, "Good Casuistry and Bad Casuistry: Resolving the Dilemmas Faced by Catholic Judges," *U. St. Thomas L.J.* 4, no. 2 (2006): 269–279; 277.

5. For a discussion of the politicization of emotion, see Michalinos Zembylas, "Mobilizing Anger for Social Justice: The Politicization of the Emotions in Education," *Teaching Educ.* 18, no. 1 (March 2007): 15–28; 17.

6. Charis Thompson describes a "monopoly of desperation" that arises from "the intersection of private struggles, the imperatives of the private sector, and autonomous medical research" that produces "extremely focused patient demand for treatment," and allows "physicians, patients, activists, and drug companies . . . to forge collective interests." Charis Thompson, *Making Parents: The Ontological Choreography of Reproductive Technologies* (Cambridge, MA: MIT Press, 2007), 240–41, 265.

7. Merriam Webster Dictionary Online, "Desperation," http://www.merriam-webster.com/dictionary/desperation

8. Herbert Hendin et al., "Desperation and Other Affective States in Suicidal Patients," *Suicide & Life-Threatening Behav.* 24, no. 4 (Winter 2004): 386–94; 388.

9. Alan Blum, "On the Phenomenology of Desperation," *Soc. Q.* 37, no. 4 (Autumn 1996): 673–98; 678.

10. Ibid., 674.

11. Ibid., 690, 694.

12. Charles L. Bosk, "Obtaining Voluntary Consent for Research in Desperately Ill Patients," *Med. Care* 40, no. 9 (Sept. 2002): 64–68; 68.

13. See note 4. See also Andrea Dworkin, "*Abortion*, Chapter 3, Right-Wing Women," *Law & Ineq.* 1 (1983): 95–120, 95; Margie Ripper, "Abortion: The Shift in Stigmatisation from Those Seeking Abortion to Those Providing It," *Health Soc. Rev.* 10, no. 2 (2001): 65–77, 66; Ruth Roemer, Editorial, "The Right to Choose Abortion," *Am. J. Pub. Health* 64, no. 8 (1974): 751; Lynn D. Wardle, "Rethinking *Roe v. Wade*," *BYU L. Rev.* (1985): 231–264, 240.

14. See www.womendeservebetter.com.

15. See, generally, Reva B. Siegel, "The New Politics of Abortion: An Equality Analysis of Women-Protective Abortion Restrictions," *U. Ill. L. Rev.* (2007): 991–1054; Reva B. Siegel, "The Right's Reasons: Constitutional Conflict and the Spread of Women-Protective Antiabortion Argument," *57 Duke L. J.* (2008): 1641–92.

16. See Jody Lyneé Madeira, "Woman Scorned?: Resurrecting Infertile Women's Decision-Making Autonomy," *Md. L. Rev.* 71 (2010): 339–410, 347.

17. Evelyn Parsons and Paul Atkinson, "Lay Constructions of Genetic Risk," *Soc. of Health & Illness* 14, no. 4 (1992): 437–455; 445.

18. Ibid., 437.

19. Martha Nussbaum, *Women and Human Development: The Capabilities Approach* (New York: Cambridge University Press, 2000), 114.

20. Martha Ertman discusses a "Plan B reality," observing that some choices "border on coercion" and that choice is not stable, so that once unattractive options can become highly desirable. Martha M. Ertman, *Love's Promises: How Formal and Informal Contracts Shape All Kinds of Families* (Boston: Beacon Press, 2016), xiv–xv.

21. See also Franklin, *Embodied Progress*, 183.

22. Sarah Franklin observed a similar growth in desire to conceive in the patients she interviewed, and noted that IVF creates hope, which then causes desperation. Franklin, *Embodied Progress*, ibid.

CHAPTER 3

1. Tami Quinn, Beth Heller, and Jeanie Lee Bussell, *Fully Fertile: A Holistic 12-Week Plan for Optimal Fertility* (Forres, Scotland: Findhorn Press 2010), 10.

2. The "vast majority" of women also believe that depression and anxiety decrease fertility. H.S. Hoff, N.M. Crawford, and J.E. Mersereau, "Mental Health Disorders in Infertile Women: Prevalence, Perceived Effect on Fertility, and Willingness for Treatment for Anxiety and Depression," *Fertility & Sterility* 104, no. 3 (Sept. 2015): e357.

3. See, e.g., Koen Demyttenaere et al., "Coping Style and Depression Level Influence Outcome in In Vitro Fertilization," *Fertility & Sterility* 69, no. 6 (June 1998): 1026–1033; E. Breuer et al., "Depression at the Beginning of Fertility Treatment and Its Effects on IVF Outcomes," *Fertility & Sterility* 92, no. 3 (Sept. 2009): S130; H. Matsubayashi, "Anxiety and Depression Are Negatively Correlated with ART Success," *Fertility & Sterility* 96, no. 3 (Sept. 2011): S153; Carolyn E. Cesta et al., "Depression, Anxiety, and Antidepressant Treatment in Women: Association with In Vitro Fertilization Outcome," *Fertility & Sterility* 105, no. 6 (2016): 1594–1602.

4. Demyttenaere et al., "Coping Style and Depression Level," 1027.

5. Ibid.

6. I. Wirtberg et al., "Life 20 Years After Unsuccessful Infertility Treatment," *Human Reproduction* 22, no. 2 (2007): 598–604.

7. Linda Tetzlaff, "Consumer Informatics in Chronic Illness," *J. Am. Med. Informatics Assoc.* 4, no. 4 (1997): 285–300; 285, 297.

8. Ibid.

9. Ibid., 285–300.

CHAPTER 4

1. Jain Tarun, Bernard L. Harlow, and Mark D. Hornstein, "Insurance Coverage and Outcomes of In Vitro Fertilization," *New Eng. J. Med.* 347 (2002): 661–666.

2. RESOLVE/Mercer Health and Benefits LLC, *Employer Experience With, and Attitudes Toward, Coverage of Infertility Treatment* (2006), at http://familybuilding.resolve.org/site/DocServer/Mercer_-_Resolve_Final_report.pdf?docID=4361.

3. Jim Hawkins, "Financing Fertility," *Harv. J. on Legis.* 47 (2010): 115–65, 119, 133–34.

4. Ibid., 133–34.

5. For example, these expectations could be subject to the halo effect (where one's overall impression of a subject influences one's feelings or thoughts about that subject's character or properties), or confirmation bias (where one is prone to understand new evidence as confirmation of existing beliefs).

6. Louise Aronson, "'Good' Patients and 'Difficult' Patients—Rethinking Our Definitions," *New Eng. J. Med.* 369 (Aug. 29, 2013): 796–97.

CHAPTER 5

1. A dilation and curettage (D&C) is a procedure that removes tissue from inside a woman's uterus, usually performed to treat heavy bleeding or to evacuate the uterine lining after a miscarriage or abortion.

2. Liberty Walther Barnes, *Conceiving Masculinity: Male Infertility, Medicine, and Identity* (Philadelphia: Temple University Press, 2014), 103, 139.

3. See generally Miriam Zoll, *Cracked Open: Liberty, Fertility, and the Pursuit of High-Tech Babies* (Northampton, MA: Interlink Books, 2013).

4. The Health Insurance Portability and Accountability Act of 1996 (HIPAA) (P.L. No. 104–191, 110 Stat. 1938 (1996)) was passed by Congress in 1996 to assist patients in keeping their health care information private.

CHAPTER 6

1. See Victoria L. Brescoll and Eric Luis Uhlmann, "Can an Angry Woman Get Ahead? Status Conferral, Gender, and Expression of Emotion in the Workplace," *Psychol. Sci.* 19, no. 3 (March 2008): 268–75; Melissa Williams and Larissa Tiedens, "The Subtle Suspension of Backlash: A Meta-Analysis of Penalties for Women's Implicit and Explicit Dominance Behavior," *Psychol. Bull.* 142, no. 2 (2016): 165–97.

2. See, generally, Carl E. Schneider, *The Practice of Autonomy: Patients, Doctors, and Medical Decisions* (New York: Oxford University Press, 1998).

3. ASRM Practice Committee, "Criteria for Number of Embryos to Transfer: A Committee Opinion," *Fertility & Sterility* 99, no. 1 (Jan. 2013): 44–46.

CHAPTER 7

1. *Schloendorff v. Soc. of NY Hosp.*, 105 N2d 92, 93 (NY 1914) (overruled on other grounds by *Bing v. Thinig*, 143 N.E.2d 3, 7–8 (NY 1957)).

2. Carl Schneider, "HIPAA-cracy," *Hastings Center Rep.* 36, no. 1 (Jan.–Feb. 2006): 10, 11.

3. Tom L. Beauchamp and James F. Childress, *Principles of Biomedical Ethics*, 5th ed. (New York: Oxford University Press, 2001), 79, 81.

4. Ibid.

5. Ibid.

6. See Nancy E. Kass et al., "An Intervention to Improve Cancer Patients' Understanding of Early-Phase Clinical Trials," *IRB Ethics & Hum. Res.* 31, no. 3 (2009): 1.

7. Ibid.

8. See Gordon Willis, "Cognitive Interviewing as a Tool to Improve the Informed Consent Process," *J. of Empirical Res. on Hum. Res. Ethics* 1, no. 1 (2006): 9–23, 9.

9. See ibid.

10. See Yarl Schenker and Alan Meisel, "Informed Consent in Clinical Care: Practical Considerations in the Effort to Achieve Ethical Goals," *JAMA* 305, no. 11 (2011): 1130–1131, 1130.

11. Rupert Hodder, *Emotional Bureaucracy* (New York: Taylor & Francis, 2011), 6, 10.

12. Margaret Gerteis et al., *Through the Patient's Eyes: Understanding and Promoting Patient-Centered Care* (San Francisco: Jossey Bass, 2002), 281.

13. Hodder, *Emotional Bureaucracy*, 181.

14. See, generally, Jody Lyneé Madeira and Barbara Andraka-Christou, "Paper Trails, Trailing Behind: Improving Informed Consent to IVF Through Multimedia Applications," *J. L. & the Biosciences* (Jan. 18, 2016): 2–38.

15. Hodder, *Emotional Bureaucracy*, 181.

16. Gerteis et al., *Through the Patient's Eyes*, 5.

17. Ibid., 5–11.

CHAPTER 8

1. Barrie R. Cassileth, et al., "Informed Consent—Why Are Its Goals Imperfectly Realized?" *New Eng. J. Med.* 302 (April 17, 1980): 896–900.

CHAPTER 9

1. *Kass v. Kass*, 696 N.E.2d 174, 180 (1998).

2. Donald Brenneis, "Reforming Promise," in *Documents: Artifacts of Modern Knowledge*, ed. Annelise Riles (Ann Arbor: University of Michigan Press, 2006), 65.

3. Ibid.

CONCLUSION

1. Yael Navaro-Yashin, "Make-Believe Papers, Legal Forms and the Counterfeit: Affective Interactions Between Documents and People in Britain and Cyprus," *Anthropological Theory* 7, no. 1 (2007): 79–98, 95.

2. Loel Kim et al., "Keeping Users at the Center: Developing a Multimedia Interface for Informed Consent," *Technical Comm. Q.* 17, no. 3 (2008): 335–357, 345.

3. Sarah A. McGraw et al., "Clarity and Appeal of a Multimedia Informed Consent Tool for Biobanking," *IRB Ethics & Hum. Res.* 34, no. 1 (2012): 9–19, 9, 14.

4. See Kim et al., "Keeping Users at the Center," 345.

5. Ibid., 346.

6. Deborah Lewis, "Computer-Based Approaches to Improving Patient Education: A Review of the Literature," *J. Amer. Med. Informatics Assn.* 6, no. 4 (1999): 272–282, 278.

7. Alan R. Tait et al., "Computer Information Program Improves Patient Understanding in Informed Consent for Cardiac Catheterization," *J. Clinical Outcomes Mgmt.* 17, no. 1 (2010): 10–12, 10; Kim et al., "Keeping Users at the Center," 349.

8. Lewis, "Computer-Based Approaches," 274.

9. Kim et al., "Keeping Users at the Center," 351.

10. Lewis, "Computer-Based Approaches," 278.

11. McGraw et al., "Clarity and Appeal," 14.

12. Ibid.

13. See, e.g., Glyn Elwyn et al., "Shared Decision Making: A Model for Clinical Practice," *J. Gen. Internal Med.* 27, no. 10 (2012): 1361–1367.

APPENDIX

1. See, generally, Juliet Corbin and Anselm Strauss, *Basics of Qualitative Research—Techniques and Procedures for Developing Grounded Theory,* 4th ed. (Thousand Oaks, CA: Sage Publications, 2014).

2. Theresa Morris, *Cut It Out: The C-Section Epidemic in America* (New York: New York University Press, 2013), 175.

3. See E. C. Haagen et al., "Current Internet Use and Preferences of IVF and ICSI Patients," *Hum. Reproduction* 18, no. 10 (2003): 2073–2078; Wouter S. Tuil et al., "Dynamics of Internet Usage During the Stages of In Vitro Fertilization," *Fertility & Sterility* 91, no. 3 (March 2009): 953–956.

4. See Y. M. Epstein et al., "Use of the Internet as the Only Outlet for Talking About Infertility," *Fertility & Sterility* 78, no. 3 (September 2002): 507–14; L. Bunting and J. Boivin, "Decision-making About Seeking Medical Advice in an Internet Sample of Women Trying to Get Pregnant," *Hum. Reproduction* 22, no. 6 (June 2007): 1662–68.

Glossary of Common
Fertility Terms

AMH (ANTI-MULLERIAN HORMONE) A hormone produced by cells in ovarian follicles. Blood levels of AMH usually provide information about a woman's ovarian reserve.

ART (ASSISTED REPRODUCTIVE TECHNOLOGY) A medical procedure in which a woman's eggs are surgically retrieved from her ovaries and combined with a man's sperm to help her or another woman to conceive. IVF is an ART procedure, but IUI is not. Other ART procedures include GIFT (Gamete Intrafallopian Transfer) and ZIFT (Zygote Intrafallopian Transfer).

BASAL BODY TEMPERATURE A temperature reading that can be used to chart fertility daily.

BLASTOCYST A stage in embryonic development reached approximately five days after fertilization.

CLOMID A medication commonly given to woman as an initial fertility treatment to help stimulate ovulation.

CRYOPRESERVATION Freezing embryos for future use.

CYCLE In IVF, an attempt to conceive using either "fresh" (recently retrieved) or "frozen" embryos. A fresh cycle has several steps: (a) a woman begins taking medications to mature her eggs; (b) her ovaries are monitored for follicle growth; (c) her mature eggs are surgically retrieved and combined with sperm to form embryos; (d) resulting embryos are transferred back into her uterus (or into another woman's) three or five days later; and (e) the woman receiving the embryos is given a pregnancy test approximately two weeks after egg retrieval. In a frozen cycle, a frozen embryo is thawed and then transferred into a woman's uterus. Cycles stopped prior to retrieval or transfer (because the patient changes her mind, becomes ill, or has immature eggs) are "cancelled."

DIMINISHED OVARIAN RESERVE A condition in which a woman's ovaries can't produce eggs normally because of medical, surgical, or age-related reasons.

DONOR EGG CYCLE A cycle in which a woman undergoes egg retrieval to "donate" her eggs to another woman who can't use her own, and then terminates her parental rights.

DONOR EMBRYO An embryo donated by a patient or couple, who terminate their parental rights.

ECTOPIC PREGNANCY A pregnancy formed when an embryo implants outside the uterus.

EGG The female reproductive cell that matures within follicles, or fluid-filled sacs, in a woman's ovaries; once released, it travels through her fallopian tubes to the uterus (also known as an ovum or oocyte).

EGG RETRIEVAL A surgical procedure to collect mature eggs from ovarian follicles.

EMBRYO An egg fertilized by sperm that has begun to divide into multiple cells.

EMBRYO TRANSFER A procedure in which embryos are transferred in the woman's uterus in IVF.

ENDOMETRIOSIS A condition in which tissue usually found within the uterine lining grows outside the uterus, potentially affecting fertility.

FALLOPIAN TUBES Two hollow tubes on either side of the uterus where the sperm combines with the egg in spontaneous, non-IVF pregnancies.

FERTILIZATION The process in which the sperm penetrates the egg's outer wall and combines genetic material, forming an embryo.

FETUS Unborn offspring from eight weeks after conception to birth.

FOLLICLE A fluid-filled ovarian sac containing a maturing egg.

FOLLICLE-STIMULATING HORMONE (FSH) A pituitary gland hormone that helps an egg to mature and instructs the body to release it; high levels of FSH indicate that a woman has lowered ability to mature eggs and poor chances of conception.

GAMETE A male or female reproductive cell.

GESTATIONAL SURROGATE A woman who agrees to gestate or carry an embryo formed from another woman's egg and carry the resulting pregnancy, and who is often contractually obligated to terminate parental rights to the infant in favor of the intended parents.

GONADOTROPIC RELEASING HORMONE (GN-RH) A hormone produced in the brain's hypothalamus that triggers ovulation. Synthetic variations are called "GnRH agonists."

HUMAN CHORIONIC GONADOTROPIN (HCG) A hormone that triggers ovulation.

IMPLANTATION When a fertilized embryo burrows into the uterine lining to form a pregnancy.

INFERTILITY An inability to conceive after a year of unprotected intercourse.

ICSI (INTRACYTOPLASMIC SPERM INJECTION) A fertility procedure useful for overcoming male infertility in which one sperm is injected directly into the egg.

IUI (INTRAUTERINE INSEMINATION) A fertility procedure that transfers sperm into a woman's uterus when she is ovulating to increase odds of fertilization.

IVF (IN VITRO FERTILIZATION) A fertility procedure in which eggs are matured, surgically removed from a woman's ovaries, and transferred into a woman's uterus to facilitate pregnancy.

LAPAROSCOPY Surgically inserting a fiber-optic camera through a small incision to view the inside of the body.

MALE FACTOR INFERTILITY Infertility caused by low sperm count or other sperm-related problems that lower the sperm's ability to fertilize the egg without assistance.

MENSTRUAL CYCLE The cycle in which a woman's body matures and releases an egg, prepares the uterus for pregnancy, and, if the egg remains unfertilized, sheds the uterine lining in a bloody discharge known as a period.

MISCARRIAGE A pregnancy that ends before 20 weeks.

MORPHOLOGY Sperm's size and shape; irregular morphology can contribute to male factor infertility.

MOTILITY Sperm's ability to move by themselves. Sperm with low motility have trouble moving forward to fertilize an egg.

MULTIPLE PREGNANCY A pregnancy in which two or more fetal heartbeats are observed via ultrasound, commonly known as a pregnancy with twins (2), triplets (3), quadruplets (4), or more. Pregnancies with three or more fetuses are termed "higher-order multiple" pregnancies.

OOCYTE/OVUM The female reproductive cell (egg).

OVARIAN RESERVE A woman's potential to conceive.

OVARIAN STIMULATION Medically stimulating ovaries to develop follicles and mature eggs.

OVULATION When a woman's ovaries release a mature egg.

OVULATORY DYSFUNCTION A condition in which a woman's ovaries aren't producing eggs normally.

POLYCYSTIC OVARY SYNDROME (PCOS) A condition in which a woman has higher than normal levels of male hormones, often causing irregular or absent menstrual cycles and small fluid-filled cysts on her ovaries. PCOS can make it harder for a woman to conceive and is also linked to skin and hair changes, obesity, and other health conditions.

PREGNANCY A condition in which a woman carries a developing fetus, as confirmed by a gestational sac in the uterus (clinical pregnancy), or tests positive on a pregnancy test (chemical pregnancy).

PREMATURE OVARIAN FAILURE A condition in which a woman younger than 40 enters menopause when her ovaries stop ovulating and producing estrogen.

REPRODUCTIVE ENDOCRINOLOGIST (RE) A physician specializing in reproductive medicine, a surgical subspecialty of obstetrics and gynecology. An RE is trained in how hormonal functioning affects reproduction.

SELECTIVE REDUCTION A surgical procedure in which drugs are injected to stop the hearts of one or more fetuses in a multiple pregnancy (also known as multifetal pregnancy reduction).

SEMEN ANALYSIS A test in which a man's semen is collected to check the sperm's number and shape.

SPERM The male reproductive cell, produced in the testes and released in a fluid known as semen.

STILLBIRTH A fetus that dies after 20 weeks.

ULTRASOUND A medical technique used to see ovarian follicles, a clinical pregnancy, or a fetus.

UNEXPLAINED INFERTILITY A medical diagnosis when a man or woman's infertility has no identifiable cause.

UTERUS (WOMB) The primary female reproductive organ where fetuses grow until birth.

ZYGOTE An early stage in an embryo's development.

Index

www.ingramcontent.com/pod-product-compliance
Lightning Source LLC
Chambersburg PA
CBHW020504270326
41926CB00008B/728